T0314993

CURRENCY POLITICS

CURRENCY POLITICS

The Political Economy of Exchange Rate Policy

Jeffry A. Frieden

PRINCETON UNIVERSITY PRESS

PRINCETON AND OXFORD

Library of Congress Cataloging-in-Publication Data

Frieden, Jeffry A.
Currency politics : the political economy of
exchange rate policy / Jeffry A. Frieden.
pages cm
Includes bibliographical references and index.
ISBN 978-0-691-16415-1 (hardcover : alk. paper)   1. Foreign exchange
rates—History.   2. Commercial policy—History.   I. Title.
HG3811.F75 2015
332.4′56—dc23   2014028533

British Library Cataloging-in-Publication Data is available

This book has been composed in Adobe Caslon Pro

Printed on acid-free paper. ∞

Printed in the United States of America

10 9 8 7 6 5 4 3 2 1

CONTENTS

PREFACE

Currencies and their values are central to the world economy. They affect international trade, investment, finance, migration, and travel. The prevailing exchange rate system often defines the international economic order. The gold standard, a global regime of fixed currencies that prevailed for over forty years before 1914, was so pivotal that the period is often known as the classical gold standard era.[1] After World War I, major governments were unable to adapt the currency order to the changed conditions, and failed exchange rate policies were a major reason why the interwar world economy tottered and eventually collapsed.[2]

In the aftermath of World War II, the Western world organized its economy around the Bretton Woods monetary order of fixed but adjustable exchange rates, with general success.[3] Since the collapse of the Bretton Woods currency system, exchange rate policies have, if anything, gained in importance.

In today's era of "globalization," exchange rate policies have played a major role in virtually all economies. The European Union has for decades attempted to stabilize the currencies of its member states, eventually leading to the 1999 creation of a single European currency— the euro. Although the eurozone has experienced massive difficulties, the single European currency remains a cornerstone of the most ambitious attempt at international economic integration in modern history.

1 Estevadeordal, Franz, and Taylor 2003.
2 Eichengreen 1992; Bernanke and James 1991.
3 See, for example, many of the essays in Bordo and Eichengreen 1993.

Elsewhere in the rich world, currency policies and movements have been a focus of political controversy both within and between nations.

Developing countries, too, have faced crucial decisions about their exchange rates. Some have linked their currencies tightly to the dollar, the euro, or other leading currencies, while others have decided to let their currencies float freely. Still others have made managing their currencies central to their economic strategies. These decisions have powerfully affected subsequent economic developments. Many countries in East Asia, in particular China, would ascribe their extraordinary economic success at least in part to systematic policies to keep their currencies relatively weak in order to stimulate export-led economic growth. On the other hand, currency crises have become commonplace elsewhere in the developing world, such as Mexico in 1994, Asia in 1997–98, Russia in 1998, Brazil in 1999, and Argentina and Turkey in 2001. Many of these currency crises led to major economic, social, and political upheavals. And currency policies have joined or even supplanted trade policies as a major source of friction among governments in today's globalized economy.

National and international currency relations are central features of the world economy, and they are largely the result of government exchange rate policies. We cannot analyze the international trading system without understanding national trade policies; likewise, we cannot analyze the international monetary system without understanding national currency policies. This has led scholars to attempt to explain government policies toward their exchange rates. Such efforts of necessity take into account both economic and political factors in the making of currency policy.

My own interest in the political economy of exchange rate policy dates back over twenty years. My research has emphasized how the distributional effects of currency policies help explain why interest groups would support or oppose particular currency measures. Almost all economic policies create winners and losers, and currency policy is no exception. My early work proposed simple divisions among socioeconomic actors, and applied them to a variety of settings.[4] While there are many other factors that go into the making of currency policy, from domestic and international macroeconomic conditions to political institutions, I continue to believe that the preferences of crucial social

4 See, for example, Frieden 1991, 1994a.

groups are an essential building block of any rounded explanation of government policy, in the monetary realm as elsewhere.

Currency Politics: The Political Economy of Exchange Rate Policy expands both the theoretical and empirical reach of my scholarship on the subject. The theoretical principles presented here go beyond my early ideas. I have been especially interested in incorporating further considerations of how exchange rates affect economic agents—a concern reflected largely in attention to *pass-through*: the extent to which currency movements are transmitted to the domestic economy by way of relative price movements. In addition, I have attempted to expand the nuance and accuracy of the socioeconomic divisions we would expect to find: exporters differ among themselves, as do those with commercial and financial interests. Other scholars have written elegantly on similar topics, and I strive to incorporate their advances in my theoretical and empirical discussions.

Theoretically, this study focuses on identifying and clarifying the distributionally motivated currency policy preferences of economic actors—firms, industries, and groups. It argues that characteristics of an industry, including its exposure to exchange rate risk and the relative price effects of exchange rate movements, determine its exchange rate policy preferences.

There are two relevant dimensions of exchange rate policy choice: the regime (fixed or floating) and level (appreciated or depreciated). With regard to the former, I contend that actors that rely heavily on international trade, investment, or financial ties will, all else being equal, prefer a stable exchange rate—the gold standard, fixed rates, dollarization, and euroization. With regard to the latter, I assert that tradables producers will, all else being equal, prefer a depreciated exchange rate. (The opposite applies: domestically oriented actors prefer a flexible rate and nontradables producers prefer an appreciated one.) These concerns are strongly influenced by the degree to which exchange rate movements are passed through to domestic prices, which in turn is a function of complex features of modern industries. Where pass-through is limited—the impact of currency movements on prices is small—concerns about exchange rate volatility rise and support for a depreciated currency declines.

Empirically, I carry out a range of studies to highlight the potential applicability of my approach across time and space. The first part of the book looks at the US experience with the gold standard in the nineteenth century—a period in which monetary politics were hotly contested within the United States, as in many other countries. The second part switches gears to explore a much more recent experience with debates over a fixed exchange rate (and beyond) among open economies—the process of European monetary integration leading toward the adoption of the euro. In the third section, I focus on the currency experiences of Latin America, which vary both in how open the economies of the region have been to the rest of the world and in the multiplicity of exchange rate policies adopted by the region's governments.

We have a long way to go before we have a full understanding of the determinants of national policies toward the exchange rate. We have even further to go before we understand how national decisions interact to create regional and international monetary orders. A wide variety of economic, political, historical, and other factors come together to affect these policies and outcomes. My hope is that the research presented here will shed light on how socioeconomic interests, whether of concentrated groups or broad segments of the population, help shape currency politics and currency policy.

ACKNOWLEDGMENTS

Over the years, I have learned from dozens and dozens of fellow scholars, and it would be futile to try to name them all. For this specific manuscript, I am particularly grateful to Lawrence Broz, Jesse Schreger, David Singer, and three anonymous reviewers, who read the entire manuscript and gave excellent comments and suggestions on it.

I owe an especially great debt to the many outstanding research assistants who have helped me over the years. I am particularly grateful to Albert Wang, who endured my foibles longest and most patiently. My other excellent research assistants have been Cynthia Balloch, Jasmina Beganovic, Ashley DiSilvestro, Andrew Eggers, Kyle Jaros, Anjuli Kannan, Rohan Kekre, Rebecca Nelson, Alex Noonan, and Andrea Woloski. I am grateful to them all, and heartened that despite having undergone the drudgery of working on my project, many of them have gone on to successful careers in academia.

For permission to reprint, I would like to thank the *Journal of Economic History* for parts of chapter 3, and *International Organization* for parts of chapter 4.

All data used in this study, along with explanations of their sources, can be accessed via http://press.princeton.edu/titles/10364.html.

CURRENCY POLITICS

Introduction

The Political Economy of Currency Choice

T he exchange rate is the most important price in any economy, for it affects all other prices. The exchange rate is itself set or strongly influenced by government policy. Currency policy therefore may be a government's single most significant economic policy. This is especially the case in an open economy, in which the relationship between the national and international economies is crucial to virtually all other economic conditions.

Policymakers who have to answer, directly or indirectly, to constituents, such as voters, interest groups, and investors, are the ones who make currency policy. Like all policies, the choices available to currency policymakers involve trade-offs. Currency policies have both benefits and costs, and create both winners and losers. Those who make exchange rate policies must evaluate the trade-offs, weigh the costs and benefits, and consider the winners and losers of their actions.

Exchange rate policy provides an extraordinary window on a nation's political economy. This is particularly true in countries whose economies are open to the rest of the world economy, because in such a situation currency policy has a profound impact on a whole range of economic activities and political decisions. Debates over exchange rate policy, and the eventual decisions made about it, tell us a remarkable amount about an economy, a society, and its political institutions.

Currency politics reflect the importance of the mass-consuming public, role of elections, organization of economic groups, power of particularistic interests, time horizons of voters and politicians, and responsiveness of political institutions to pressures along with virtually all other features of a national political economy. In some ways, exchange rate policy requires a government to make a relatively simple decision: to fix the currency or allow it to float, to try to keep the currency strong or weak. But these simple decisions reflect extraordinarily complex structures, motives, and pressures. Currency politics summarize many features of a national political economy, for those who make currency policy must take into account the impact of their decisions on almost everyone in society.

Currency Choices

Currency policymakers face two interrelated choices. The first is the desired exchange rate *regime*, and especially whether to fix the exchange rate against either some other nation's currency or a commodity such as gold. The second is the *level* (price) of the exchange rate.[1]

The exchange rate regime has two common meanings. The first refers to the prevailing international monetary arrangements. The gold standard, Bretton Woods gold-dollar standard, and contemporary floating are international monetary regimes; the European Monetary System (EMS) was a regional monetary regime. In this sense, regime choice involves joint decisions by several countries. No one nation can single-handedly create an international monetary regime, given that such a system exists only to the extent that more than one nation adheres to it.

The second meaning of the exchange rate regime is simply the method by which an individual government manages its currency. In this context, a nation can choose a variety of ways to organize its own

---

1 The economics literature on exchange rates is enormous. For a recent survey of the state of the art, see Engel 2014. For two excellent surveys of previous generations of the literature, see Isard 1995; Sarno and Taylor 2002.

exchange rate in relation to those of other currencies. A *fixed* exchange rate regime commits the monetary authorities to maintain the value of the national currency against a commodity such as gold or another national currency. Sometimes a currency is fixed against a basket of currencies, but this is less purely fixed as it implies substantial variability in exchange rates relative to individual currencies. In addition, if (as is common) the composition of the basket is not announced publicly, the government can alter the exchange rate by altering the basket. In limiting cases, a government can choose to adopt the currency of another country, such as the US dollar, or create a multicountry currency union, such as the euro.[2]

With a *fixed but adjustable* or *adjustable peg* regime, the government promises to keep the exchange rate constant at any given point, yet makes it clear that it will change the exchange rate as deemed desirable. This provides the benefits of short-term exchange rate stability without completely eliminating the ability of national politicians to affect policy. The uncertainty associated with a currency whose value could be changed at any point, however, can make such a regime less than fully credible.

A *floating* exchange rate is one that the monetary authorities do not try to support at a preannounced level. The currency's value is determined on foreign exchange markets, and national policymakers do not commit to defend a particular rate. This does not preclude attention by policymakers to the exchange rate. The authorities might intervene to stabilize the currency or try to keep it from falling (or rising) more than they think acceptable. And national monetary policies—such as interest rate policy—might be undertaken with an exchange rate stance in mind. But there is no explicit public promise to sustain any particular exchange rate.

In addition to the exchange rate regime, monetary authorities make policies that influence the *level* of the exchange rate—the currency's value. A currency can rise in value—appreciate or revalue—in relationship to other currencies or decline in value—depreciate or devalue. Exchange rates can move differently against different currencies. The best summary measure is the *effective exchange rate*, a country's ex-

---

2 Although some observers regard these last cases as qualitatively distinctive, due to the greater difficulties associated with leaving such a regime—de-dollarizing or exiting the euro, for example—here I consider them as special cases of a fixed rate. After all, there are always costs in abandoning a fixed exchange rate, and the only difference is in the extent of the costs.

change rate against other currencies weighted by their importance in the country's trade. Movements in the *nominal* exchange rate, which simply measures the relative value of the currency, are often less meaningful than changes in the *real exchange rate*, which adjusts for inflation differentials between countries. If the home country has no inflation while the foreign country has 20 percent inflation, with exchange rates held constant, this is the equivalent of a *real depreciation* of the home country's currency: the foreign-currency price of home goods has gone down relative to the foreign-currency price of foreign goods, while the domestic-currency price of foreign goods has risen relative to the domestic-currency price of home goods. It is also equivalent to a *real appreciation* of the foreign currency, as prices of its goods expressed in its own currency have risen relative to those of the home country.

The real exchange rate reflects the impact of the exchange rate on the country's trade and payments. Policymakers, businesspeople, journalists, and others frequently refer to a currency's impact on "competitiveness"—such as to complain that the currency value is making it difficult for home industries to compete with imports or to export. In these cases, what they are complaining about is the real exchange rate. Some industries gripe about an "overvalued" (appreciated or "strong") currency, while others may grumble about an "undervalued" (depreciated or "weak") one.[3]

The real value of the currency is crucial to every open economy because it affects the prices of national goods and services relative to those abroad. As a result, policymakers, economic agents, and others care deeply about the real exchange rate—often expressed as the country's competitiveness. And this in turn makes nominal exchange rate policy key, for in almost all circumstances nominal currency movements have a real effect. To be sure, the effect may vary among countries, among goods, and over time; in fact, this variation can play an important role (more on this below). While scholars disagree on how effec-

---

3   Some scholars dislike such terms because of their indeterminacy: it is not clear what the currency is over- or undervalued relative to. The reference point is typically some notional equilibrium level of the exchange rate. This might be its *purchasing power parity* (PPP) level, at which the actual ability of currencies to purchase domestic goods and services is roughly equivalent, or a level adequate to secure "internal and external balance"—that is, a noninflationary domestic monetary policy and rough balance in the current account. Although there is some subjectivity to the terms, they are commonly used, and in most cases descriptive enough to make sense.

tive exchange rate policy can be, most accept that nominal currency movements have a significant real impact, at least in the short and medium run.[4]

For our purposes, the key point is that policymakers can affect both the exchange rate regime and level of the exchange rate. They can do so by many means, from altering interest rates to intervention in currency markets. Currency values also have a powerful impact on the well-being of important economic actors—and indeed, the fate of national economies more broadly. Currency policy is just about as powerful as any single national economic policy can be. And the choices that it presents to policymakers and the public are equally crucial.

Currency Trade-offs:
One Trilemma and Two Dilemmas

Like all policies, currency policies involve trade-offs. The starkest is most colorfully known as the trilemma.[5] The trilemma—also dubbed the Unholy Trinity, Inconsistent Trio, and other phrases of varying catchiness—says that only two of the following three are possible: financial integration, a fixed exchange rate, and monetary independence. Most important for our purposes, this means that in a financially open economy, the government must choose between a fixed exchange rate and monetary policy autonomy. The idea is central to the Mundell-Fleming approach to balance-of-payments adjustment developed in the 1960s.[6] When financial integration allows capital to move freely among countries, domestic interest rates are given by world interest rates. If the exchange rate is fixed, a monetary expansion (or contraction) has *no effect*, as its impact is negated by a countervailing outflow (or inflow) of funds. For example, if the monetary authority lowers the domestic interest rate in order to stimulate the economy, funds flow out until the domestic interest rate has risen back to the world rate.

---

4 For a recent survey of studies on the relationship between exchange rate movements and prices—including the real exchange rate—see Burstein and Gopinath 2014.

5 The literature on the trilemma is enormous. For two important recent contributions, see Obstfeld, Shambaugh, and Taylor 2005; Aizenman, Chinn, and Ito 2010.

6 For the original statements of the approach, see Mundell 1960, 1963; Fleming 1962; McKinnon 1963. For critical summaries, see also Mussa 1979, 1984.

In a financially open economy, then, policymakers must choose *either* a stable exchange rate *or* the ability to have an independent monetary policy; they cannot have both. It is also the case that policymakers could choose to limit capital mobility—this is the third leg of the trilemma—although contemporary international financial markets and contemporary technologies may make this a less viable option for all but the most authoritarian regimes. This effectively reduces the trilemma to a dilemma with respect to the choice of exchange rate regime. (I return to closed economies, including instances in which financial integration is not a given, below.)

Policymakers face difficult choices and real trade-offs in making currency policy. This is because there are advantages to both fixed and floating rates as well as both strong and weak currencies. How policymakers weigh these effects depends, among other things, on how their constituents weigh them. And constituency preferences are in turn a function of the expected economic impact of the choices in question. In an economically open economy, there are two dimensions along which these options can be evaluated—two sets of dilemmas, so to speak, on whose horns currency policymakers find themselves.

Regime: Stability versus flexibility. When choosing a currency regime in a financially open economy, in line with the trilemma, the trade-off is between the monetary stability that a fixed rate brings, and the policy flexibility that a floating or adjustable rate allows. A fixed exchange rate makes cross-border trade, payments, finance, investment, and travel more predictable, removing most or all foreign exchange risk from cross-border transactions. It can also bring domestic monetary stability: if the currency is pegged to that of a low-inflation partner, a fixed exchange rate holds domestic inflation roughly at the level of the partner. But this cross-border and internal monetary consistency comes at the expense of national policy autonomy. The currency cannot be devalued (depreciated) to make national goods cheaper than foreign goods, nor can national monetary policy be loosened beyond that of the currency's anchor. After 1998, Argentine farmers and manufacturers found themselves priced out of local and foreign markets, but the Argentine authorities could do nothing so long as they were bound by a currency fixed to the dollar. Ireland's macroeconomic conditions were dramatically different from those of Germany in the 1990s—Ireland was booming, and Germany was stagnating—but Ireland's commitment to peg the Irish pound to the deutsche mark (DM) required Irish monetary policy to be identical to that of Germany. And such peripheral European countries as Spain and Portugal would have been much better off with monetary policies tailored to their own conditions during the financial crisis that began in 2007, but their membership in the eurozone made this impossible. The trade-off, then, is between monetary stability and predictability, on the one side, and monetary independence and flexibility, on the other.[7]

Level: Purchasing power versus "competitiveness." Choosing a fixed exchange rate means forgoing national control of the currency's nominal value.[8] But even if the monetary authorities retain autonomy, there are difficult choices about the desired strength of the currency. On the one hand, a strong (appreciated) currency increases national purchasing power, allowing domestic residents to buy more with their money. This is the *income effect* of an exchange rate movement: a currency appreciation increases effective national income. On the other hand, a strong currency raises the relative price of domestic products. This makes it harder for national producers to compete with foreigners on domestic or international markets; it also reduces local-currency earnings from foreign sales or profits. This is the *substitution effect* of an exchange rate movement: when a currency appreciates, consumers at home and abroad substitute foreign for domestic products. The trade-off here is as stark as with regard to the regime: a weak-currency exchange rate policy to improve the competitive position of domestic producers reduces the purchasing power of domestic residents, while a strong-currency exchange rate policy that improves the effective income of national consumers puts competitive pressure on national producers.

On both the regime and level dimensions, there are no unambiguous welfare criteria to guide policymakers, even if they were purely benevolent social planners. Exchange rate choices are not typically among policies that are better or worse for aggregate social welfare.[9] A country

---

7 For an excellent survey of the economics of regime choice, see Corden 2002.

8 Policymakers can engineer a real appreciation or depreciation even with a fixed exchange rate by acting to raise or lower domestic prices. For now, for simplicity, I focus on nominal exchange rate movements with real effects, which in any event are normally far easier to engineer and far more common. In the empirical applications, I analyze examples of real appreciations and depreciations within a fixed rate regime.

9 The literature on optimal currency areas, discussed below, has some implications for aggregate welfare—it indicates whether welfare can be improved by giving up or maintaining the national currency—but this is something of a special case. It cannot be applied directly to the choice of floating or fixing, and is not relevant to the level of the exchange rate. For literature

could thrive (or stagnate) with a fixed or floating currency, or with a strong or weak one. The principal factors involved in the choice of currency regimes and values are how different options affect the constraints and opportunities available to policymakers, and how they affect economic agents in society. In this, exchange rate politics differs from many other economic policies. In trade policy, for example, there is a clear, generally agreed-on welfare baseline: free trade is the optimal policy, and scholars attempt to explain deviations from it. There is no similar welfare baseline in exchange rate policy, which means that in some sense exchange rate policy is *entirely* the result of political economy factors.

One potential exception to this rule is the literature on optimal currency areas (OCAs), which does in fact suggest clear welfare criteria. Indeed, economists have a well-developed theoretical apparatus to evaluate the desirability of two countries sharing a currency. For our purposes, this could be relevant inasmuch as a currency union is an extreme variant of a fixed exchange rate—one end of the continuum that stretches from freely floating exchange rates to a union that makes the (former national) currency as close to "irrevocably fixed" as is conceivable. The analysis of the OCAs thus can be relevant to the choice of exchange rate regimes. Robert Mundell and others developed this approach in the early 1960s.[10] Previously seen as something of an intellectual curiosity, this literature is now regarded with more respect, in large part because of its relevance to monetary unification in Europe.[11]

The OCA approach weighs the benefits of giving up a national currency against the costs of forgoing the ability to devalue or revalue in response to changing economic conditions. The *benefits* of currency union are rarely clearly stated in the literature, but can be assumed to be the stabilization of expectations with respect to cross-border transactions. The *costs* of currency union depend on the impact of a govern-

---

that emphasizes the developmental advantages of a weak currency, see Rodrik 2008; Bhalla 2012. I return to this last argument in chapter 7.

10 For the original statement, see Mundell 1961. See also McKinnon 1963; Kenen 1969. For surveys of the approach, see, for example, Tavlas 1993, 1994; Masson and Taylor 1993; Goodhart 1995.

11 The analysis of European monetary integration has generally been carried out, at least as a first cut, in OCA terms. For a summary and interpretation, see Eichengreen and Frieden 1994. For two early European applications, see Bayoumi and Eichengreen 1992; De Grauwe and Vanhaverbeke 1993. For a survey of the vast literature on Europe, see Eichengreen 1993. For a summary of the experience, see Gros and Thygesen 1998.

ment's giving up the exchange rate as a policy tool. These costs in turn are a function of both the actual *effectiveness* and *desirability* of an independent monetary policy. To evaluate the effectiveness of monetary policy, the OCA approach focuses on factor mobility: the more factors are mobile between countries, the less effective monetary policy will be. If labor can move freely between two nations, any attempt to stimulate (contract) one country's economy will lead to an inflow (outflow) of labor and—much as with financial market integration—dilution of the policy's impact. To weigh the desirability of independent policy, the OCA approach considers whether the countries are subject to the same exogenous shocks. If two economies have identical structures and face identical external conditions, they have no (national welfare) reason to pursue different exchange rate policies. The national welfare is improved by giving up the exchange rate as a tool when the countries in question have similar structures or integrated factor markets, or face correlated exogenous shocks. This conclusion has motivated many studies of whether these conditions hold in prospective currency unions.

OCA analyses are entirely oriented to discovering the *aggregate social welfare* effects of currency policy. This is a major consideration, and analytically the proposition that governments do what is best for their countries is certainly worth considering. It is a proposition lacking in firm microfoundations, however, and also (unfortunately) empirical support. Indeed, almost all attempts have shown that the founding members of the EMS, and the later Economic and Monetary Union (EMU), did not constitute an OCA. This reinforces the significance of understanding sources of policy other than national welfare, including the role of politicians themselves and domestic interest groups.

The two dimensions of currency policy require policymakers to make critical decisions about the national economy. On one dimension, they must decide whether a predictable economic relationship with the rest of the world economy is more important than the ability to manage the national macroeconomy in line with domestic concerns. On the other dimension, they must decide which groups in society—consumers, debtors, international investors, manufacturers, and farmers—will be helped and which hurt by the real exchange rate. There is no obviously "right" decision for both sets of choices; both involve weighing costs and benefits that can be—and are—evaluated differently by different people and groups.

The analysis of exchange rate policy requires central consideration of political economy factors. In particular, we can concentrate on the *political* impact of currency policy—that is, how it affects the incentives for politicians and policymakers—and its *distributional* impact—how it influences the fortunes of socioeconomic groups.

The Politics of Currency Policy

Just as exchange rate policy in general reflects virtually every aspect of a nation's political economy, it also reflects virtually every aspect of a nation's political institutions. Politicians make currency policy, and to do so must account for the impact of this policy on their political constraints and opportunities. Scholars have paid quite a bit of attention to how the expected impact of exchange rate policies might influence the behavior of politicians and their appointees.[12] One obvious question is how politicians might expect different exchange rate policies to affect their electoral prospects.

Many scholars, for example, anticipate that politicians with stronger incentives to manipulate monetary conditions for electoral purposes would be more likely to opt for a flexible exchange rate regime that allows an independent monetary policy. For some, this implies that democracies in general will incline more toward flexibility than will authoritarian regimes. By extension, political systems in which politicians are more likely to be able to claim credit for favorable economic conditions may be associated with more flexibility. By this logic, inasmuch as multiparty coalition governments make it difficult for any one party to take credit for economic performance, the benefits to currency flexibility may be more limited. And since electoral systems based on proportional representation are particularly likely to give rise to multiparty coalition governments, some have argued that these systems will incline toward fixed rates. On another dimension, insofar as a strong real exchange rate raises the purchasing power of consumers, the more sensitive governments are to consumer interests in the electorate, the more likely they may be to engineer a real appreciation in the run-up to an election. Such other political institutional variables as parties, inde-

---

12 For a survey of the literature on the political economy of exchange rate policy, including that on political institutions, see Broz and Frieden 2006.

pendent bureaucracies, and electoral structures have been suggested to have systematic effects on national exchange rate policies.[13]

Exchange rate policy is closely related to domestic monetary policy, so that the enormous literature on the political economy of (typically closed-economy) monetary policy is relevant. In this light, many scholars have brought the institutionalist tools used to analyze domestic monetary policies to bear on exchange rates. More broadly, scholars have investigated government choices of exchange rate policies as part of an integrated array of monetary policy choices.[14]

One strand of this literature focuses specifically on the use of a fixed exchange rate regime as an anti-inflationary commitment device. The idea is that a fixed exchange rate can serve as a nominal anchor for national monetary commitments, raising the costs of inflationary policies; it thus can help the government overcome the time inconsistency of monetary commitments.[15] A government in search of anti-inflationary credibility, for instance, can establish either an independent central bank or fixed exchange rate.[16] This makes the exchange rate primarily valuable as a commitment mechanism.

There is no question that political institutions affect the making of currency policy. Differences between dictatorships and democracies, presidential and parliamentary systems, and other more nuanced characteristics of national political institutions influence the way that politicians think about policy choices. In this study, I consider such factors as they arise. My main focus is elsewhere, though, on the relationship between currency policy and *distributional* (rather than political-institutional) features of national political economies. For example, the use of a fixed exchange rate as a nominal anchor for credibility-enhancing purposes is undoubtedly part of the story in many cases, but

---

13 For particularly good examples of analyses of institutional, especially partisan, factors, see Bernhard and Leblang 1999; Bearce 2003, 2008; Bearce and Hallerberg 2011.

14 See especially the special issue of *International Organization* 56, no. 4 (Fall 2002), which has several articles along these lines. This issue was republished as a book (Bernhard, Broz, and Clark 2003). See also Bodea 2010.

15 On monetary credibility generally, see Blackburn and Christensen 1989; Persson and Tabellini 1990. For an analysis of the use of the exchange rate as a nominal anchor for the gold standard, see Bordo and Kydland 1995. For an analysis for the EMS, see Giavazzi and Pagano 1989; Weber 1991. For explicit extensions to exchange rate policy, see especially Bernhard, Broz, and Clark 2003.

16 For example, J. Lawrence Broz (2002) suggests that in developing countries, dictatorships are more likely to fix, in large part because they have more limited abilities to commit credibly to low inflation. See also Steinberg and Malhotra 2014.

even here attention must be paid to distributional factors. After all, policymakers have to weigh the decision to fix the currency for credibility purposes against the expected societal demands for changes in the exchange rate, and without a clear picture of these demands, it is hard to know how to assess the commitment value of a fixed rate against the alternatives.

The Distributional Politics of Currency Policy

The theory presented here emphasizes the role of economic interests in the making of exchange rate policy. It concentrates on how different policy choices, both with regard to the currency regime and its level, are expected to affect economic agents. While I accent the position of particularistic interests, I also underscore the impact of currency policy on broader groups, such as consumers or foreign-currency debtors.

The theoretical approach taken here is common in studies of the making of foreign economic policy.[17] We begin with some theoretically grounded principles about the policy's expected distributional impact, from which we derive the anticipated policy preferences of those who would be helped or harmed by the result. On this basis, we examine the potential role of these distributionally relevant interests in the making of the policy in question. This way of thinking about economic policies in general and foreign economic policies in particular is commonplace. Nobody, say, would attempt to explain a country's trade policy without homing in on the role of interest groups in favor of or opposed to trade protection. This book's core argument is that we need to think about currency policy in similar ways, accounting for the interests and influence of economic interest groups. Trade theory is a useful starting point to understand the structure of international trade, but it needs to be supplemented with an analysis of the political economy of trade policy. In the same way, open-economy macroeconomics is a useful jumping-off place to understand international monetary relations, but it needs to be supplemented with an analysis of the political economy of currency policy.

My theoretical approach to the distributional politics of exchange rate policy is presented in full in chapter 1. To be sure, my emphasis on

---

17 The approach has been dubbed "open economy politics." For a review, see Lake 2009.

this aspect of currency politics is not meant to rule out the importance of other sociopolitical factors. In empirical applications, I note the relevance of other considerations as appropriate. But I stress the position of economic interests, and because the exchange rate affects virtually all interests in society, this is both complex and critical enough as a starting point.

Currency Policies in Open and Closed Economies

Much of the discussion up to now has implicitly or explicitly highlighted the character of currency policy in financially as well as commercially open economies. This is appropriate given the prominence of the policy in open economies along with the many open economies both historically and today. Indeed, in the contemporary globalized international economy, exchange rates are clearly among the most important policies undertaken by national governments. Yet economic openness is far from a constant: there have been many periods over the past two hundred years in which the world economy has been quite closed, and even in eras of generalized openness, some countries have remained shut off from the rest of the world economy. It is crucial to recognize the theoretical and empirical significance of variation in economic openness, both over time and among countries, for the making of currency policy.

The economics and politics of monetary policy are different in a closed economy. Both financial and trade closure change the policy environment, albeit in different ways. In a financially closed economy, monetary policy has only indirect and long-term effects on the exchange rate, so that fixing the currency's value does not constrain short-term monetary autonomy. Monetary policy in a closed economy operates by way of interest rates, which in turn affect real variables. For example, a monetary expansion increases real money balances and lowers interest rates, and lower interest rates stimulate expenditure for investment and consumption. By the same token, a monetary contraction leads to higher interest rates and lower expenditures.[18]

18 This presumes *some* short-term real effect of monetary policy, and is not meant to challenge the

There is a systematic difference between the impact of monetary policy in closed and open economies. In the former it affects interest rates, and through them, aggregate economic activity. In a financially open economy, interest rates are given by world conditions rather than set at home, so that monetary policy is either ineffective if the exchange rate is fixed, or operates by way of the exchange rate: an expansion leads to depreciation, and a contraction to appreciation.

At the same time, an economy closed to trade has fewer tradables producers, and fewer firms exposed to currency risk and affected by a currency movement. It is not surprising that when few economic agents are engaged in cross-border (thus cross-currency) business, interest in the exchange rate is lessened. Conversely, it is not startling that in economies open to trade—such as the small open economies of Europe or the Caribbean—the exchange rate is of great interest.

Although most of the analysis in this book is of open economies, a comparison between closed- and open-economy macroeconomic policies has interesting implications for the politics of monetary policy in the two types of economies. In a closed economy, monetary policy largely implicates the interest rate. The impact of interest rates is typically on such macroeconomic aggregates as inflation, unemployment, and growth. The rates also have direct distributional effects on borrowers and savers, but these are broad categories. Many people may in fact be unclear about the net impact on them of interest rate movements; after all, a mortgage holder may also have pension funds. There are important groups made up of borrowers and savers (or creditors), and there are industries that depend particularly on interest rates. The housing construction industry is especially sensitive to interest rates, as are some small businesses. Nevertheless, the principal impact of interest rate movements is broad and macroeconomic, rather than narrow and distributional. This implies that the political pressures associated with monetary policy in a closed economy will be broad and diffuse. Indeed, most of the scholarly and other analyses of monetary policy that focus on closed-economy effects emphasize such general national-level factors as political instability, the partisan composition of the government,

more modern, rational expectations notion that monetary policy has no real *long-term* impact. If nominal monetary or exchange rate policy had no real impact at all in either the short or long run, its politics would hardly be worth studying—except perhaps as an illustration of mass hysteria. For a much more complete treatment, see, for example, Cumby and Obstfeld 1984.

and the level of unemployment as determinants (or results) of monetary policy.[19]

Open-economy conditions make monetary policy directly relevant to more intensely concerned, concentrated groups than interest rates. Exchange rates have a much more immediate impact on some economic actors than do interest rates. The exchange rate directly affects the relative price of domestic and foreign goods. If the price of wheat is set on world markets, wheat farmers will see the domestic-currency price they receive rise and fall as the exchange rate moves. Import competers will face more or less foreign competition as the currency falls or rises. In this way, open-economy monetary policy implicates the interests of relatively well-defined, concentrated groups of producers and consumers. Individuals may not know whether they are net debtors or net creditors. But exporters, import competers, foreign investors, multinational corporations, and foreign debtors are well aware of their position in international trade and payments, and how movements in the exchange rate affect them.

I anticipate that monetary politics in an open economy will more closely resemble interest group politics than in a closed economy. Better-defined and more concentrated segments of society will be drawn into the political fray to contest the exchange rate than will attempt to influence interest rates. Exchange rate politics will involve particularistic interests, especially those intensely affected by currency movements. And because more economic agents are exposed to the direct effects of monetary and exchange rate policy in an open economy, I expect monetary policy in such an economy to be more politically contentious.

None of this is meant to imply that the difference between closed- and open-economy monetary politics is one of night and day. For one thing, the purely economic differences between them should not be exaggerated: both interest and exchange rates matter in both closed and open economies, and broad and particularistic interests are affected in both settings. The difference is of degree, not kind.

Nonetheless, there should be a noticeable difference between the politics of monetary policy in closed and open economies. In closed economies, it should be more a matter for public opinions, electoral

---

19 For three surveys, see Lohmann 2006; Franzese and Jusko 2006; Alesina and Stella 2011. For two early classics, see Alesina 1989; Grilli, Masciandaro, and Tabellini 1991.

politics, and national political institutions—for the expression and consideration of concern for national macroeconomic developments. In open economies, it should have a powerful and differentiated impact on well-defined groups, leading to something much more similar to special interest politics. How these differences play themselves out in national political institutions will vary along with these institutions, of course. The principal point is that there will be a predictable and recognizable distinction; in a globalized economy, well-defined groups will hotly contest the exchange rate. While the empirical analyses in this book are largely about open economies, there are enough instances of more closed economies to allow at least some comparisons.

Currency Politics Applied across Time and Space

In the remainder of this study, I present and apply a theory of preferences over exchange rate policy to a wide variety of empirical settings. Most of the applications are to relatively open economies. The first two studies concern the United States in the late nineteenth century and Europe since the 1970s. Both episodes cover open economies in an open world economy, and in both instances, the principal exchange rate issue was whether to adopt and sustain a fixed exchange rate—the gold standard in the US case, and a peg to the DM (and eventually a single currency) in the European case. These investigations allow us to see the common features of the politics of exchange rates in distinct settings.

The third set of studies covers Latin American currency policy since the 1970s. To some extent this, again, involves open economies in an open world economy, especially since the 1990s. But the Latin American experience has an important feature. Until the 1980s, almost all Latin American countries had high trade barriers and substantial controls on cross-border capital movements, so that by most standards they were financially and commercially closed. Over the course of the 1980s, most Latin American governments substantially liberalized trade and financial flows. This allows us to explore the effects on the political economy of currency policy of going from a closed to an open economy.

The periods and regions analyzed here are highly varied. This may appear to be a drawback, as the idea of comparing the United States in the 1870s to the European Union in the 1990s may seem foolish. I prefer to think that this allows for a more rigorous evaluation of my theoretical propositions. And I also believe that there are many similarities—often unrecognized ones—among the many and highly varied national experiences with currency politics. Indeed, one of the purposes of this study is to suggest that a common analytic architecture can help us understand such seemingly unrelated experiences as the classical gold standard, euro, and Argentine currency board.

Plan of the Book

Currency Politics analyzes the politics of exchange rates. It has both theoretical and empirical ambitions. Theoretically, this study focuses on identifying the distributionally motivated currency policy preferences of economic actors—firms, industries, and groups. Empirically, the book evaluates the accuracy of its theoretical arguments in a variety of historical and geographic settings. From a historical perspective, it looks at the politics of the gold standard, particularly in the United States. In a more contemporary mode, it examines the political economy of the process of European monetary integration. And it also analyzes the politics of Latin American currency policy over the past forty years.

Chapter 1 sets forth a theoretical framework for the analysis of the politics of exchange rates, emphasizing the sources of special interests with regard to currency policy. It provides analytic expectations about the sorts of patterns we should observe in exchange rate politics. The book then looks in depth at various settings to see the extent to which these expectations are borne out. It does so by concentrating on carefully delimited instances of exchange rate politics. The analyses are both narrative and, where possible, statistical. Chapters 2 and 3 focus on the United States during the gold standard era, and the complex and conflicted politics of gold in the United States between 1865 and 1896. The frequent congressional votes on currency policy issues allow me to evaluate the impact of some of the factors I argue help determine exchange rate policy preferences.

The subsequent chapters explore more recent instances of exchange rate politics, again with a mix of narrative and statistical analysis. Chapter 4 describes and analyzes the lengthy process of European monetary integration, which began in the early 1970s, culminated in the 1999 adoption of the euro, and continues today. The following two chapters examine Latin America. Chapter 5 gives an overview of Latin American currency policy since the early 1970s and then provides a statistical analysis of exchange rate choices. Chapter 6 focuses on the daunting problem of currency crises, which have been a frequent and debilitating feature of the Latin American economic scene, with a detailed discussion of the recent experiences of Mexico, Argentina, and Brazil. Chapter 7 considers some broader implications of the analysis in the book, after which I conclude with a summary of its findings.

A Theory of Currency
Policy Preferences

This study emphasizes the distributionally motivated currency policy preferences of economic actors—firms, industries, and groups. It argues that characteristics of an industry, including its exposure to exchange rate risk and the relative price effects of exchange rate movements, determine its exchange rate policy preferences. Because in an open economy the exchange rate affects all national economic actors, understanding the making of currency policy requires a more or less complete map of the national political economy.

There are two relevant dimensions of exchange rate policy choice: the regime (fixed or floating) and the level (appreciated or depreciated). With regard to the former, I contend that actors that rely heavily on international trade, investment, or financial ties will, all else being equal, prefer a stable exchange rate—the gold standard, fixed rates, dollarization, and euroization—which reduces the currency risk associated with their international activities. With regard to the latter, I maintain that tradables producers will, all else being equal, prefer a depreciated exchange rate, which raises the relative price of their products, while producers of nontradable goods and services have opposing interests. I expect that the degree to which exchange rate movements are passed through to local prices will have an important impact on policy preferences. Producers of goods with limited pass-through (due to substantial product differentiation, for example) will be more favorable to a fixed exchange rate and less favorable to a depreciated currency. There are many ways to add nuance and complexity to this analysis, but I will try to rely on these three factors—*international exposure*, *tradability*, and *pass-through*—to explain as much of currency policy preferences as I can. I believe that this can provide building blocks for a broader analysis of the politics of exchange rates.

The rest of this chapter develops my argument in detail. It starts with a statement of the things I am trying to explain—the dependent variables of the study. I then present my reasoning and the empirical expectations that flow from it. This is followed by a brief summary of other scholarly studies of the economics and politics of exchange rates in order to situate this study within the broader literature

The Dependent Variable: Interests in the Exchange Rate

I am interested in explaining the currency policy preferences of domestic socioeconomic groups. This is a limited goal. Even were it fully achieved, it would not supply enough information to clarify national government policy preferences, which also depend on national political institutions and domestic political bargaining. Nor is it sufficient to explain policy outcomes, which depend on national conditions and international circumstances. But understanding the policy preferences of socioeconomic actors, especially firms, industries, and other economic interest groups, is a necessary first step.

The literature on the politics of trade policy offers a parallel. Trade policy, too, is the result of the preferences of domestic socioeconomic actors, domestic and international political and economic institutions, interstate strategic interaction, and a myriad of other things. Yet nobody would question the centrality of understanding how different trade policies affect firms, workers, and other social groups. Indeed, a massive literature on the political economy of trade focuses on how best to understand the distributional impact of different trade policies.[1]

In the same way, I am interested in understanding the differential impact of international monetary policies on society, given that a proper understanding of the interests of social actors is essential to further analysis. We cannot understand the motivations of policymakers without knowing the pressures and demands they face from their constituents. However we analyze international monetary policy, we need some notion of how policy affects society.

The need for microfoundations for the analysis of international monetary policy can be seen in many contexts. For example, it is common for analysts to assert that a particular currency is "unsustainable." But no nominal exchange rate is technically impossible to sustain: the national economy can always be forced to conform to the exchange rate by driving wages and prices down; in fact, it was common for governments to do this to stay on the gold standard. What is typically meant by unsustainability is that such attempts would be *politically* impossible to maintain in the face of domestic opposition. This implies that the analyst has some notion of what these political constraints are. And the constraints vary from place to place and time to time: one government may not be able to sustain an exchange rate that might well be sustained by another one.

An understanding of the societal interests affected by international monetary policy is central to any analysis of such policy. The goal of this book is to help specify the societal interests that form the building blocks of national currency policies and international monetary systems.

Determinants of Exchange Rate Policy Preferences

I derive the exchange rate policy preferences of economic actors from their economic characteristics. As above, the issue can be divided into two dimensions: the currency regime and its level. The two dimensions are interrelated in practice—a fixed currency cannot be devalued, of course—but can be treated separately for ease of exposition.

---

1 For excellent surveys, see Milner 1999, 2013.

Preferences over the Exchange Rate Regime

Those who consider currency risk as more important will, all else being equal, favor a fixed exchange rate; those who view currency risk as relatively less of a consideration will prefer a floating rate. This means that *exposure to exchange rate volatility* is a principal determinant of support for a fixed currency. Stabilizing exchange rates is primarily significant to those who deal with cross-border trade and payments. On the other hand, those whose businesses are entirely domestic have little reason to want the government to tie its hands to stabilize a price—that of the currency—that is of no direct importance to them.

Exposure to exchange rate volatility usually depends on involvement in international trade, finance, and investment. An enterprise that relies heavily on earnings from exports or foreign production, or is a substantial user of imported inputs or capital, can be hard hit by exchange rate fluctuations. Multinational corporations with facilities in several currency areas can have their business disrupted by unexpected exchange rate movements. In addition, investment planning can be hampered by uncertainty about the exchange rate. If foreign labor costs in a host country, measured in the home currency, rise substantially solely because the exchange rate moves, it can be costly for a multinational firm.

In all these instances, the time horizon of currency exposure matters. So too does the availability of opportunities to ensure against foreign exchange risk, especially forward-currency markets. Small and poor countries typically have thin forward markets, so that hedging is difficult, expensive, or impossible. Even where forward markets are well developed, they cannot inexpensively provide complete protection against currency movements.[2] This means that in virtually all circumstances, the most serious risks are borne by those with long-term nominal commitments in foreign currency. These commitments might be explicit or implicit contracts to deliver or purchase goods in return for a fixed amount of foreign currency, or debt contracts denominated in foreign currency. Substantial exchange rate movements can be risky in these cases. On the other hand, firms whose goods are traded on spot

---

2 The development of complex swaps and other derivatives has improved the ability of major banks and corporations to protect themselves, but at a cost. And as mentioned, these instruments are typically only available for the major currencies.

markets or investors with assets that can be liquidated easily are less exposed to currency risk. So firms with long-term currency exposure will be concerned to stabilize exchange rates. These firms include, most prominently, exporters or importers with long-term contracts denominated in foreign currency, and those with long-term foreign-currency investments.[3] This gives rise to the following empirical implications, all of which require the usual "all being else equal" modifier:

- The greater a firm's involvement in cross-border trade and investment, the greater its support for a fixed exchange rate
- For a firm heavily engaged in international trade and investment, support for a fixed exchange rate will increase with
  - its reliance on long-term implicit or explicit contracts denominated in foreign currency
  - the length of its investment horizons

These implications can be translated into more descriptive expectations. Exporters of complex manufactured products, multinational corporations, and international banks can all be expected to be particularly interested in policies to stabilize exchange rates, as can foreign-currency debtors. The empirical work that follows evaluates as many of these expectations as can be assessed given the state of the data.

Preferences over the Level of the Exchange Rate

Whether the national currency is fixed or floating, or something in between, is an important decision; so too is the *level* of the currency's value. More accurately, it is the real exchange rate—the relationship between domestic and foreign price levels—that has to be amenable to government policy for policy preferences to make any difference. If national price levels adjusted quickly to nominal exchange rate move-

---

3 At a high enough level of cross-border diversification, however, currency movements become irrelevant. A firm with fixed investments proportionately distributed among all countries would be protected against exchange rate movements: the rise in one currency would be counteracted by the decline of others. These factors mean that cross-border investors will be especially worried about currency volatility if they hold relatively immobile assets abroad, as do almost all foreign direct investors, and if the investor is less than fully diversified among countries.

ments—as they have in societies with long-term high inflation or a full indexing—then exchange rate policy would have little or no impact on relative foreign as well as domestic prices. Whether this holds in other societies is an empirical question.

In fact, there is overwhelming evidence for substantial deviations from *purchasing power parity* (PPP)—the relationship between the domestic and foreign price levels that would make national consumption baskets roughly equal in price—for long periods of time. Recent estimates indicate that the half-life of deviations from PPP—the period in which prices and exchange rates change to eliminate half the difference in the two countries' price levels—range from about three to over seven years.[4] Even the shorter period is a long time in macroeconomic terms, and an eternity—or election—in political terms.

There is also strong evidence that nominal exchange rate movements are major causes of these substantial real exchange rate changes.[5] All of this is simply to say that government policy is capable of affecting the real exchange rate for a long enough time to matter to economic agents and the economy as a whole. This is important for our purposes, because if national policy did not have this capability it would be hard to justify a study of it.

Understanding firm interests in the currency's level is simplified with a survey of basic exchange rate economics. The standard approach to exchange rates, used as the foundation for the analysis here as well, is the Mundell-Fleming-Dornbusch framework.[6] Typically, it regards the national currency as an asset, and assumes that asset prices adjust more rapidly than goods prices. Thus, currency markets adjust more quickly to news about monetary policy than do goods markets. Another crucial and related component of the model is that monetary policy leads the currency to *overshoot*, which implies both interest rate and exchange rate effects of monetary policy.

When, for example, the monetary authorities increase the rate of growth of the money supply, interest rates decline and investors sell off the currency. In the Dornbusch overshooting model, the currency falls by more than the change in monetary policy would imply, so that investors now expect a future currency appreciation. This makes investors

---

4 For two leading surveys on PPP and the relevant citations to a range of empirical studies, see Burstein and Gopinath 2014; Froot and Rogoff 1995.
5 See, for example, Clarida and Gali 1994; Eichenbaum and Evans 1995.
6 See especially Dornbusch 1973a, 1973b, 1976.

willing to hold the currency at the lower prevailing interest rate, as they will be compensated for the interest rate differential between home and foreign markets by the capital gain reaped when the currency rises in value. This approach, which is widely enough accepted to be the standard fare of most textbooks, shows how monetary policy can lead to changes in nominal exchange and interest rates, and (along with the assumption of sticky prices) demonstrates how currency movements can have real effects on relative prices.

Economic analysis goes on to investigate the macroeconomic impact of currency movements. There are *income* effects, which induce expenditure reduction, as well as *substitution* effects, which induce expenditure switching. The former effects operate as a decline in the currency's value (in the case of a depreciation) to reduce real purchasing power in world prices, so that real disposable income is lower and domestic expenditures go down. The latter effects run through the relative price impact of a depreciation, thereby leading consumers to substitute domestic products for previously imported (now more expensive) goods, switching consumption from imports to domestic output. The aggregate macroeconomic impact of the two effects depends very much on the country's economic structure and starting position.

Exchange rate economics is only raw material for our concerns. Given that the authorities can affect the real exchange rate, we want to know its impact on relative prices, and how this influences economic agents. For this purpose, an approach to the real exchange rate based on the relationship between tradable and nontradable goods and services is particularly useful.

The real exchange rate (*RER*) is usually expressed as the relationship between the national and foreign price levels, expressed in the home currency, as follows:

$$RER = e\frac{P}{P^*},$$

where *e* is the nominal exchange rate expressed in units of foreign currency per unit of domestic currency, *P* is the domestic price level, and *P** is the world (foreign) price level.[7] As this indicates, the real exchange rate can change because the nominal exchange rate changes. The real

---

7   I express it in this manner so that an increase is an appreciation. Often the numerators and denominators are reversed (the "Latin American" version), but this seems more intuitive.

exchange rate can also change without a nominal currency movement, when the relationship between the national and foreign price levels change. A rise in the local price level relative to world prices leads to a real appreciation, while a rise by less than that of world prices leads to a real depreciation.

Alternatively, the real exchange rate can be expressed in terms of tradable and nontradable goods and services. *Tradable* goods are those that enter freely into world trade, while *nontradable* goods and services are those consumed where they are produced. Tradability can be the result of transport costs or other inherent features of products that make them difficult or impossible to sell across borders. Housing, restaurant meals, education, health care, and haircuts are typical examples. Tradability is relative, not absolute. Belgians buy homes in the Netherlands and commute, Southern Californians get their hair cut in Mexico, and foreigners come to the United States for medical and educational services. In addition, many nontradables use substantial tradable inputs, such as construction materials in housing, which can lead their prices to be linked. Much evidence exists, however, that the tradables/nontradables definition of the real exchange rate captures many of the relevant relative price characteristics of exchange rate movements.[8]

In this framework, the prices of tradable goods are set in world markets, while the prices of nontradable goods and services are set domestically. In other words, national policy cannot affect the world price of tradables, expressed in foreign currency; tradables prices are thus an anchor for the real exchange rate. When the national currency depreciates (appreciates), tradable prices expressed in the home currency go up (down) proportionately. When the peso-to-dollar exchange rate is twenty to one, and a lamp trades for ten dollars on world markets, it costs two hundred pesos; if the peso is devalued to thirty to one, the lamp costs three hundred pesos.

Currency movements affect the relative price of tradables and nontradables because typically nontradable prices adjust slowly to changes in the domestic-currency price of tradables. In the case of a depreciation, for example, tradables rise immediately (leaving aside for now such complications as incomplete pass-through) while nontradables lag. Because tradables producers use nontradables as inputs—worker wages, for instance, are heavily influenced by the price of housing—

8 Giovannini 1988; Alogoskoufis 1990.

input costs rise more slowly than output prices. Tradables producers receive more for their products while paying less for inputs into the production process. The real exchange rate—the competitiveness of the currency, in common parlance—has increased.

Expressed in terms of tradables and nontradables, the real exchange rate (RER) is as follows:

$$RER = e\frac{NT}{T},$$

where, as above, e is the nominal exchange rate, T is the price of tradables, and NT is the price of nontradables.[9] As above, movement in either the nominal exchange rate or the relationship between tradables and nontradables prices can alter the real exchange rate. Of course, the two can counterbalance each other: there will be no change in the real exchange rate if the nominal exchange rate movement is offset by an equivalent movement in the tradables-to-nontradables price ratio.

We can now examine the currency policy concerns of economic agents.[10] Firm profits, all else being equal, are increasing in output prices and decreasing in input prices. Input prices can be separated into three components: nontradable goods and services, tradable goods, and interest rates. Output is solely of nontradables and tradables, leaving the financial sector aside for now. Firms differ in the composition of their inputs and output.

Firm interests in the exchange rate are a function of the structure of their inputs and outputs: the more output is tradable and the more inputs are nontradable, the stronger the preference for a weak currency. At one extreme, a firm that produces tradables and uses only nontradable inputs stands only to gain from a real depreciation: as tradables prices rise against nontradables, the price of the firm's output rises unambiguously relative to its inputs. At another extreme, a firm that produces nontradables and uses tradable inputs (and no domestic finance) has diametrically opposed interests.

The more realistic setting is one in which firm outputs and inputs vary on a continuum. Some produce more goods that are tradable, and

---

9 Again, I express it in this manner so that an increase is a real appreciation.
10 The general discussion here is based on the models in Branson and Love 1988; Hooper and Mann 1989; Bodnar and Gentry 1993; Campa and Goldberg 1995; Goldberg and Campa 1996. Those interested in mathematical derivation of the simple implications presented here can consult these works, especially Goldberg and Campa 1996.

some produce more nontradables; inputs range similarly in the degree to which they include nontradable goods and services. This leads to simple expectations about preferences over the level of the real exchange rate. All else being equal,

- the larger the share of tradable goods in a firm's output, the stronger its support for a relatively lower (more depreciated) exchange rate
- the larger the share of nontradable goods and services in a firm's inputs, the stronger its support for a relatively lower (more depreciated) exchange rate

Of course, this applies conversely: firms with more nontradable output and more tradable inputs will prefer a stronger (more appreciated) exchange rate.

The interests of international investors are ambiguous with regard to the level of the exchange rate (as opposed to its stability). A strong home currency allows investors to purchase overseas assets more cheaply, but reduces the local-currency value of foreign earnings. Ideally, international investors would buy low and sell high—have the home currency appreciate when they want to buy foreign assets and depreciate when they are receiving foreign earnings—but this hardly seems a realistic policy position. There are identifiable patterns, though. International financial institutions typically prefer their home currency to be strong: some of their international business is associated with the international standing of their home currency, and they have privileged access to deposits in their own currency. The international use of a currency tends to benefit the banks based in the issuing country. This has been called a desire for "denomination rents," as financial institutions whose home currencies are preferred denominations for international assets have an advantage over others in international financial intermediation.[11] Still, while international financial institutions may prefer a strong currency, these preferences are likely to be weak relative to the desire for currency stability.

Another pattern with regard to cross-border capital flows is more important, and that is the interest of those with foreign-currency liabilities. While currency movements do affect the home-currency value of

11 Alexander Swoboda (1968) coined the term.

foreign investors' assets and earnings, those with substantial foreign-currency debts face more dire consequences. A firm with such debt earns money and owns assets in local currency, but has substantial liabilities in foreign currency and can easily be made insolvent by a depreciation. So those with substantial foreign-currency debts can be expected to oppose a depreciation.[12] All else being equal,

- the larger a firm's net foreign-currency liabilities, the weaker its support for a relatively lower (more depreciated) exchange rate

Inasmuch as the level of the exchange rate effectively determines relative prices within an economy, it is not surprising that economic actors will support policies that move relative prices in a direction favorable to them. In the case of a depreciation, it is to be expected that producers of tradables will be favorable and those with net foreign-currency liabilities will be unfavorable. Nonetheless, it is worth making the relationships and their sources explicit. In what follows, I discuss an important qualifier to these relative price considerations: the extent to which exchange rate movements are in fact reflected in domestic price changes.

The Impact of Exchange Rates on Prices and Implications for Policy Preferences

Goods prices do not respond immediately and completely to exchange rate movements. The responsiveness of prices to currency movements has gotten a great deal of attention from economists, and the issue is of direct importance to our purposes. After all, most economic agents do not care about the exchange rate in itself but rather only as it affects the prices they confront. For any good, this makes the elasticity of price with respect to the exchange rate a crucial determinant of policy preferences, and this elasticity is known to vary enormously among industries and goods.

---

12 The problem is more complex, of course. Typically, when a currency appreciates, domestic agents borrow more in relatively cheap foreign currency. If they fully internalized the likelihood of an eventual depreciation, they would borrow up to a level appropriate to the devaluation risk. There is a nontrivial likelihood, however, that firms with external debts multiplied by an exchange rate collapse will be bailed out, so excessive borrowing may take place for quintessential moral hazard reasons. For a detailed analysis of the issue, see Walter 2008.

Economists began to focus on this issue in earnest in the wake of the sluggish response of US trade to the major dollar depreciation of the late 1980s. Studies found that exchange rate changes were not fully reflected in higher import prices, so that US imports did not decline as rapidly as anticipated. As the yen rose by well more than 50 percent against the dollar between 1985 and the early 1990s, for example, the prices of Japanese cars exported to the United States did not increase anything like 50 percent; in fact, they may not have risen at all. Analyses of other national experiences have shown that currency movements are often not reflected in price movements. More generally, the degree to which this is true varies substantially across countries and industries.[13]

Exchange rate pass-through, as noted earlier, is the extent to which changes in the exchange rate are transmitted to domestic prices. It is well established that pass-through is frequently limited, even over relatively long time horizons, and that there is great variation among goods and industries. The sources of the phenomenon are less well understood, although several explanations exist. One of the most prominent interpretations ascribes limited pass-through to "pricing-to-market" behavior by firms.[14] Pricing to market is strategic behavior by exporters, given characteristics of the markets into which they are selling. This prominent explanation of limited pass-through is worth describing in more detail.

An exporting firm in a perfectly competitive market has no choice about pricing its goods. Of course, the prices in question are expressed in national currencies, so that when currency values change, prices change accordingly. Take the example of Argentine wheat and a world market price of wheat set in US dollars. Argentine suppliers constitute a small enough share of the market that nothing they do can affect the world price of wheat in dollars. If the peso appreciates against the dollar, this does not influence the dollar price of wheat, only its counterpart in pesos; it simply lowers the amount received by the exporter. The

---

13 For a few examples of the early development of this enormous literature, see Hooper and Mann 1989; Feinberg 1989; Feenstra 1989; Lee 1997; Parsley 1995. Further citations are provided below as the discussion is extended. For a useful survey, see Goldberg and Knetter 1997. The literature has continued to develop, probably beyond what is essential for the purposes here. See, for example, Campa and Goldberg 2005; Engel 2006.

14 For the quintessential statement of this, see Krugman 1987. For a more general statement, see Dornbusch 1987.

same is true of a depreciation: if the peso falls against the US dollar, Argentine wheat exporters—given that the dollar price of wheat is fixed—see the Argentine price of wheat rise, so that they earn more in pesos for each bushel of wheat sold. In this case, in which the exporter takes the foreign-currency price as given, the exchange rate change is fully passed through to the home-currency price. A depreciation is passed through to the seller in higher unit prices, while an appreciation leads to lower unit prices paid to the seller. The same is true of analogous Argentine *imports*—let's say of foreign computers whose prices are set on the world market in dollars. A peso depreciation is passed through fully by the foreign seller to the Argentine buyer, leading to an increase in the peso (Argentine) price of computers, while an appreciation leads to a decrease in their price.[15] In other words, in competitive markets, exchange rate changes are passed through directly to changes in goods prices, so that a depreciation (appreciation) leads to an increase (decrease) in the local-currency price.

But when the exporter is large enough to affect the price of its product in the foreign market, the exporter has to devise a conscious pricing strategy—both in general and specifically in the face of a currency movement. An export producer might choose to absorb a favorable exchange rate movement and keep prices constant, or counterbalance an adverse currency movement by raising prices. For instance, an exporting firm whose currency depreciates could maintain preexisting foreign-currency prices on its product in order to increase returns. In a competitive market, if the dollar declined against the peso, peso prices of US goods would fall; if the dollar rose, peso prices of US goods would rise. But where exporting firms have market power, due to market structure or product differentiation, these relationships can be affected. As the dollar declined against the peso, for example, a US computer software producer might keep the Argentine price of its software constant, which would imply earning more money in dollars as the peso rises against the dollar. On the other hand, an exporting firm whose currency appreciates might decide not to raise foreign-currency prices so as not to drive away business. If the dollar rose against the peso, a US software company might decide to hold steady the peso price of its software sold in Argentina—even though this would lower

---

15 This may seem peculiar to many, used to thinking of a depreciation as reducing the foreign price of domestic goods—"making exports more competitive"—but such a setting is inconsistent with perfectly competitive markets in which the exporter has no market power.

the dollar price received per unit. In either case, firms are clearly not price takers, otherwise their prices would not be amenable to their decisions, and they are making pricing policy in a strategic (rather than perfectly competitive) setting.

Why might producers not pass exchange rate changes on to customers? Presumably, when a foreign producer does not lower its price when its currency depreciates, the reason is that the foreign seller is convinced that it will not lose many buyers to competitors who *do* lower prices. This market power might be due to highly differentiated products, high entry barriers, or something else that allows the producer to charge more than the competitive price for the good. In the opposite case—where a foreign-currency appreciation is not passed through to the local buyer in higher prices—the firm is typically attempting to moderate prices in order to avoid losing business. This is presumably driven by a concern about market share, which is rational if the product is one where customer loyalty and reputation are important, such that a temporary loss of market share could have substantial long-term effects. One explanation of Japanese automobile pricing behavior in the example mentioned above—in which prices of Japanese cars exported to the United States were constant even as the yen rose by more than 50 percent against the dollar—is that Japanese producers were concerned that passing through the yen appreciation to US consumers would cost them market share that they had worked laboriously to build up and was in their longer-term interest.

There is strong evidence that pricing to market is common.[16] It varies substantially by product, firm, and country, as one would expect in the case of behavior contingent on a particular strategic environment. But there appear to be many industries in which producers absorb the price effects of exchange rate movements rather than passing them on to consumers.

There are other possible reasons for incomplete pass-through. One is invoicing behavior, in which those trading goods across borders can

---

16 For early studies of the phenomenon, see Fisher 1989; Froot and Klemperer 1989; Knetter 1989, 1993; Marston 1990. Work has continued on the process. For some of the more recent advances, see Gopinath and Itskhoki 2010; Gopinath, Itskhoki, and Rigobon 2010. In the bargaining theory of Linda Goldberg and Cédric Tille (2013), exporters with market power can get contracts written in their own currency. Raphael Brun-Aguerre, Ana-Maria Fuertes, and Matthew Greenwood-Nimmo (2013) show that such exporters are able to have prices respond asymmetrically, always to favor the exporter.

use either producer- or local-currency pricing. Pricing to market is one form of local-currency pricing; Japanese auto manufacturers regarded the prices of their cars sold in the United States as set in local currency (dollars), not producer currency (yen). There are other reasons why goods are invoiced in one currency or another—oil and many other commodities are typically invoiced in dollars no matter where they are produced—and this affects pass-through. So too can menu costs, inventories, and long-term contracts make it difficult to change prices quickly when currencies move.

Whatever the reason, it is well established that while some goods prices directly and immediately incorporate currency movements, others do so slowly, if at all. At one extreme, the local price of a basic commodity or simple manufacture—wheat, coffee, iron ore, basic steel, or apparel—is essentially its world market price times the exchange rate; any change in the exchange rate is reflected in the local price. At the other extreme, the local price of complex differentiated products—telecommunications equipment, machine tools, or airplanes—reflects complex pricing decisions by manufacturers and marketers, and responds to the exchange rate slowly, if at all.

Full pass-through implies unitary elasticity: a one-to-one relationship between the exchange rate and local-currency price of a good traded on world markets. And this is surprisingly hard to find empirically. While there are theoretically grounded reasons why this might be the case, for our purposes all that matters is that it is true and obeys certain regularities. That it is true is unquestioned; the regularities are more debatable, but the general patterns are relatively clear. First, tradability increases the responsiveness of prices to exchange rates. This is at the core of the tradables-nontradables interpretation of the real exchange rate: tradables prices adjust more rapidly than nontradables prices to currency movements, such that after a nominal depreciation, nontradables prices lag tradables to create a rise in the relative price of tradables. Second, among tradable goods there is also variation in local price elasticities with respect to the exchange rate. More concentrated industries in which products are highly differentiated generally have less pass-through; more competitive industries with more standardized products usually have more pass-through.

This lengthy detour is relevant because the extent to which currency movements are passed through to prices affects exchange rate policy preferences. Firms care about the relative price effects of policies;

if a devaluation is not reflected in higher prices for imports, it will not help local import competers. Local automobile or machinery manufacturers concerned about foreign competition will support a devaluation if it raises import prices; if it does not, they have to find other means to achieve these ends. Limited pass-through also affects concerns about currency volatility, for it shifts exchange rate risk among producers and their customers. In the case of local-currency pricing, generally associated with low pass-through, an exporter bears the currency risk if its currency appreciates. The exporter cannot raise local prices and must accept lower home-currency earnings (as the Japanese auto producers did in the case of their US sales after 1985). Other sources of limited pass-through similarly increase exposure to currency risk by one or another of the parties to the transaction, and heighten concern about exchange rate volatility.[17] The fact that limited pass-through forces one party to bear the currency risk is exacerbated by the fact that limited pass-through is primarily a feature of highly differentiated goods for which there are few or no forward markets. In wheat or copper markets, pass-through is nearly complete and forward markets are well developed; while there is currency risk associated with trade in wheat or copper, it is easily hedged. In the market for specialized auto parts or machinery, pass-through is much more limited and there are no real forward markets, and thus either the producer or customer is forced to bear a currency risk that cannot be hedged on the product markets themselves.[18]

I argue that pass-through must be factored into any analysis of exchange rate preferences—just as, for example, the elasticity of import demand is a crucial consideration for the political economy of trade policy. Limited pass-through dampens preferences over the level of the exchange rate and heightens concerns over currency volatility. This means that the expectations stated above, relative to the international exposure of firms and tradability of their products, must be tempered by consideration of the degree to which exchange rate movements are

17 To be sure, every loss is counteracted by an analogous gain, but increasing the currency risk of a sale or purchase is likely actually to reduce the probability that it takes place. So, for example, exporters in markets in which the customer takes the exchange risk (say, with producer-currency pricing) may find demand for their goods dampened as a result.

18 Of course, the currency risk itself can be hedged, but as already mentioned, forward markets for many currencies are expensive and their time horizons are usually quite limited—which is especially a problem for specialized manufactures that are typically contracted for over a relatively long time horizon.

reflected in sectoral prices. Specifically, I expect that the more incomplete a firm's pass-through,

- the greater its support for a fixed exchange rate
- the weaker its preferences over the level of the exchange rate

This implies that concern over the level of the exchange rate will be concentrated in sectors with full or nearly full pass-through, while concern over exchange rate risk will be concentrated in sectors with incomplete pass-through.

The group most likely to find its interests affected by pass-through is exporters, who have conflicting exchange rate policy preferences. Exporters, on the one hand, have international interests, and this leads them to prefer a fixed rate. On the other hand, they are tradables producers, and this leads them to prefer a weak currency, which usually implies not fixing (in order to be able to depreciate). So an exporter must weigh the value of a stable currency against the value of a currency that can depreciate to improve its competitive position. Pass-through is an important determinant of how this trade-off is weighed. If pass-through is complete—the good is raw steel, wheat, or copper—concern over the level is heightened and concern over the regime is dampened, so demand for a weak currency trumps demand for a stable one. If pass-through is incomplete—the good is a machine tool or commercial aircraft—concern over the level is dampened and concern over the regime is heightened, so demand for a stable currency trumps demand for a weak one. Exporters in high pass-through industries will tend to prefer a depreciated floating rate; exporters in low pass-through industries will tend to prefer a fixed rate.

Certainly the incorporation of pass-through (and other factors that influence the price effects of exchange rate movements) is a real complication to any economic or political economy analysis. Nevertheless, it is central to a contemporary understanding of exchange rates, and I believe that it needs to be just as key to our analyses of the political economy of exchange rate policy. While it does complicate analysis, so too do considerations of factor supply and import elasticities in trade policy, asset specificity in contractual analyses, or entry barriers in regulatory policy. Further work on the political economy of exchange rates should build on (and contribute to) our understanding of the relationship between exchange rates and prices, just as work on the political economy of trade builds on other work concerning affected industries.

Observable Implications

Up to now, the analysis has remained at a relatively high level of abstraction. Empirical application depends on translating these conceptual guidelines into observable implications. In what follows I associate values of the explanatory variables explored above with the sectoral characteristics of particular economic activities. Perhaps the easiest way to organize the discussion is to indicate who the strongest supporters of identifiable currency policies are likely to be, and why.

Above I separated the regime and level dimensions for purposes of simplification. But in reality the two are usually linked. A currency cannot, after all, depreciate if it is fixed, so that supporters of a depreciated exchange rate typically also oppose a fixed rate. By the same token, it is difficult for supporters of a fixed exchange rate to also argue for an appreciation or depreciation.[19] So in practice, there is often a single dimension along which exchange rate politics are organized: supporters of a depreciated flexible currency against supporters of a fixed exchange rate. For the former, support for a depreciation outweighs whatever preferences they may have over the regime; for the latter, support for a fixed rate outweighs preferences over its level. This is more empirical observation than theory, yet it allows me to specify the groups most likely to find themselves in each camp.

The principal supporters of a fixed exchange rate are, I anticipate, to be found among those who face substantial foreign exchange risk (high international exposure or limited pass-through). Such supporters are those with important international economic ties: international investors, international financial institutions, multinational corporations, and exporters of specialized manufactured products. The last are worth highlighting, as their presence on the list is due to limited pass-through.

---

19 The exchange rate could depreciate (appreciate) and then be fixed, locking in a depreciated (appreciated) rate. Yet it is likely that those who want a depreciation (appreciation) at one point in time anticipate wanting one again (especially inasmuch as the real depreciation or appreciation may eventually be eroded by domestic price increases or declines); as such, the more common pattern is linked support for a depreciated currency and opposition to a fixed one.

Also supportive of a fixed rate will be, I expect, those with substantial net foreign-currency debts. There are nuances appended to each of these assertions, but the general expectation is that most support for a fixed rate will be drawn from these ranks.

The principal supporters of a depreciated currency are tradables producers (high tradability and high pass-through). Those that compete with imports have unambiguous preferences for a weak, floating exchange rate; both the level and volatility dampen import competition. Tradables producers that produce for export have to weigh the positive effects of a weak currency against the negative effects of currency volatility. As noted above, those in sectors with high pass-through gain more from a depreciation and lose less from volatility. This implies that producers of standardized commodities and manufactured goods will tend to support floating and depreciation, while producers of complex, differentiated manufactures will tend to support a fixed rate.

Many further complexities could be added—as is the case with the derivation of virtually all policy preferences. But this is a reasonable approximation to allow for substantial empirical evaluation. I anticipate an interest group lineup roughly like the following:

> *In favor of a fixed exchange rate*: International investors, international financial institutions, multinational corporations, exporters of specialized manufactures, and those with net foreign-currency liabilities
>
> *In favor a depreciated exchange rate*: Tradables producers, especially import competers as well as producers of simple commodities and manufactures

In the empirical work that follows, I attempt to evaluate the extent to which these expectations are borne out in a wide variety of historical and geographic settings, constrained by limitations of the data.

Other Factors Relevant to Exchange Rate Policy Preferences

Although my primary focus in this book is on these sources of policy preferences, currency politics involves many other considerations.

Some of them are related to those presented above and are worth highlighting.

Exchange Rates in Closed and Open Economies

As I have already discussed above (see the introduction), financial and commercial openness is relevant to the making of currency policy. In line with the trilemma, when capital is mobile across borders, governments must choose between a stable exchange rate and monetary policy independence.

There is another sense in which economic openness heightens the trade-offs involved in exchange rate policy choices. In open economies, the exchange rate is of great interest to a wide variety of economic agents: many of them are exposed to foreign competition in trade, whether in domestic or overseas markets, while others are exposed to the financial effects of currency movements. It is not surprising that in the limiting cases of countries that are inherently exposed to trade—such as the small open economies of Europe or the Caribbean—there has long been a great sensitivity to currency movements. In this sense, in open economies there is likely to be substantial interest in exchange rate policy, and hence substantial real or potential political pressures on policymakers. This makes it important to evaluate the politics of currency policy in light of the degree of financial and commercial openness of the economy in question. While many of the empirical cases are in open economies, some are not, and the differences are well worth noting. The extent of financial and commercial openness affects the macroeconomic effects of currency movements as well as the sensitivity of economic agents to these movements.

Exchange Rate Policy and Trade Policy

Exchange rate and trade policy both affect the relative prices of domestic and foreign goods, so they are potential substitutes. A sector unable to achieve its goal with regard to policy of one type may attempt to influence the other policy. One could think of many reasons why success might be more easily attained on one policy dimension than on another. First, there is the problem of aggregation. A trade barrier affects (in the first instance) only producers and consumers of one good; a currency movement touches almost everyone. This has both advantages and disadvantages for the sectoral interest: there will be little opposition to sector-specific protection, but little support for it either. A steel manufacturer demanding a tariff has only to worry about steel consumers, typically a weak and disunited bunch, but by the same token, it has only its fellow steel manufacturers to ally with. If the steel manufacturer can build a society-wide coalition of all tradables producers in favor of a depreciation, it will have much more powerful supporters, yet at the same time a depreciation is likely to implicate more powerful opponents as well.[20]

This suggests that one consideration in assessing interest group action on the exchange rate is the relative difficulties associated with organizing for and obtaining a favorable currency or trade policy. If an industry is well organized and powerful on its own, and has few coalitional ties with other industries, trade protection would presumably be a more achievable goal than a devaluation. On the other hand, if there is broad support among industries for a devaluation, a coalition in its favor might be easier to organize and more likely to succeed than a series of sector-specific protectionist measures.[21]

Another factor to consider in the substitutability of trade and currency policy is whether other commitments might bind one or the other of the policies. A preexisting trade agreement, for example, can force a sector that would, all else being equal, prefer a sectoral tariff to opt for the second best—a depreciation.[22] But this, too, can go in both directions. For instance, when two countries have signed an agreement to reduce trade barriers between them, one is unlikely to look favorably on another's use of currency depreciation to improve the competitive position of its producers.[23] Both trends are widely observed. The trade liberalizations of the 1980s and 1990s in Latin America stimulated a burst of political economy pressures on the exchange rate, as producers previously protected by trade barriers now refocused their lobbying en-

20 For an excellent survey of the political economy of trade policy, which also raises issues parallel to those mentioned here, see Rodrik 1995.
21 Joanne Gowa (1988), starting from this point, argues that as a result we should expect little interest group activity on currencies compared to trade.
22 For a strong case for this connection, see Copelovitch and Pevehouse 2013.
23 Of course, in principle the depreciation's impact on the partner's economy is ambiguous and might be positive—it provides cheaper imports, after all—but in reality the demands of affected import competers usually outweigh those of import consumers.

ergies on the currency. On the other hand, in the context of the Mercosur regional trade agreement, Brazil's devaluation of 1999 led many in Argentina to argue that the Brazilians were violating the agreement's spirit by using an active exchange rate policy to improve their competitive position. The Brazilians did not respond as Argentine demands grew for increased trade protection, until Argentina finally followed Brazil in devaluing the peso.

All this implies that there will be an interaction between the political economy of a country's trade policy and its currency policy. This applies to the domestic setting—the interest group and institutional lineup for the making of the two policies. It also applies to the international setting—the range of prior commitments or other constraints on one or the other policy instrument. Full analysis of the politics of exchange rates will take the relationship between trade and exchange rate policy into account.

International Factors

My focus has been on the formation of domestic policy preferences. This would seem to ignore the international strategic dimension of national currency policy. After all, one country's exchange rate is only meaningful in relation to that of other countries. There is a long history of international agreements, negotiations, and conflicts over currencies, all of which require systematic analysis of the strategic setting. For this analysis, the preferences of domestic socioeconomic actors are simply raw material—essential raw material, but only one component of the broader picture.

Links to gold or the dollar are only meaningful as they affect the relationship between the home currency and other currencies, and this relationship depends on the decisions of *other* governments. A country that ties the currency to gold alone among nations is in a different position than a country that does so at a time when a worldwide gold standard exists. An explicit link to the dollar means one thing if US monetary conditions are stable, and something quite different if the United States itself is experiencing rampant inflation and currency depreciation. And of course the actual level of the exchange rate is only relevant as it affects its value relative to other currencies, such that one currency's depreciation or appreciation is entirely contingent on what other currencies are doing. The dollar can only decline against the yen, say, if the Japanese currency does not drop by more than the dollar.

There is in fact a substantial literature on the political economy of international monetary regimes themselves, largely cast in terms of understanding the strategic interplay of nation-states with different interests.[24] There is also a literature about how international monetary policies are affected by and affect other relations among countries, whether economic (trade and investment) or not (military and ideological).[25] Most of these studies employ game-theoretical tools to understand the circumstances that would make it more or less likely for self-interested governments to come together to create international monetary arrangements.[26] One common argument, made especially with regard to the classical gold standard, is that there are substantial network externalities associated with a common monetary regime, especially one of fixed nominal rates.[27] An associated contention is that formal as well as informal cooperation among national authorities has been important to the creation and maintenance of such a regime, whether the gold standard or Bretton Woods.[28]

These international analyses have crucial domestic implications. The network externalities associated with a common fixed-rate standard may have a domestic reflection, as those concerned with reducing currency volatility will be more insistent when the gains to associating with an existing zone of monetary stability are greater. Where there is no system of fixed rates with which to affiliate—such as in the early 1930s—demands to stabilize the currency are likely to be weaker; but where a large number of countries have created such a system—whether under the classical gold standard, Bretton Woods, or in the EMS— these demands are likely to strengthen.[29]

No analysis of exchange rate policy outcomes can ignore these international considerations. One way of incorporating this is to assume or assert that domestic actors internalize the strategic (international) implications of their proposed policies. This may be accurate in some instances, but not in others; the question is largely empirical. More

---

24 See Cohen 1977; Eichengreen 1989, 2009; Gallarotti 1995; Kirshner 2003; Oye 1992.
25 See Cohen 1994; Helleiner 2003; Kirshner 1995.
26 For surveys of some of these approaches, see Broz and Frieden 2001, 2013.
27 See, for example, López-Córdova and Meissner 2003.
28 See Eichengreen 1992.
29 See Frieden 1993, 1994b.

generally, though, even those primarily concerned with exploring strategic monetary interaction among governments need to be able to posit the goals of the individual national governments—how highly they value currency stability, how much they prize monetary autonomy, or how strong they would like the national currency to be—before carrying out their analysis. And these national preferences, so to speak, are in turn strongly affected by the interests of domestic groups. In other words, studies that focus on international factors can be seen as *complements* to the work presented here: advances in understanding the domestic politics of currency policy would improve our understanding of interstate interactions, and vice versa.

Credibility

While I have emphasized the distributional effects of currency policy on relative prices and their volatility, it is also the case that in some situations, governments have used the exchange rate importantly or even primarily as a device to signal the government's anti-inflationary resolve. In fact, there have been a number of prominent instances of these so-called exchange-rate-based stabilization programs.[30] If currency policy is used first and foremost as a commitment device, particularistic interest group considerations are likely to be less relevant. There are certainly circumstances in which hyperinflation or broad sociopolitical demands to reduce inflation might dominate special interest concerns. These are best evaluated empirically as they arise, and I attempt to consider them as appropriate.[31]

Other Related Work

Many scholars have addressed the political economy of exchange rate policy in the past twenty-five years. Some of them build on an approach similar to that here, while others develop it in a somewhat-different direction.[32] There has been substantial scholarship on particu-

30 See Alfaro 2002.
31 For an analysis of the anti-inflationary credibility associated with different exchange rate policy announcements, see Guisinger and Singer 2010.
32 For similar approaches, see, for example, Hefeker 1997; Walter 2008, 2013. C. Randall Hen-

lar features of exchange rate policy, such as its connection with immigrant remittances.[33] And there have been many studies of specific episodes in exchange rate history, such as the end of the Bretton Woods system or interwar collapse of the gold standard.[34] And many scholars have analyzed currency politics in particular countries or regions.[35]

Perhaps the single currency experience that has received the most concentrated attention by historians, economists, and political scientists is the gold standard. Indeed, the longest-lived international currency regime in modern history was the classical gold standard, around which the international economy revolved for over forty years, from about 1870 until the 1930s, with an interruption for World War I and its aftermath. This experience is relevant to our purposes, for several reasons. Most obviously, it is a prominent case of the politics of currency policy, since the gold standard was politically controversial for much of its history (I analyze the US controversy over it in chapters 2 and 3). More generally, the gold standard provides an excellent laboratory to evaluate the impact of many of the factors discussed in this study.

The potential contemporary theoretical and empirical relevance of the gold standard has not been lost on social scientists, who have reexamined the economics and political economy of the pre-1914 international monetary regime in recent years. Recent scholarship on the international and domestic causes as well as consequences of the commitment to gold supplies an important background for the work done here.[36]

All these factors and scholarly contributions need to be incorporated into the analysis of exchange rate policy. My emphasis on the distributional preferences of domestic economic actors is not meant to replace but instead complement this work.

---

ning (1994) focuses on relations between banks and industry. Gerald Epstein (1991) takes a class-analytic viewpoint, emphasizing the potentially different interests of labor and capital.

33 See Singer 2010.

34 On Bretton Wood, see Gowa 1982. On the gold standard, see, for example, Eichengreen 1992; Simmons 1994.

35 For an analysis of Latin America, see Roett and Wise 2000. For explorations of transition economies in particular, see Markiewicz 2006; Frieden, Leblang, and Valev 2010. The literature on Europe is far too extensive to cite here; see chapter 4.

36 For prominent examples among these studies, see Eichengreen 1992; Simmons 1994; López-Córdova and Meissner 2003.

Other Scholarship Relevant
to Exchange Rate Policy

In addition to literatures aimed directly at explaining international monetary policy, there are associated literatures of relevance. These include, most prominently, work done by economists about the economic sources and effects of a variety of exchange rate policies. This work underpins many of my arguments and is worth presenting in some detail. In most cases, this scholarship helps illuminate the economic sources and effects of currency policy, without having immediate or direct implications for the formation of the policy preferences on which I focus.

OCAs

I have already noted the large economic literature on OCAs. The most directly relevant conclusion of this literature is that it specifies the conditions under which a nation's welfare would be improved by giving up its own currency. As mentioned above (see introduction), useful as this may be as a notional baseline for policy, it is somewhat limited. First, its explanatory power depends on the extent to which governments pursue maximizing aggregate social welfare. Second, there are continuing debates over the theory and measurement of the principal OCA criteria. Third, most currency policy debates are about measures that fall far short of giving up the national currency. Nonetheless, inasmuch as the OCA literature is the only economic literature of direct relevance to currency choice, it is important to keep in mind.

Trade and Exchange Rates

Much of my argument rests on assertions about how currency movements might affect international trade. For example, I contend that those favorable to commercial integration will be more likely to support a fixed exchange rate to stabilize currency values; for this to hold, it should be the case that in fact stable currencies do increase trade among countries.

Economists have evaluated the impact of exchange rates on cross-border trade and investment. Until relatively recently, many economists assumed or asserted that currency risk was empirically unimportant for economic activity. Forward markets and a wide variety of other financial instruments, it was argued, provide opportunities for firms and others to protect themselves against exchange rate volatility. Indeed, most estimates of the static welfare effects of the adoption of a single currency by EU countries calculated the total benefits to be at most a couple percentage points of European output. More recent research, however, has tended to establish that currency risk has a significant impact on trade. The most striking result is that of Andrew Rose (2000), who found that sharing a currency roughly tripled trade between two countries. While this magnitude is controversial, most recent work finds a substantial effect of currency volatility on international trade. For example, Michael Klein and Jay Shambaugh (2006) found that a currency peg increased bilateral trade by 36 percent—an appreciable quantity.

There may be many reasons for the impact of currency volatility on trade and investment. Forward contracts can be costly, especially in minor currencies, and typically do not extend to the medium and long term (over three years) more relevant to firms engaged in complex trade, investment, and other strategic decisions.[37] There may also be network externalities associated with the use of a common (or fixed) currency. In any case, whether currency volatility is costly to particular economic agents is an empirical question. The general claim that support for fixed rates comes especially from those heavily involved in international trade and payments is one that can be evaluated by looking at the politics of currency policy.[38] The growing literature on the economic impact of currency movements is a useful background to this.

---

37 For two economic arguments that exchange rate volatility is costly, see Hefeker 1997, especially chapter 4; Neumeyer 1996. The former stresses the costs of hedging and uncertainty to particular firms; the latter focuses on the impact of currency volatility on the efficiency of financial markets.

38 Evidence that this is indeed the case should lead some economists to consider how this fact might be incorporated into their macro- and microeconomic models. In fact, approaches that concentrate on irreversibilities in investment do help explain the impact of exchange rates, and I make use of both theoretical and empirical studies in this vein below.

Pass-Through and the Impact
of Exchange Rates on Prices

The explanations presented here emphasize the impact of pass-through on the politics of currency policy, which makes the literature on pass-through and related topics important to the present study. Over the past twenty-five years, in fact, there has been a tremendous increase in the analysis of the impact of exchange rate movements on sectoral prices—either directly or as seen through their influence on employment, production, profitability, or investment. These analyses tend to show that the factors discussed above do indeed have a significant impact on industry-specific reactions to exchange rate movements.

Among the most detailed empirical analyses are those that Linda Goldberg and her coauthors carried out.[39] They look at the response of sectoral investment to exchange rate movements in several countries over nearly thirty years. For example, José Campa and Goldberg (1995) examine the US experience from 1972 to 1986. They distinguish between the impact of export exposure and imported input exposure by industry—how crucial foreign sales and foreign inputs are, respectively, to the industry. The scholars also differentiate between low- and high-markup industries; a high markup over costs should be closely correlated with the degree of pricing to market or other pass-through-reducing behavior. Low-markup sectors are those typically associated with simple manufactures. In the United States, they are primary and fabricated metals, transportation equipment, food and kindred products, textiles, apparel, lumber, furniture, paper, petroleum and coal products, and leather products. The authors do indeed find the expected effects. A depreciation (appreciation) of the US dollar increases (decreases) sectoral investment the more the industry exports, and decreases (increases) it the more the industry uses imported inputs. Perhaps more important, high-markup sectors show little or no responsiveness to exchange rate movements, while low-markup sectors are quite responsive. Results differ across the countries they examine, which demonstrates the importance of market and industry structures. Other work along these lines has similarly demonstrated significant

---

39 See, for example, Goldberg 1993, 1997; Goldberg and Kolstad 1995; Goldberg and Campa 1996; Campa and Goldberg 1995, 1999. On related issues, see Goldberg and Tille 2008, 2013.

differences in the ways in which exchange rate movements affect industries.[40]

A related body of work focuses on documenting and understanding the relative nonresponsiveness of prices to exchange rate movements. Foremost in this vein has been the work of Charles Engel and his coauthors.[41] Engel (2002, 231–32) and his collaborators have shown convincingly that, as he puts it, "Consumer prices in rich countries are not much affected by nominal exchange rate changes in the short run." Detailed studies demonstrate that the effects vary by country, by good, and in line with other factors. One of the considerations that Engel and others have recently underscored is the currency denomination of international trade, in which there is a choice between setting prices in the currency of the producer or local currency, with obvious implications for susceptibility to exchange rate movements.[42]

There is no need to go into more detail on these issues here, other than to conclude that there is a large and growing literature that investigates the extent to which prices move in response to currency movements. And while it may seem daunting that understanding the impact of currency movements on industries requires a detailed knowledge of the country's and industry's economic structure and organization, this does not make exchange rate policy different from trade policy—and most regulatory policies. In all cases, the particular impact of policy depends on a myriad of factors. Were the policies in question of trivial importance, some might question the justifiability of an analytic enterprise that requires such detailed knowledge, but actuality these policies have a substantial impact on national economies. Indeed, the differentiated impact of currency movements on industries is crucial for a wide variety of macroeconomic, microeconomic, and distributional concerns. Thirty years ago there was virtually no information available about the economic effects of exchange rate movements; now there is a wealth of data and analysis. This can only assist those interested in studying the *politics* of currency policy in greater depth.

---

40 For a summary of much of the literature, see Burstein and Gopinath 2014. For other examples, see Anderton 2003; Eusufzai 1997; Forbes 2002a, 2002b; Kandil and Mirzaei 2002; Lee 1997; Parsley 1995. While the findings are not always consistent across investigations, regularities do emerge, as indicated in the text.

41 For examples and surveys, see Engel 2000, 2002, 2014; Devereux and Engel 2002; Engel and Rogers 2001.

42 See also Bacchetta and van Wincoop 2005.

All these literatures are critical to the accurate analysis of the politics of exchange rate policy. It is impossible to do all of them justice in one study, but further work in this area will need to incorporate the insights of scholars working in all these areas and more.

Conclusions

The preferences of socioeconomic actors are a key component of any attempt to explain national exchange rate policies. In this study, I start with the expected distributional effects of the choice of exchange rate regime along with the level of the real exchange rate to project the anticipated policy preferences of firms, industries, and groups. I argue that support for a stable, including fixed, currency will be increasing in the extent of an economic agent's involvement in cross-border economic activities as well as its reliance on long-term contracts in foreign currency, including foreign-currency debt. I also contend that support for a depreciated currency will be increasing in the tradability of an actor's output and the nontradability of its inputs, yet decreasing in the degree of its foreign-currency liabilities. Both dimensions of these policy preferences are affected by the extent of pass-through—the degree to which currency movements are reflected in domestic prices. The greater the pass-through is, the weaker are preferences over both the stability and level of the exchange rate. On this basis, I anticipate that the principal supporters of a fixed exchange rate will be found among international investors, international financial institutions, multinational corporations, exporters of specialized manufactured products, and those with substantial net foreign-currency debts. The main supporters of a depreciated currency will be found among tradables producers, particularly producers of standardized commodities and manufactured goods. The remainder of this book is devoted to analyses of the making of currency policy in practice, as an attempt to evaluate the accuracy of these theoretically grounded expectations.

The United States: From Greenbacks to Gold, 1862–79

For much of the late nineteenth and early twentieth centuries, the United States was a hotbed of exchange rate controversy. A succession of US movements for international monetary alternatives—paper currency (greenbacks), a silver standard, bimetallism, and a variety of related schemes—were the global focal point of opposition to the gold standard. US currency activists sponsored a series of international monetary conferences that attempted to create a counterpoint to the international gold standard. Several presidential elections revolved around gold, and two significant third parties were formed to oppose it. The victory of the progold candidate in 1896 was a watershed in international monetary developments, signaling the triumph of the gold standard and paving the way for its adoption in most of the rest of the developing world.

The politics of gold, silver, and greenbacks in the United States was central to the nation's political and economic development. Since the nation's founding, its economy had been oriented toward agricultural exports, but its urban industrializing, commercial, and financial sectors were growing rapidly. The US political economy was riven by conflicts between these two powerful blocs, which often took on regional characteristics, pitting the Northeast and Midwest against the South and West. After the Civil War settled one great divide, slavery, US politics revolved largely around the country's connection to the world economy, particularly the closely linked exchange rate and trade policies. From the 1860s through the 1920s, this great complex of policies—the gold standard and tariff—was the central dividing line of US economic policy debates.[1]

From the standpoint of currency politics, the US experience is a canonical example of the political economy of exchange rate regime choice. The debates took place in a classical open economy, during the "first era of globalization" in the decades before 1914. The policy alternatives ran the spectrum from a floating (paper) currency to a fixed (gold) standard, with the typical trade-off implied by the trilemma, between stability and flexibility. The political debates were protracted and divisive. This allows us to evaluate the theoretical arguments made in chapter 1 against the rich US historical record. Between the 1860s and the 1930s, debates over US currency policy were frequent and frequently bitter; there is a great deal of electoral and legislative evidence about the divisions over the country's exchange rate regime. This is valuable evidence for the assessment of the sources of exchange rate policy preferences.

The theoretical perspective developed in chapter 1 focuses on three factors: exposure to exchange rate risk, tradability, and pass-through. US foreign trade interests in the late nineteenth century were dominated by producers of commodities and simple manufactures—the country was almost exclusively an exporter of raw materials—and what little evidence exists indicates that pass-through was substantial, so that variation on this dimension is unlikely to have mattered much. But the other two factors should have been central to the debates. I expect that those with substantial international exposure—the international finan-

---

1 This is closely related to Richard Bensel's (2000) central thesis in his masterly study with broader interpretative ambitions than my work here, but whose emphases are consistent with mine.

cial and commercial sectors—would have been strong supporters of a fixed rate under the gold standard; those without international exposure, nontradables producers, should have been largely indifferent and perhaps even hostile to the fixed-rate gold regime. The hostility of nontradables producers may have been tempered by the fact that a depreciated dollar would have moved relative prices against them.

By the same token, I expect tradables producers to have been the core constituency for devaluing, which implied going or staying off gold, given the expected benefits they would receive from the relative price effects of a dollar depreciation. Trade policy was a potential alternative. Tradables producers for which protection was economically and politically feasible, such as import competers organized enough to obtain tariffs, had less reason to worry about the exchange rate.

I find substantial support for the theory. The principal supporters of the gold standard in the United States were the international financial and commercial communities of the country's large cities. Gold's principal opponents were in the tradables sectors: manufacturing, agriculture, and mining; nontradables producers also mobilized against gold at times. The position of manufacturing is especially interesting. In the early years of the debates, before 1873, import-competing manufacturers were at the forefront of antigold (progreenback) sentiment. After 1873, farm prices began to decline; meanwhile, manufacturers concentrated their political efforts on obtaining tariff protection. This path was not open to the country's export-oriented farmers and miners, who remained the main proponents of a depreciated currency and floating rate against gold.

In this part of the book, I provide both qualitative and quantitative evidence to these effects. In the current chapter, I survey US currency policy from the Civil War until the country returned to the gold standard in 1879. The next chapter deals with the 1890s. In each chapter, I present both a chronology and analysis of events, and an examination of electoral and legislative behavior that permits a statistical evaluation of the strength of my argument. Congressional votes on antigold (and progold) bills are particularly instructive.

Whether one looks at the 1860s, 1870s, or 1890s, the country appears clearly divided. Globally exposed progold forces, on the one hand, were concentrated in the international financial and commercial centers. On the other hand, there were the tradables producers, especially export producers in the nation's agricultural and raw materials sectors.

Manufacturers' interests evolved over the sixty-year period. For one thing, US industry became more productive as well as more internationally oriented. For another, those manufacturers concerned about their competitive position were able to get tariff protection that dampened their desire for a depreciated dollar. There were, to be sure, many other factors at work—partisan, regional, coalitional, and otherwise. But the pattern of winners and losers from exchange rate regime choices identified in chapter 1 holds up well, and illuminates the period. It also allows us to view this foundational period in US political development in much broader historical, comparative, and economic perspective.

Analytic Expectations

The classical gold standard was the quintessential fixed-rate currency regime, in a quintessential integrated world economy. The government of a country "on gold" committed itself to exchange its currency for a fixed amount of gold on demand. A currency that was thus "as good as gold" stood in a predetermined relationship to all other gold-backed currencies. The advantages of being on gold were severalfold. First, international financial markets regarded membership in the gold club as indicative of financial probity; countries on gold had better access, at lower interest rates, to the booming loan markets of London, Paris, and Berlin.[2] Second, the gold link's stability made international trade, investment, travel, and migration more predictable. Countries on gold were more tightly integrated into the booming world economy on almost every level.

These were powerful attractors for the United States in the nineteenth century. In this period, the United States relied heavily on capital inflows from abroad and sales of primary products—such crops as cotton, tobacco, and wheat, and such minerals as copper and silver—to Europe. Although US industry was growing, the country was overwhelmingly agrarian, and its agriculture was heavily export oriented. The international financial sector specialized, in fact, in selling US investments—the bonds of local, state, and federal governments as well as the bonds and stocks of major private corporations—to European

2   Bordo and Rockoff 1996.

savers. Not surprisingly, the sectors of the economy that relied on international financial and commercial intermediation—especially the nation's banking and trading centers—were strong supporters of the gold standard.

But there were costs to being on gold. The "gold price"—the exchange rate—could not be varied without losing the confidence of the international community. This effectively removed monetary policy from control of the government: the currency's value could not be changed, and given the high levels of capital mobility, national interest rates had to simply follow world rates. These costs were not insubstantial, particularly as during the late nineteenth century, prices of many goods—and especially primary products—declined dramatically. Today, when a country's principal commodity's price declines significantly, the consensus advice is to cushion this term of trade shock with a devaluation to keep the domestic price of the shocked commodity more stable. This policy was not available to a country on gold. And this in turn is almost certainly why, faced with the trilemma, virtually every commodity producer chose a flexible exchange rate. Practically every country whose economy depended on commodity exports was off the gold standard for most of the late nineteenth century. The only exceptions were the British Dominions—Canada, Australia, New Zealand, and South Africa—with their imperial ties to London, and the United States.

The trade-offs between monetary stability and monetary autonomy, and between a stable exchange rate and a "competitive" one, were acutely felt in the United States. The arguments presented in chapter 1 lead to the expectations that those most exposed to currency volatility should have been the strongest supporters of the gold standard, while tradables producers (assuming substantial pass-through) should have been its strongest opponents. To apply this accurately to the US context between the 1860s and 1890s, we need to know about the country's economic structure, which evolved over these thirty years. We nonetheless can make two broad generalizations. First, the most internationally exposed economic groups were the nation's large financial and commercial sectors based in the urban Northeast. The international financial community was largely oriented toward foreign borrowing, for which being on the gold standard was crucial.[3] Second, the tradables

3 Ibid.

producers most concerned about the level of the exchange rate were primary producers. Pass-through was effectively complete in agricultural and mineral products, and the country was a substantial net exporter of primary commodities, so that tariff protection would be of limited value to these producers because much of what they produced was sold on foreign markets. Pass-through was probably also substantial in manufactured goods (data are hardly available), but more important was the fact that many manufacturers competed with imports and could benefit greatly from trade protection—if they could get it.

One reason the battle over gold was so bitter in the United States, and its outcome so often in doubt, was that the country's economic structure made both of the principal sets of protagonists powerful. The United States was the world's leading primary producer, with enormous exports of farm products and raw materials. At the same time, the nineteenth-century United States was the world's largest debtor, and the country's international financial sector was vital and powerful. The gold standard pitted the Wall Street of August Belmont, J. P. Morgan, and their colleagues against the Main Streets of countless farming and mining communities. The outcome was never certain; the political clout of the nation's agrarian majority could not be ignored, nor could the influence of the country's financial and commercial classes.

Many scholars have explored the US movements against gold; specifically, the Populist movement of the 1890s has been the focus of a great deal of attention.[4] Yet scholars have typically treated the movements' economic and political economy components only superficially, centering instead on regional, class, cultural, and religious factors. And most of the historical analyses deal with the movements as if they were purely US phenomena.[5] This would no doubt have seemed strange to the Greenback and Populist activists themselves, whose grievances were almost entirely economic and whose perspective was international. Even when scholars do notice the economic aspects of the struggle over gold in the United States, it is usually to concentrate on closed-

---

4 For one of the earliest examples of this scholarship, see especially Goodwyn 1976.
5 An exception is the relevant portion (chapter 6) of Bensel's (2000) study of US industrialization. His treatment is outstanding, viewing this as an important episode in the country's political and economic development. The older historical literature on the Greenback era, especially by Irwin Unger and Robert Sharkey, is better informed economically than the later literature on the Populist period. But even these last two pay little or no heed to the international aspects of the phenomenon.

economy monetary considerations, such as to assert that it pitted proinflation debtors against anti-inflation creditors.

Scholars have mostly ignored two central features of the conflicts. For one, the US controversies were global in nature; they were the local reflection of similar conflicts going on in almost every country. Second, the main policy target of all sides in the debates was national exchange rate policy.

The various forms of exceptionalism applied to the study of US populism and similar movements against the gold standard downplay the general, comparable, and global features of the movements. This is to ignore most of the political economic context at home and abroad, and separate artificially the issue of US adherence to the gold standard from what was a worldwide dispute over exchange rate policy. The empirical analyses in this chapter and the next allow not only an evaluation of my argument but also a comparison to the applicability of other common ones, such as that the division was primarily between debtors and creditors, or that economic factors were of little importance to it.

In what follows, I trace the course of the US politics of the gold standard from the Civil War to 1879; in the next chapter, I look at the period from the 1880s through the 1890s. In so doing, I evaluate the applicability and usefulness of the above assertions, and when possible, subject them to more rigorous statistical tests.

From Civil War to Contraction, 1865–69

Although it is well known that Americans engaged in heated political battles over the gold standard during the Populist era of the 1890s, it is less widely understood that these continued a conflict that began after the Civil War and lasted from 1865 until 1879. The earlier controversy was, at least initially, one of the "purest" monetary debates of the gold standard era, for the policy choice was between two textbook extremes. On one side were supporters of a paper currency not backed by specie (precious metal), with a floating rate against gold-backed currencies; on the other side were supporters of a return to the pre–Civil War fixed rate to gold. This conflict is also significant, both politically and economically, because the Greenback period, during which the United States was off gold, was the reference point for subsequent debates over the gold standard: both pro- and antigold forces looked back on these

TABLE 2.1
Dollar-to-sterling exchange rates, 1862–78

1/31/1862	5.0399	6/30/1870	5.435
6/30/1862	5.3076	1/31/1871	5.4078
1/31/1863	7.7802	6/30/1871	5.4992
6/30/1863	7.1267	1/31/1872	5.3499
1/30/1864	7.6373	6/29/1872	5.5323
6/30/1864	12.0428	1/31/1873	5.5295
1/31/1865	10.0516	6/30/1873	5.6208
6/30/1865	6.8158	1/31/1874	5.4229
1/31/1866	6.834	6/30/1874	5.4078
6/30/1866	7.4634	1/30/1875	5.5023
1/31/1867	6.5821	6/30/1875	5.6968
6/29/1867	6.731	1/31/1876	5.502
1/31/1868	6.8345	6/30/1876	5.4717
6/30/1868	6.8254	1/31/1877	5.128
1/30/1869	6.6279	6/30/1877	5.1251
6/30/1869	6.6701	1/31/1878	4.9638
1/31/1870	5.9006	6/29/1878	4.8998

fifteen years for an indication of what it would mean to be off the gold standard.

The issue was joined because during the Civil War, the United States went off gold and the federal government financed part of the war effort by issuing fiat currency (greenbacks)—paper money not backed by gold.[6] By 1865, this and related measures had driven the money supply up to about 215 percent of its 1862 level, and prices rose accordingly (at their high point in early 1865, wholesale prices were also 215 percent of their 1862 level). The price of gold—that is, the nominal exchange rate of the greenback—skyrocketed, reaching 285

6   There are several major sources on the politics and economics of the greenback period. The most important are two outstanding studies: Unger 1964; Sharkey 1959. The account that follows draws primarily on these two, with supplementary material from Weinstein 1970; Friedman and Schwartz 1963, 15–88; Sundquist 1983, 106–33; Barrett 1931; Calomiris 1988; Ritter 1997. Because Sharkey and Unger in particular are so complete, and I have relied on them so heavily, I eschew specific references except to particular facts or citations. Sharkey's analysis, which I found especially impressive, stops in 1870. The Milton Friedman and Anna Jacobson Schwartz treatment is detailed and complete, but focuses on the macroeconomic issues rather than their connection to politics. In what follows, I ignore many of the important and fascinating economic issues of the episode—such as the interrelationship of the exchange rate, interest rates, and the payments balance—which are dealt with in the economics literature.

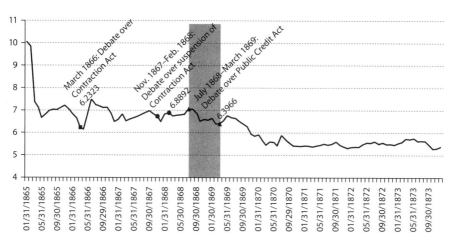

Figure 2.1 Dollar-to-sterling exchange rate, 1865–73. *Source*: Table 2.1.

percent of the prewar parity in 1864. Another way of seeing this is through the nominal exchange rate of the greenback against the pound sterling, which averaged $4.86/£ before the Civil War, but had dropped to a low point of $12.04 in June 1864 (see table 2.1 and figure 2.1).[7] The fact that the country was on a pure fiat currency system (greenbacks) meant that monetary policy was made by the secretary of the treasury, who could manage the money supply in line with the government's macroeconomic and fiscal goals. This task was simplified by the passage of the 1863 National Banking Act, which gave the federal government greater powers over bank regulation and the character of bank reserves.

Another major source of war finance was borrowing, and by 1865 the federal government had amassed a debt of $2.8 billion, equal to one-half of the US gross national product. A large proportion of the bonded debt was in so-called 5–20s (the government had the option to call them in five years and was required to redeem them after twenty) at 6 percent interest. The bonds' issuing documents specified that interest was to be paid in gold (which at the height of the greenback depreciation, meant that effective interest payments were well over 12 percent), but they were ambiguous as to whether the principal was to be repaid in gold-backed or paper currency.

7   For one set of data for the greenback period, see Officer 1981, 649.

It was generally accepted that governments at war would suspend convertibility to gold to allow inflationary financing of the war effort, avoid war-driven speculation against the currency, or both. Once the war ended, the government had to devise a policy to restore normalcy to the country's monetary standard. This set of problems was, along with Reconstruction, the key dividing line in US politics from 1865 until 1879.

The Issues

After the Civil War ended, the federal government faced two interrelated macroeconomic issues. The first one had to do with the monetary standard. The country was on a fiat currency with a floating exchange rate against the pound sterling and other gold-backed currencies, and the government had several options. It could continue the greenback standard indefinitely, keeping the country on a floating exchange rate. This had the advantage of giving the government the ability to affect macroeconomic conditions, but it deviated from the prevailing financial and monetary orthodoxy inasmuch as it implied a peacetime decision to stay off gold.

On the other hand, the government could restore the pre-1862 gold value of the currency ("resume" dollar convertibility to gold at the prior rate). To do so meant forcing prices down approximately to their 1862 levels, implying a severe deflation. A return to gold at the prewar parity would signal fiscal and financial responsibility to investors, especially the foreign investors and lenders on which the US economy depended heavily, yet would make it impossible for the government to use monetary policy for macroeconomic purposes.[8]

There were several intermediate options. One was to go back to gold, but at a depreciated exchange rate. This would avoid deflation, allowing prices to remain at the level to which they had risen during the war, although it would not have provided one of the principal benefits of going back to gold—attractiveness to foreign investors—as the depreciation meant that pre–Civil War assets would be reduced in value. Another intermediate option was to stay on greenbacks, but keep their supply constant. In the context of a rapidly growing economy, this

8 On the signaling value of the gold standard, see Bordo and Rockoff 1996.

implied a restrictive monetary policy, and would have led prices to decline continually, but at a gradual rate. After ten or fifteen years, prices—including the market price of gold—would have returned to 1861 levels, and the dollar could at that point go back to gold. (The debate became even more complicated after 1873, with the rise of the silver issue, which I'll explore more below.)

There was merit in all the monetary proposals. Greenbacks provided monetary flexibility, which was especially valuable for a rapidly growing economy whose main products were primary commodities with volatile prices. Gold supplied a nominal anchor and a signal to foreign investors whose capital was desperately needed. A rapid deflation would restore the country to gold quickly, but would impose substantial adjustment costs; a more gradual deflation would reduce the costs, yet also limit the immediate benefits of going back to gold. Of course, each of the options had substantially different distributional implications and gave rise to conflicting sets of political pressures.

There was a second, related macroeconomic policy question: whether to pay the principal on the bonded debt in (depreciated) greenbacks or the more valuable gold-backed dollars. The 5–20 bonds issued by the federal government could, in principle, be redeemed either in greenbacks or "gold dollars." The difference to a bondholder between being paid off in greenbacks or in gold dollars depended on the price level as well as on the exchange rate. Gold dollars were always more valuable than greenbacks, so holders of government bonds had a strong interest in recognition of their bonds in gold dollars. Again, there were valid arguments on both sides. The bonds had been purchased with depreciated greenbacks, so redeeming them in greenbacks made sense. On the other hand, the federal government was anxious to restore its creditworthiness, and recognizing the gold value of its bonded debt was sure to help. The bond and monetary questions were linked: although it would have been possible in theory for the government to service these bonds in gold dollars without returning to the prewar gold parity, it is hard to see how that could have been justified, while servicing them in greenbacks would have injected more paper currency into the money supply. So Greenbackers tended to oppose gold payments on bonds, while gold bugs tended to support them.

The terms of the controversy are somewhat unfamiliar to modern ears. The relative value of the greenback was typically measured as the gold price or in gold dollars, despite the fact that gold dollars existed solely as a unit of account; economic agents knew how much the pre-1862 dollar was worth in gold (and pounds sterling, for example) and quoted greenbacks at a discount against the gold dollar.[9] So there are common references to the dollar trading at some fraction of parity or a discount against gold, or gold trading at a premium (over greenbacks). These were simply ways of expressing the value of the paper currency against gold. Perhaps the most common form was to speak of the gold price or the "gold premium"—that is, the premium of gold dollars over greenbacks. A decline in the gold price (premium) was an appreciation of the greenback, for the lower the gold price (premium), the closer the greenback's value was to the value of a gold dollar. The relationship with imports and exports was as clear then as it is today, when we would speak of depreciation and appreciation. For instance, an 1872 retrospective on the early postwar experience explained (quite accurately) "the extraordinary increase in the exportation of many articles of domestic produce" as due to "the fact that the premium on gold often rose with great rapidity"—in other words, the greenback frequently depreciated substantially against gold, "the effect of which was to increase the purchasing power of the foreign consumer . . . or, what was the same thing, to decrease the relative cost of such articles of American product as were available for export and sale in a foreign market."[10]

The matter is simplified by expressing the dollar's value in terms of the pound sterling, which was fixed to gold throughout the period. Table 2.1 presents the nominal dollar-to-sterling exchange rate for this time, showing the dramatic depreciation during the Civil War and variegated course of appreciation after the war ended. Figure 2.1 displays the exchange rate movement graphically, and also indicates the timing of important debates over monetary legislation.

Another term of significance to the debates is *contraction*. This was the policy of reducing the money supply to force prices down and was a necessary prerequisite to Resumption. Contraction was, in other words, the monetary policy that had to be followed in order to restore the United States to gold. It implied strong deflation, and was associ-

---

9 Gold coins were minted, but they did not circulate except in the Far West, where they were valued solely in terms of the market price of their gold content.

10 Quoted in Sharkey 1959, 150n33. Frank D. Graham (1922) includes a fascinating discussion of the impact of the exchange rate on price movements of what he calls export, import, and domestic commodities, confirming the relative price movements examined here.

ated with depressed business conditions, high unemployment, and other recessionary trends. Supporters of gold regarded contraction as either necessary and salutary, or a necessary evil; opponents regarded it as both evil and unnecessary.

International Factors

The US debate took place in the context of the first truly integrated international economy, of which the gold standard was a central component. Great Britain and its colonies had been on gold since 1717, with a break for the Napoleonic Wars. Over the course of the nineteenth century, Britain's international economic predominance meant that the gold standard exerted a powerful pull on other nations that were engaged in, or wanted to be engaged in, international trade and investment. For several decades, most other countries were on a bimetallic standard in which gold and silver traded at a set rate. In the late 1860s and early 1870s, though, major silver discoveries began to drive the price of silver down against gold. The prospects of instability in the gold-to-silver price led most governments to decide in favor of one or the other. After some attempts to negotiate an international bimetallic standard—attempts in which the United States participated—most industrial countries switched to gold. By 1875, Germany, Norway, Sweden, Denmark, and the Netherlands had adopted the gold standard, and France, Belgium, and Switzerland were moving toward it. At this point it was clear that participation in the gold standard was central to full membership in the club of developed nations that dominated the classical open world economy.

The US implications of these international trends were contradictory. On the one hand, the industrialized nations at the center of the world economy were committed to gold; as a rich industrializing nation, the United States might be expected to comply. On the other hand, the movement toward gold coincided with the beginning of a long-term decline in prices of primary products, and as a result, almost all commodity producers remained on silver or paper money in order to be able to counteract the adverse price trends with currency depreciation. As the world's most important commodity producer and exporter, the United States might be expected to go along with countries with similar production profiles (say, Latin America and Russia).

The US debates reflected a fundamental set of choices over what kind of political economy it was or wanted to be. Like every other country, the United States had to decide what to do about the emergence of a fixed-rate international monetary system. Unlike most other countries, the United States was a hybrid: both a powerful industrial nation and massive primary producer. Each feature of the country was associated with particular regions and groups, and the battle over gold divided the nation more or less evenly. Rejecting the gold standard meant rejecting the vision of globalization represented by British industry and finance; accepting it meant adopting the British notion of a liberal international political economy. The US debate over gold reflected a much broader national and global conflict.

The Interests

The debate over Resumption was about both the currency regime and its desired level. Those who wanted to return to gold wanted both a fixed exchange rate and real appreciation in order to restore the pre–Civil War parity. Which issue was predominant varied over time and among groups. While the most committed monetary activists on both sides tended to support gold or greenbacks on principle, most participants focused on more pragmatic issues, which changed over the fifteen years during which the issue was debated. What follows summarizes the interest group lineup in the context of the arguments made in chapter 1.

Internationally oriented commercial and financial interests. These interests were the strongest and most consistent supporters of gold. Their economic interests were closely tied to the country's integration into the British-led international order, and they backed both free trade and the gold standard. The New York Chamber of Commerce complained about the risk attached to a floating exchange rate: "Prudent men will not willingly embark their money or their merchandise in ventures to distant markets ... with the possibility of a fall [in gold] ere their return can be brought to market."[11] This is clearly consistent with the expectation that exposure to exchange rate risk—which an Eastern business newspaper called "almost as uncertain as a ticket in a lot-

---

11 Quoted in Unger 1964, 151.

tery"—would be associated with support for a fixed rate.[12] For the international financial sector, whose business consisted of intermediating between foreign investors and the US economy, adherence to the gold standard was crucial: it was an important determinant of a country's access to foreign capital, and thus the size of its business.

Nontradables producers. Two crucial nontradables groups were significant in their opposition to gold: railroad magnates and businesspeople from the interior. There was a railroad-building boom after the war ended, and when it slowed the railroad owners blamed—probably with some justification—the restrictive monetary policies of contraction. As one newspaper declared in 1874, "The strongest influence at work in Washington upon the currency proceeded from the railroads. . . . The great inflationists after all are the great trunk railroads."[13] Railroad workers, the largest segment of the embryonic labor movement, also tended strongly toward greenbacks. The railroad hub of Toledo, Ohio, for example, was a stronghold of the greenback movement, and within it neighborhoods with large numbers of railroad workers were the most fervently progreenback.[14]

More generally, businesspeople far from the coasts, whose operations were entirely domestic—in wholesale and retail trade, small-town banking, real estate, and the like—were early supporters of paper currency. They regarded the gold standard as irrelevant or harmful to their interests. As a Chicago merchant put it, "These gentlemen on the seaboard base all their calculations on gold, to bring them to par with foreign countries, leaving us in the West to take care of ourselves."[15] Economic activity in the interior was not exposed to exchange rate movements; the gold standard implied a surrender of monetary independence, which was not appealing; and the return to gold required a real appreciation and contractionary monetary conditions, for which nontradables producers saw no reason.

Tradables producers. All else being equal, I expect tradables producers to support a depreciated currency, opposing the appreciation necessary for the United States to return to gold. This might be tempered for

---

12 Quoted in Unger 1959, 47.
13 Quoted in Unger 1964, 222.
14 John Wegner (1995, 136–40) shows that in the fifth ward, where over one-quarter of the adult male population was constituted of railroad workers, the Greenback Party's candidate for governor received 59 percent of the vote in 1877.
15 Quoted in Unger 1964, 157.

producers of goods with incomplete pass-through concerned about exchange rate volatility, but these would almost certainly have been rare in the nineteenth-century United States. In fact, almost all tradables producers strongly opposed the return to gold, with varying degrees of vehemence among themselves and over time. Three broad groups of tradables producers are relevant: manufacturers, farmers, and miners.

Only some portions of US manufacturing were sensitive to import competition or concerned about exporting. Transport costs made many imports prohibitively expensive, and many US industries grew up precisely because distance from Europe provided natural protection. Tariffs were also quite high, especially after the Civil War. To some extent these tariffs were for revenue purposes, but they had a protective effect. This meant that many US manufacturers did not have to worry about foreign competition (and there were virtually no manufactured exports).

Nonetheless, as US industrialization took hold, some of the country's key industries faced significant import competition. The country's two most important industries had strong views on monetary matters. Both textiles and iron were large, geographically concentrated—in New England and Pennsylvania, respectively—and politically active.

US iron makers were particularly staunch supporters of greenbacks and opponents of Resumption. They saw a depreciated currency as a complement to trade protection, which they had long demanded. Henry Carey, the country's best-known economic thinker and a stalwart protectionist whose ideas were extremely popular among the manufacturing interests, agitated continually for greenbacks. He gave the example of how a floating currency protected the United States from the effects of the 1866 Overend-Gurney panic in London: "The crash was terrific, yet it never affected our domestic operations for even a single hour. Our monetary independence had been established. Our machinery of exchange being a non-exportable one, we had no use for gold, and if it were needed abroad, we could say 'Why let it go!'"[16] More to the point, the ironworkers' trade journal complained in 1867, "If gold is at a premium [i.e., the currency is depreciated], then iron can be made to profit, but if it descends much below its present point [i.e., appreciates], then can the British come in at prices that render its pro-

16 Quoted in Sharkey 1959, 154.

duction unprofitable."[17] The iron manufacturers were firm opponents of gold and contraction. One of the most active leaders of the progreenback forces in Congress, in fact, was Pennsylvania's William D. Kelley, known as "Pig Iron" Kelley because of his close association with the iron industry.

The import-competing industrialists, not surprisingly, saw the gold standard as a tool of their principal competitors, the British. Joseph Wharton of Bethlehem Iron Company charged: "The contraction and resumption policy was probably urged upon [Treasury Secretary Hugh] McCulloch by our English enemies." Then the return to gold was "nothing more in the interest of those . . . enemies and more deadly to the soldiers and champions of the nation who are in mine, mill and farm desperately fighting for her independence." Another industrialist pleaded: "What we want is *rest*, breathing time . . . to develop our resources—*dig out* our coal and *iron* and manufacture our iron into rails and machinery."[18]

New England manufacturers appear to have been mixed in their views. As one of the country's industrial strongholds, the region had many manufacturers sympathetic to a depreciated currency. The important textile industry, however, appears not to have been a redoubt of greenback sentiment.[19] There seem to have been several reasons for this. First, the textile industry was of much longer standing than the iron makers, and many textile manufacturers were competitive on world markets—even to the point of being favorable to free trade. This may have made them more sympathetic to concerns about currency volatility. Second, the United States so dominated world cotton production that the country's market power meant that any movement of the US dollar affected the raw materials costs of all the world's cotton textile manufacturers. A depreciation of the dollar made cotton cheaper to British as well as US industrialists, mitigating the positive impact on US cotton goods' competitiveness.[20] Nonetheless, on the whole US manufacturers were opposed to the hard-money position.

Trade policy could provide the same sort of competitive edge to US manufacturers as a depreciated currency. There were virtually no manu-

17 Ibid., 158.
18 Quoted in Unger 1959, 53.
19 Evidence on this is spotty, although Unger and Sharkey both mention it.
20 Unger 1964, 144–47; Sharkey 1959, 160–64. During this period, the United States accounted for between 65 and 75 percent of British cotton imports (Ellison [1886] 1968, 86).

factured exports, so the issue was about competition in the US market. Like gold, tariffs were politically controversial, although the defeat of the free trade South in the Civil War reduced the opposition to protection. Many in the country, though, remained hostile to trade protection for manufacturing. Importantly, one of the principal sources of hostility to protection—farmers—was favorable to a depreciated currency. This meant that manufacturers and farmers could make common cause in opposing the gold standard while they would be opposed to each other on trade policy.

The US agricultural sector was generally hostile to the gold standard. Cotton and tobacco farmers were reliant on their overseas sales, and after the late 1860s, wheat farmers became increasingly export oriented. This gave farmers a strong interest in a depreciated currency; pass-through was nearly complete, so that there was little concern about currency volatility.

Through the 1860s, most farmers were relatively inactive on monetary issues, as manufacturers and other businesspeople led the charge in favor of greenbacks. After 1870, however, farmers became increasingly vocal in opposing the return to gold. The reason is simple: farm prices were quite favorable for the first few years after the Civil War. Wheat prices approached the unheard-of apex of three dollars a bushel in 1867, and generally farm prices between 1865 and 1870 were at levels not again reached until World War I. But US wheat, cotton, and other agricultural prices began to fall in the late 1860s. This was part of the global decline in primary prices that continued until 1896 and became known as the Great Depression due to the depressed nature of prices internationally for over twenty years. After 1873, farmers were among the more forceful and committed opponents of the gold standard, in the United States as elsewhere. Although the secondary literature makes no mention of this, my argument would lead to an expectation that farmers producing solely for the domestic market—such as in dairy and orchard products—would have interests like those of other nontradables producers, while farmers in the export sectors would have strong interests in depreciation.

The minerals sector was concerned primarily about export prices, and shared the concern of manufacturers and farmers with contraction and real appreciation. The important coal producers were closely tied to Pennsylvania's iron manufacturers, and the coal miners and iron makers were often politically active as a coalition; the nation's new oil industry, also based in Pennsylvania, often joined them. Other miners—especially the country's large silver-mining industry that was growing rapidly in the West—were more like farmers, doing reasonably well through the 1860s, but experiencing price declines after 1870. Silver prices in particular were driven down as European countries embraced a monometallic gold standard and sold off their silver stocks, and as rich new silver deposits were discovered. The silver miners, like farmers, eventually became central to the antigold movement in the middle and late 1870s.

The greenback movement did not have the radical tinge that its Populist successor sometimes took on. Historical studies of the period from 1865 to 1879 make it clear that the initial social base of opposition to gold was among industrialists, railroad magnates, and the middle classes of small-town America; in the words of one scholar, "The earliest Greenback support ... appeared to rest on middle-class and other 'genteel' reformers."[21] Eventually farmers, miners, and laborers came to be important members of the antigold coalition, and there were some social radicals in the movement. But opposition to gold after the Civil War was broad based and included large segments of the business community.

Bondholders. As mentioned, debates over specie resumption ended up implicating the form in which the US government would service its bonded debt. Supporters of gold wanted both principal and interest paid in gold; supporters of greenbacks wanted at least principal and perhaps interest as well paid in greenbacks. Bondholders had an interest in the progold view, which would earn them far more than payment in greenbacks. Inasmuch as a bondholder might also be a member of one of the groups discussed above, this would complicate their policy preferences. The two issues could be separated, as in fact was attempted by Jay Cooke. Cooke, one of the country's leading businesspeople, was heavily committed to government bonds—both as an investor and as a Philadelphia banker who had brought them to market—but he was also a prominent railroad entrepreneur. His involvement with the railroads led him to oppose contraction and a return to gold; his involvement with government securities led him to support full bond payment in gold. Many businesspeople found it more difficult to support two somewhat-contradictory policies. In any case, the fact that a large portion of the business community in particular and investing classes more

---

21 Wegner 1995, 140.

generally had bondholdings was important in drawing in more supporters of gold than would otherwise have been the case.

Leaving the issue of bonded debt aside, the lineup of interests was largely as expected by the approach presented in chapter 1, based on *exposure to currency risk* and *tradability*. Those most concerned about exchange rate risk, the northeastern financial and commercial sectors, were the strongest supporters of a gold standard regime. Nontradables sectors, especially railroads and interior businesses, with little or no such exposure, supported the floating paper currency. Tradables sectors generally—manufacturing, farming, and mining—favored a depreciated paper currency and opposed an appreciated gold-backed dollar. It is worth noting that farm and mine opposition to gold gained strength only after farm and minerals prices began to decline; so long as they were moving favorably, farmers and miners were quiescent.

Politics and Policies

The debate over whether, when, and how the United States would return to the gold standard was central to the broader question of what kind of country it would be—agrarian or industrial, rural or urban, "globalized" or self-sufficient. As a result, the process by which the United States returned to gold was bitterly contested. The international context, domestic interest group lineup, and domestic partisan and other political developments interacted in complicated ways.

The secretary of the treasury at war's end was Hugh McCulloch, a financial conservative who had been the country's first comptroller of the currency under the 1863 National Banking Act. He took office in March 1865, and was kept on by Andrew Johnson after Abraham Lincoln's assassination. Almost immediately, he began retiring greenbacks to reduce the supply of paper money, by twenty-five million dollars between July 1865 and February 1866. McCulloch's annual report, issued in December 1865, made it apparent that contraction and an early return to gold were priorities for him. McCulloch had supporters in Congress, especially among urban Republicans and the traditionally hard-money Democrats. In February 1866, McCulloch's supporters presented a bill that would have given him sweeping powers to contract the money supply. The bill was extreme enough that it was voted down in mid-March 1866; a moderate version passed a week later, and in

April 1866 Johnson signed the Contraction Act into law. After appreciating 15 percent against sterling between November 1865 and April 1866, the clear signal of congressional resistance to contraction led the dollar to depreciate by over 20 percent during May and June 1866, as indicated in table 2.1 and figure 2.1.

McCulloch's position was weakened as President Johnson's unpopularity led to big losses for his supporters in the midterm elections in November 1866. But the biggest challenge to contraction was unfavorable macroeconomic conditions. Over the course of 1866 and into 1867, the economy weakened considerably.

The choices available were underscored by the impact of the Overend-Gurney crisis in mid-1866, referred to in the Carey quote above. The panic in London led gold to be shipped from the United States to Europe. This, along with the clear indication that Congress would not stand for contractionary efforts to defend the dollar, led to a substantial dollar depreciation. This depreciation was widely seen to have improved economic conditions and raised prices, counteracting the negative effects of contraction. It was obvious to all that in the absence of the depreciation—which of course would not have been possible with the dollar on gold—the domestic recession would have been worsened by the London crisis.

McCulloch was implementing a restrictive monetary policy. Between 1865 and 1868, by one measure, the money supply contracted by 18 percent. Some data make the contraction smaller, but this was in the context of a generally growing level of economic activity, so that output was 26 percent higher in 1868 than in 1865 with a substantially smaller money supply. As a result, from early 1865 to early 1868, prices declined by 14 percent even as the dollar appreciated by 32 percent against sterling (from \$10.05/£ to \$6.83/£) (see table 2.1). While the general deflationary environment is relevant, for our purposes it is especially important to see how relative prices of different goods and services evolved. Table 2.2 and figure 2.2 show how some representative prices moved over the 1864–79 period; metal products are indicative of manufactured prices, while building materials are classically nontradable. The table illustrates that prices of manufactured goods plummeted between 1865 and 1869, while farm prices dropped by much less, and nontradables prices declined by even less. This is the macroeconomic backdrop to the late 1860s' centrality of manufacturing to the antigold movement.

TABLE 2.2
Representative relative price indexes, 1865–79

	Farm Products	Metal products	Building material
1865	100	100	100
1866	95	91	108
1867	90	81	102
1868	93	74	98
1869	87	74	93
1870	76	65	86
1871	69	66	86
1872	73	84	91
1873	70	79	90
1874	69	34	86
1875	67	57	76
1876	60	51	71
1877	60	46	68
1878	49	41	61
1879	49	44	63

Contraction became increasingly unpopular as 1867 wore on, and McCulloch came under continual attack for "burning greenbacks"— that is, retiring paper currency in preparation for a return to gold. The *Chicago Republican* accused McCulloch of being "fully determined to paralyze the industrial interests of the country"; his "insane contraction policy" was, the newspaper wrote, proof that McCulloch was a "tool of Wall Street brokers and capitalists." Opposition to contraction came to span the political spectrum, at least outside the urban Northeast. As the editor of the influential *Chicago Tribune* declared, "The four million a month burning up of greenbacks is severely condemned by all men of both parties in the West. That policy finds no supporters in any party."[22]

Meanwhile, McCulloch's plan to pay off the federal debt in gold came under attack. Radical opponents of gold wanted to pay off all government debts in greenbacks, but the more moderate Pendleton Plan presented by a leading Ohio Democrat called only for greenback redemption of the 5–20 bonds. The more radical proposals smacked of outright repudiation, yet it was a reasonable interpretation of the 5–20s' legal status that gold should be used to pay the interest and greenbacks for the principal. It seemed fair to repay the 5–20s in the currency in

22 Quoted in Sharkey 1959, 92, 96–97.

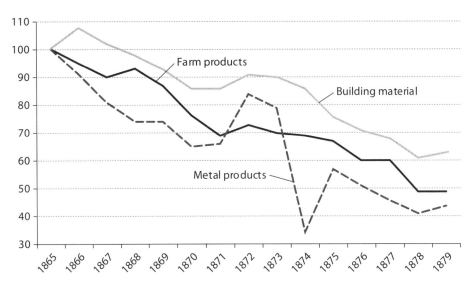

Figure 2.2 Representative relative price movements, 1865–79. *Source*: Table 2.2.

which they had been bought, which was after all the nation's legal tender—a popular slogan was "the same currency for the plough-holder and the bondholder."[23] The use of greenbacks for debt redemption would also serve to expand the money supply.

Political conditions favored the opponents of contraction. Supporters of President Johnson were punished by voters in the 1866 election, due to both disagreements about Reconstruction and contraction. The results of the 1867 Ohio state election were even clearer, as the previously dominant Republicans lost the state legislature and almost lost the governorship. Most observers, and most Republicans, ascribed the setbacks to the party's association with contraction and the commitment to gold. Consequently, many Republicans hurried to distance themselves from the hard-money position of the Johnson administration, while many Democrats attempted to profit from the unpopularity of contraction by supporting soft-money alternatives to McCulloch's policies.

By the end of 1867, McCulloch's progold policies were so unpopular that Congress acted to block them. The House of Representatives passed a bill in December suspending the secretary of the treasury's

23 Ibid., 100.

authority to withdraw greenbacks from circulation. A compromise bill was passed by the Senate and became a law in February 1868 (without Johnson's signature, but with the plain knowledge that a presidential veto would be overridden). The votes in both the House and Senate were overwhelming. The secretary of the treasury in the new Grant administration that took office in 1869 was George Boutwell, a congressman from a Massachusetts manufacturing district who was a prominent opponent of gold.

With contraction halted, the battleground shifted to the issue of how to repay bondholders. The character of the debate was somewhat different from that over the gold standard itself: it had some monetary implications, as repaying bondholders in greenbacks would have increased the money supply and depreciated the currency, but it also had implications for the rights of bondholders and creditors more generally.[24] Businesspeople and investors indifferent to the gold standard—or even hostile to it—might be indignant at the suggestion that the government could reduce its obligations to investors by decree. Advocates of gold payments condemned the greenback payments plan as repudiation and confiscation—words that evoked a radicalism that frightened many in the business community and investing classes. The 1868 Republican platform called for full payment in gold, while the Democrats continued to try to take advantage of soft-money sentiment by leaving open the possibility of greenback payments. The sweeping Republican victory—while no doubt due largely to the popularity of Ulysses S. Grant—seemed to indicate the defeat of the antigold forces. Once the Forty-First Congress took office in March 1869, it passed a Public Credit Act committing to specie payment on the bonded debt. The bill mentioned a return to gold favorably, but without proposing a course of action. Meanwhile, a series of controversial Supreme Court cases first threatened and then eventually sanctioned the legality of the greenback as legal tender.[25]

Agitation over greenbacks as well as gold paused after the repeal of contraction and recognition of the bonded debt in gold. Although the dollar appreciated and prices declined between 1868 and 1873, both trends were gradual and took place in a period of general prosperity. As

24 The government could conceivably have serviced its debt in greenbacks, yet counteracted this injection of liquidity, so that it had no net monetary effects, but this would have been a highly unusual move.

25 See Dam 1981.

table 2.2 indicates, most prices did decline, but nontradables (cf. building materials) remained less affected by contraction. The early battles over the currency standard had led to something of a compromise. The initial attempt to get the dollar back to gold quickly had created a backlash that took the restoration of the gold standard off the political agenda, yet government bonds would be paid in gold. This reflected the unpopularity of a return to gold with industry, interior businesspeople, and others along with the unpopularity of imposing capital losses on government bondholders.

Figure 2.1 puts together the movement of the nominal exchange rate of the dollar against the pound sterling with the political debates of the period. It can be seen, for example, that debate over the Contraction Act led to a gradual depreciation of the currency—not surprisingly, inasmuch as it represented a defeat of the hard-currency policy. Indeed, the dollar generally depreciated (with some volatility) from the Contraction Act debate until discussion began on the Public Credit Act. The passage of the Public Credit Act, however, was followed by a graduate appreciation given that it represented a general victory for hard-money policies.

For our purposes, apart from the intrinsic interest of this episode of high political conflict over the monetary standard, several points are worth making:

- The interest group lineup was largely as would have been predicted by the framework examined in chapter 1. International exposure was associated with support for a fixed rate: the international financial and commercial sector favored gold, and the nontradables sectors favored greenbacks. Tradability was associated with support for depreciation and thus opposition to a fixed rate: manufacturers were generally supporters of greenbacks. Farmers and miners, although sympathetic to greenbacks, were less active as prices of their products performed relatively well.
- The conflict cut across political parties. Both Democrats and Republicans were divided on gold and greenbacks. The issue was often played for partisan advantage, as when Ohio Democrats attempted to capitalize on the unpopularity of the national Republican administration's support for gold by favoring

greenbacks. But in the main, partisan divisions were much more fluid than the underlying interest group cleavages.

- The evolution of relative prices was related to debates on gold. Participants in the debates appear to have had a clear sense of the implications of currency policy for them; manufacturers in particular related exchange rate policy and movements to their competitive position. Relative price movements also affected the extent of political mobilization on the subject. The favorable relative prices of farm and mine goods led farmers and miners to be less active than manufacturers.

From Panic to Resumption, 1873–79

Following several years of relative quiet, the currency issue exploded again after 1873. The date was significant for several reasons. First, by then it was apparent that there was a worldwide movement toward gold, as Germany and Scandinavia had joined the gold standard, and other European countries were debating it. Second, by 1873 it was evident that farm and mine prices were trending downward as the Great Depression began. Third, a serious panic erupted in September 1873, bringing new attention to macroeconomic policy.

The Issues

The question of whether to move toward a resumption of specie payments came back to the fore after the Panic of 1873. Gold supporters saw the financial difficulties as due in part to uncertainties about the country's monetary system, while gold opponents saw them as proof that excessive commitment to gold was tying the government's hands in reacting to a crisis. The battle raged until the country joined the gold standard at the beginning of 1879. The general contour of the issue was as it had been—hard-money supporters wanted to return to gold, and soft-money supporters wanted to stay off it—but the focus now shifted to a silver standard as the soft-money alternative.

The rise of silver. Before 1873, US currency politics had pitted supporters of a paper currency against supporters of gold, but after 1873 the division was largely between supporters of silver and supporters of gold. This shift deserves discussion. Much of the world had been on a bimetallic gold and silver standard before the early 1870s, with the gold-to-silver ratio at approximately sixteen to one. Yet in the early 1870s, the price of silver began to decline—in part due to silver discoveries and in part due to the (endogenous) movement of European countries toward a monometallic gold standard, which led them to buy gold and sell silver. As the market price of silver fell, the gold-to-silver ratio rose—to eighteen to one in 1880, twenty to one in 1890, and thirty-two to one in 1895.[26] This was of little interest to anyone but silver miners—and countries on a silver standard. As the price of silver declined (meaning that the gold-to-silver ratio rose), the price of such silver-based currencies as those of Japan, Russia, China, Mexico, and India also declined, depreciating against currencies on gold.

The United States, too, had been bimetallic before the Civil War. If specie payments had been resumed on the prior basis, the US dollar would have been convertible into *either* gold or silver, at a sixteen-to-one ratio. This would have driven gold out of circulation: the market price of gold coins would have been higher than their face value, so that they would be melted down and sold. This in turn would have put the United States on a silver standard, and the dollar exchange rate against gold standard currencies would simply have followed the declining price of silver. While the calculations are complex (if the United States had been on silver, the resultant increase in demand for silver would have raised its price above what in fact prevailed), Milton Friedman has estimated a hypothetical silver price that implies that at its low point, a silver-based dollar would have depreciated against gold-backed currencies by almost 50 percent between 1873 and 1896 (as in actuality happened to the silver-based Mexican and Japanese currencies).[27]

For the United States to return to gold, silver (at least at the sixteen-to-one rate) had to be removed from the currency standard. The Coinage Act of 1873 effectively "demonetized" silver, ending its use for major coinage. The act was barely noticed at the time—the country was

---

26 The gold-to-silver ratio is presented in the standard format; see also Friedman 1990, 1180–81. While it would probably be somewhat more accurate to transform the gold and silver prices into common quotations in, say, pounds sterling, the debates were all couched in terms of the gold-to-silver ratio ("free silver at 16:1").

27 The Japanese experience is particularly relevant. Japan went from paper currency to silver in 1886, then to gold in 1897. Between 1885 and 1897, the yen depreciated by one-third against the currencies of its trading partners (the nominal effective exchange rate) and even more against gold standard currencies.

on paper, and the gold-to-silver ratio had been stable—but when a resumption of specie payments was contemplated, the act's implications were clear. Were silver to share legal status with gold, at the old sixteen-to-one ratio, the government would have had to coin silver freely and supplanted gold, putting the country on a silver standard. Hence the Silverite activists raised the slogan "Free [coinage of] silver at 16:1," which would have forced the government to turn as much silver into coin as the market demanded. The Coinage Act became known to antigold activists as "The Crime of 1873," intended to force the country off silver surreptitiously. Some historians believe that this was the intent of the act's proponents, who knew that silver prices were declining.[28] Still, whatever the intention, the result was to make the adoption of a silver standard the principal goal of antigold activists.

Both silver and inconvertible paper currency meant a floating exchange rate against gold, and both also implied a depreciation. But there were several reasons that silver rather than paper currency became the rallying cry of the gold opponents. First, there was a long-standing distrust on the part of many Americans—especially those in the Jacksonian agrarian tradition—of paper money coupled with a belief in the desirability of precious metals as money. Second, and more to the point, there was concern that a paper currency could be manipulated *against* the interests of its supporters. The great attraction of paper was, in the words of one supporter, "that money can be created by the Government in any desired quantity, out of any substance, with no basis but itself."[29] This was also a problem, though, for it meant that the executive could pursue a tight monetary policy that led to an appreciation of the currency, as indeed Treasury Secretary McCulloch had done. This was a reasonable fear: throughout this period, the executive tended to be much more sympathetic to gold than Congress, thereby prompting charges that the executive branch was a tool of Wall Street and London, and sparking battles between the president and Congress. Soft-money advocates tried to counter this with legislation that specified exactly what to do with the currency—how much money to issue, what bank reserves to require, and so on—but the Treasury was much better positioned to run monetary policy. A specie standard based on silver had the great advantage of taking discretionary control of monetary

---

28 See, for example, O'Leary 1960; Friedman 1990.
29 Quoted in Hicks 1931, 316–17.

policy away from a government that soft-money advocates did not trust and guaranteeing a depreciating currency.[30]

Third, tying soft money to a silver standard—and thus increasing the demand for silver—was popular with silver miners, as it would raise the price of silver. Silver miners were moderately influential in their own right; perhaps more important, their political position was pivotal and inflated. Silver miners' influence was inflated because they were largely located in the sparsely populated Rocky Mountain states (Colorado, Nevada, Utah, Idaho, etc.), so that a disproportionate number of senators had powerful silver-mining constituents. The silver-mining states were pivotal because they were largely Republican, and in an era of Republican ascendancy they constituted a strong soft-money lobby within the mostly hard-money Republican Party. For these reasons, enlisting the support of silver miners for the antigold cause made good political sense.

Some in the United States toyed with an intermediate position between gold and silver, known as international bimetallism. This would entail an internationally negotiated bimetallic fixed rate, which implied a modest devaluation of the dollar and refixing against gold. International bimetallism would have required agreement from other major countries, and US currency activists sponsored international monetary conferences to attempt to achieve this, but they had no success.[31] This left a unilateral silver standard as the only real alternative to gold.

The macroeconomic context was no longer that of the early postwar period. Two crucial things had changed. For one, the contractionist policies of McCulloch had produced a real appreciation of the dollar (i.e., movement of the greenback toward the prewar exchange rate), which continued at a more gradual pace after 1869. The exchange rate between 1871 and 1873 had been in the $5.50/£ range, so that a further appreciation of less than 15 percent was necessary to reach $4.86/£. While this made a return to gold less difficult, it did not eliminate the underlying currency issue.

---

30 I admit to being unconvinced of the importance of the first motivation. There are few indications in contemporary debates that soft-money advocates disliked paper money per se. I incline toward the second view as an *explanation* for the first, but I present them both in deference to the historical literature.

31 For an excellent study of the four major conferences in the latter part of the century, see Reti 1998.

Second, the global price decline associated with the Great Depression of 1873–96 had begun. All US prices continued to decline after 1873 (see table 2.2), but as before tradables prices were more depressed than nontradables prices. Farm prices in particular, which had declined more slowly than manufactured goods prices during contraction, started to drop more quickly after 1869. This, along with the previous development, shifted the issue away from the difficulties of returning to gold and toward the currency standard best suited to deal with the country's economic problems.

The Interests

The battle over the return to gold continued to reflect the turbulent and contested nature of the US political economy. With the South once more represented in Congress and increasingly in the hands of Democrats, the antigold forces remained powerful. More and more land in the Midwest and Great Plains was being brought into wheat production, augmenting the export-oriented farm complex. Rapid industrialization was bringing ever more manufacturers, especially of iron and steel, to the forefront. While most of them continued to be a source of antigold sentiment, trade protection muted many of the manufacturers' concerns. The railroad owners continued to oppose gold, particularly after the bursting of the industry's boom. The commercial and financial sectors concentrated in the great northeastern port cities remained the strongest supporters of gold. Their views solidified as the country's finances matured and the international gold standard was adopted by more and more countries.

Manufacturers. As before, industrialists tended to oppose the gold standard. Industrial concerns about the currency were softened by the adoption and entrenchment of high protective barriers, reaching an average of 47 percent. During the Civil War, tariffs had been raised for both protective and revenue purposes, and after the war debates continued over whether to remove them. Agitation for trade liberalization was moderately successful. In 1870, tariffs on some raw materials were eliminated, and tariffs of manufactures were cut by 10 percent in 1872. But the free traders were defeated—the 1872 tariff cut was rescinded three years later—and it was evident that high trade barriers would protect US manufacturers. This made currency depreciation a less pressing issue. While manufacturing interests were largely as they had been, the success of their demands for trade protection dampened the intensity of their concerns over exchange rate policy.

Farmers. Unlike industry, the agricultural sector's involvement in currency politics grew dramatically after 1873. Even as farm prices began trending down significantly, the country's wheat farmers were becoming more reliant on exports. The United States had exported virtually no grain before the Civil War. But improvements in land and water transport, especially the expansion of the railroads, meant that by 1869 about one-tenth of the country's wheat output was exported, and by 1879 this was up to about one-third. The country remained overwhelmingly agrarian, but its typical farmers were less and less southern cotton planters, and more and more family wheat farmers in the Midwest and Great Plains.

Wheat production was growing rapidly, so that US wheat exports skyrocketed from 28 million bushels in the late 1860s to 140 million bushels in the early 1880s, and then 180 million bushels in the mid-1890s.[32] The increasing orientation of US farming toward wheat exports had several implications, both in the 1870s and over the following decades. First, wheat prices dropped rapidly, especially as the Great Plains, Canadian prairies, and Argentine pampas were opened for production. The Liverpool price of a bushel of wheat, a good indicator of world market prices, averaged $1.52 in 1868–72, $1.31 in 1880–84, and $0.88 in 1895–99.[33] Moreover, while farmers producing for the domestic market could be aided by trade protection, those selling into world markets could not; only a depreciation would help them.[34] And finally, the expansion of export-oriented farming from the cotton and tobacco South to the Midwest and Great Plains wheat regions had important sectional political effects. It was in the years after 1873 that the general pattern was established that would hold until the 1930s, in which farmers in the South, Midwest, and Great Plains were the principal opponents in the United States of the gold standard.

Miners. Second only to the farmers among the ranks of the anti-gold forces were US miners, both of silver and other metals (apart from gold, of course). The United States was a major producer and exporter

32 See Harley 1980.
33 Ibid.
34 Or export subsidies—a possibility that was never really contemplated in the nineteenth century.

of a large number of minerals, from lead and copper to silver, and as with farm goods, world mineral prices were declining quickly. A silver standard's boost to silver miners was obvious, and they were a large enough group to matter politically.

Politics and Policies

The battles that began in 1873 implicated both interest groups and partisan considerations. The partisan aspects were complex, as there were pro- and antigold interests in both parties. Republican presidents during this period overrode their own party's congressional delegations, using the veto and patronage to secure a return to gold.

In April 1874, Congress passed soft-money legislation that became known as the Inflation Bill. Northeastern hard-money interests mounted a furious campaign to get the bill overturned, and President Grant indeed vetoed it. This was politically dangerous for the Republican Party, as support for the bill included much of its membership. In fact, divisions over the legislation were more sectoral and regional than partisan, pitting western and southern industry, trade, and agriculture against eastern trade and finance. The House vote was illustrative: the East (minus Pennsylvania, home to the iron and steel manufacturers) was against it, 59–3; the West (including Pennsylvania) and South were for it, 85–26 and 51–14, respectively. Democrats split 35–37 against, while Republicans voted 105–64 for the bill.[35] Grant's veto was widely blamed for having lost the Republicans the midterm elections of 1874.

After the Inflation Bill and its veto, President Grant and other gold supporters were keen to demonstrate that the country could successfully return to gold. The Republican Party leadership, given the 1874 electoral debacle, was itself eager to show that the party could act in a unified manner—and that Grant had the party's support. As a result, in January 1875, Grant and the party leadership pressured the lame-duck Republican Congress to pass the Resumption Act, calling for a return to gold on January 1, 1879. This infuriated the soft-money supporters, who had succeeded in passing the Inflation Bill and whose numbers were set to increase in the incoming Congress. Congress repeatedly

---

35 Unger 1964, 410. The Pacific states voted 3–1 against the bill, and there was one independent congressperson.

repealed the Resumption Act, but the two-thirds majority necessary to override the presidential veto was not forthcoming.

The frustration of some antigold forces led to the creation of the Greenback Party in 1875. The next year, the party ran US industrialist Peter Cooper for president in a largely symbolic effort (he was eighty-five years old), but in the 1878 midterm election it brought together antigold forces, working-class activists, and other insurgents to garner about a million votes and elect quite a few congresspeople.[36] The third party served primarily to discipline the two major parties in areas where soft-money sentiment was strong, and the pull of party discipline might otherwise have led major-party candidates to dampen their support for greenbacks and silver. The Greenback electoral threat was an effective component of the powerful popular pressure on Congress.

Against this backdrop, congressional antigold activism continued. In February 1877, Congress passed a moderately Silverite bill that required the government to purchase small amounts of silver, yet did not remonetize it. President Rutherford B. Hayes vetoed this Bland-Allison Act, but the veto was overridden. His treasury secretary, John Sherman, had in fact found that a compromise such as Bland-Allison was the probable price of defeating the Resumption Act's repeal. In any event, Sherman recognized that the bill would have little impact on monetary conditions. In late 1877, an attempt to repeal the Resumption Act was defeated, and the country went back to gold at the beginning of 1879.[37]

The twists and turns of policy are reflected in the movement of the dollar against sterling, as demonstrated in figure 2.3. The veto of the Inflation Bill led to an appreciation of the dollar, but the currency weakened as the fight over Resumption went on and its conclusion seemed unsure. It was not until attempts to repeal the Resumption Act had been decisively defeated by a presidential veto that the dollar began to appreciate again, which it did more or less gradually and continually until 1879.

---

36 The numbers are subject to interpretation, because there were also quite a few related insurgent parties and independents running on platforms similar to that of the Greenbackers as well as fusion Democrats. The estimated number of congresspeople elected range from fourteen to twenty-six. The estimates of the total votes range from about 800,000 to approximately 1.6 million; the latter figure was something like one-fifth of the total popular vote (Unger 1964; Lause 2001; Ritter 1997).

37 Just barely, though: it passed the House and failed by one vote in the Senate. Hayes would have vetoed it, however, and antiresumptionists were far short of enough votes for an override.

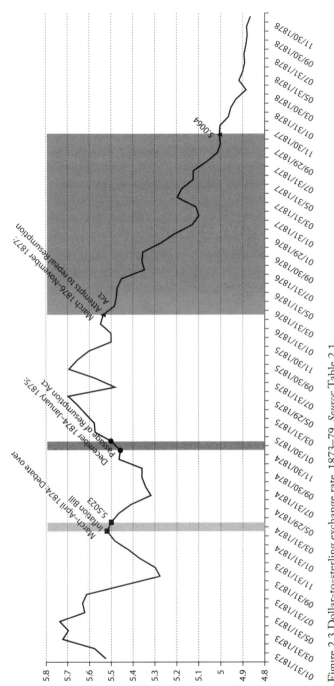

Figure 2.3 Dollar-to-sterling exchange rate, 1873–79. *Source:* Table 2.1.

The United States chose a fixed exchange rate, the gold standard, after a long series of acrimonious political battles. The currency was at the center of domestic political debates in the 1860s and 1870s, splitting the two major political parties and prompting a modestly successful third-party movement. In addition to what was noted above, we can make the following observations about the relevance of this episode to the arguments presented in chapter 1 (and vice versa).

- The general interest group positions on gold were as they had been before 1873, but after that date manufacturers were less important to the antigold movement, while farmers and miners were more significant. This was due to the particularly adverse movements in farm and mine prices along with the availability of high tariffs to assist manufacturers.
- The demand for the free coinage of silver at a sixteen-to-one rate against gold came to replace the demand for paper currency. "Free silver" would have put the United States on a silver standard, with an exchange rate that would depreciate and float against gold.
- Congress tended to be much more sympathetic to soft-money arguments and interests than the executive branch. Whether by presidential veto, persuasion, or patronage, presidents Grant and Hayes were central to the return to gold between 1868 and 1880.

The Political Economy of Gold and Greenbacks: A Statistical Analysis

Up to this point, my theoretical expectations have only been illustrated by a historical narrative. Given the nature of the evidence, of course, alternative historical paths are difficult to analyze. I look here at other evidence about the politics of US currency policy in this period for a more systematic evaluation of my argument. Specifically, I analyze congressional voting on a series of legislative initiatives of relevance to US adherence to the gold standard to see if the interest group lineup I expect is borne out by the evidence.

Over the course of the late 1860s and 1870s, Congress voted hundreds of times on issues that were directly or indirectly related to the country's currency policy. Most of these votes had clear implications for both the exchange rate and exchange rate regime. Debates over contraction pitted those who wanted to appreciate the currency to allow a return to gold against antigold forces who wanted to maintain a depreciated paper currency and minimize the possibility of a return to gold. The Resumption Act and attempts to repeal it were specifically about the currency standard. This gives us a unique opportunity to assess the sources of legislators' preferences over exchange rate policy. To the extent that legislators represent the views of their districts, it also allows us to explore the sources of districts' disparate views on monetary and currency policies in this period. In particular, we can attempt to see the relationship between economic activity and exchange rate preferences.

The purpose of this exercise is to see if the economic characteristics of Americans—in this case, grouped by congressional district and represented by their members of Congress—were reflected in their views toward monetary issues. There are, however, many possible confounding effects between this relationship and what can be seen in the voting as well as economic data. The data available to us are only partial and only tangentially related to the hypotheses I have set forth. The relevant census—that of 1870—had limited economic information, and it is typically in a form difficult to associate with modern economic ideas or the kinds of economic activities relevant to my argument. Perhaps most unfortunate, there are really no data available that could be related to involvement in international financial or commercial activities, or mining.

Although congressional voting gives some sense of the underlying policy preferences, the relationship is hardly transparent. Some constituents and districts undoubtedly cared much more than others about the issue, and yet we cannot easily categorize votes by the preference intensity of either the constituents or their legislators. It is possible that some districts and members of Congress were largely indifferent, which would have made their votes more likely to be swayed by partisan considerations, patronage, or vote trading. And nothing is to say that members of Congress necessarily voted the interests of their districts. In addition, Reconstruction and its aftermath complicated congressional voting in this early period, so that the states of the former Confederacy were either not represented in Congress, or were represented by officials whose electoral base shifted radically over the course of Reconstruction and its reversal.

A wide variety of strategic behavior, involving everything from logrolling to partisan politics, also usually affects the voting behavior of members of Congress. Finally, while some of the legislation in question is easy to classify as either favorable or unfavorable to gold, there were many compromise bills presented and voted on—and the compromises sometimes were opposed by both extremes. Nonetheless, the congressional votes supply us with an unusual opportunity to examine the relationship between the economic characteristics of particular districts and expressed legislative preferences of the districts' representatives.

In what follows, I provide a statistical analysis of many dozens of congressional votes. As I use the same approach here and in the next chapter, it is worth going into some detail about the data and statistical methods.[38] I group the votes by decades, since congressional district borders were redrawn after the 1870 census. Because there are far more congresspeople than there are senators, and we have economic data at the level of the congressional district, I look only at votes in the House of Representatives.[39] Roll call voting data are readily available, but as noted it is not always apparent how to interpret the votes. In each group of votes on an issue, I have tried to select votes that would most clearly separate those who supported hard money—in particular, the gold standard—from those who supported soft money—in particular, a paper or silver standard. I use twenty-four votes for the decade of the 1860s, covering voting between 1866 and 1869 on the Contraction Act, Suspension of Contraction, and Public Credit Act. I use seventeen votes for the decades of the 1870s, covering voting between 1874 and 1877 on the Inflation Act, Resumption Act, and attempts to repeal the Resumption Act. I use two statistical approaches:

1. I pool all votes on the subject. This means that the vote of the member of Congress from each congressional district is counted numerous times, one for each vote. The unit of analysis is the congressional district, not the member of Congress, whose identity might change over the course of the period.

38 For more detailed information on the data and methods, see http://press.princeton.edu/titles/10364.html.

39 In an earlier work (Frieden 1997), I explored Senate votes as well in the 1890s' Populist period.

This has the advantage of taking each vote as an observation (which is obviously accurate), but the disadvantage of simply repeating the data on each congressional district. By pooling, I hope to reduce the impact of such idiosyncratic factors as log-rolling, absences, or indifference, yet the method has pitfalls. In any case, standard errors are clustered by congressional district, which may ameliorate some of the disadvantages of this approach.

2. I look at the proportion of the votes on the subject on which the member of Congress from the congressional district voted in favor of hard money. For example, if there were ten votes, and the member of Congress voted for the hard-money position eight times, the proportion would be 0.8. The advantage of this approach is that it can give some sense of the depth of feeling about the topic; a member of Congress who voted for hard money 90 percent of the time can be assumed to be more fervently progold than one who did so 60 percent of the time. Nevertheless, this turns a binary variable (a yes–no vote) into a continuous one in ways that may obscure some political considerations.

The principal purpose of trying the two different methods is to get around the clear problems with analyzing roll call votes, whether this has to do with imperfect representation, logrolling, the use of patronage to buy votes, or varying levels of preference intensity, in addition to the problems created by limited economic data. Neither of the methods is perfect, but together they provide a reasonable picture.

The main explanatory variable I investigate—strictly limited by data availability—is the importance of certain economic activities in the congressional district. These economic data are available in the census by county, and I have aggregated them up to the level of the congressional district. Some nuance is undoubtedly lost in this translation (choices have to be made when county and congressional district borders do not match), but the relatively detailed nature of the economic data is valuable.

Unfortunately, in 1870 most modern notions of economic activity were only embryonic at best. Output data in dollar terms are only readily available for manufacturing, and I use manufacturing output per capita for each congressional district. Output numbers for agriculture are by weight or volume (pounds, bushels, gallons, etc.). I have converted the output of the main agricultural products (not all of them) to dollars at the prevailing national prices; again, I use them per capita for each district. There are no output data on services, and employment data (typically grouped by job category rather than sector of employment) are not useful for my purposes.

Given the nature of my argument, it seemed useful to differentiate among tradable and nontradable farm products. I have thus divided agricultural products into those most likely to have entered into world trade—cotton, wheat, tobacco, and rice—and those least likely to be traded—orchard products and the products of market gardens. This allows me to see if farmers producing export goods had different policy preferences than those producing solely for the domestic market. Both sets of farmers might be expected to oppose the gold standard: producers of tradable farm products due to the direct effect on prices they received, and producers of nontradable farm products due to the sacrifice of monetary independence implied by the gold standard. I expect export farmers to have stronger policy preferences than other farmers, though. To study this possibility, I look first at the proportion of the farm output in the district that was tradable, controlling for total agricultural output there, and then omit total farm output to simply examine tradable and nontradable farm output per capita in each district.[40] All voting data are taken from Howard Rosenthal and Keith Poole's online data; all economic data are from the decennial census.[41] I now turn to an analysis of voting on monetary matters between 1865 and 1879.

The 1860s

Congress voted (many times) on three important sets of issues between 1866 and 1869. The first issue was the Contraction Act. Early in 1866,

---

40 Again, note that this is not all agricultural output but instead the output of the crops I have converted to dollar terms. This certainly covers only a portion of the total agricultural output, yet it does include the most important crops that US farmers produced.

41 For the voting data, see http://voteview.com/. For the census data, see http://www.icpsr.umich.edu/icpsrweb/landing.jsp. For detailed information on all data as well as methods used for this and all statistical work in my study, see http://press.princeton.edu/titles/10364.html.

as the implications of Treasury Secretary McCulloch's policy of rapid contraction became clearer, a bill to expand his powers to contract the money supply was voted down in the House. Eventually a compromise was hammered out, but along the way there were several controversial votes.

Within a month of the passage of the compromise Contraction Act, the Overend-Gurney failure caused a British and more general financial panic that lasted for much of the rest of 1866. Almost immediately, members of Congress began trying to force the secretary of the treasury not only to stop contracting the money supply but instead to expand it. As soon as Congress came back into session in December 1866, bills were introduced to curtail the Contraction Act; by the end of 1867, opposition had grown to the point where the House of Representatives actually repealed the compromise act, now seen as too contractionary. The Senate passed the bill to repeal in January 1868 and, at least for the moment, attempts to return to gold were dead. Contraction had led to a strong appreciation of the dollar against sterling, from over $10/£ early in 1865 to $6.50/£ at the end of 1866. With the suspension of the Contraction Act, the dollar stopped rising and in fact depreciated to around $7.00/£, where it stayed during most of 1868.

The third set of votes of interest in this period had to do with whether to redeem government bonds in gold or paper. Almost as soon as the Contraction Act was suspended, this closely related issue was brought to the legislature. As previously noted, there was some ambiguity about whether some of the federal bonds issued during the Civil War should be paid on maturity at the prevailing paper-currency rate or prewar gold standard one. With the dollar trading at around $7/£, as opposed to the prewar rate of $4.86/£, this made a substantial difference to bondholders (and the federal government). Over summer 1868, Congress debated a variety of measures related to a proposed Public Credit Act, all of which involved whether to honor the bonds' principal in gold or paper money, with the predictable division between hard- and soft-money supporters. Partisan considerations were crucial here; with both the executive and legislature in Republican hands, there was concern that refusing to honor the debt in gold would reflect badly on the financial probity of the Republicans. Nonetheless, both parties were divided: typically Democrats were three to one against, and Republicans were three to one in favor, although the count varied from vote to vote. Eventually, in March 1869 both the House and Senate agreed on payment in gold, but many of the roll call votes along the way were hotly contested. In the House, many of the votes were decided by a five- or ten-vote margin out of around two hundred sitting members of Congress.

I start by analyzing the voting behavior on these sets of measures. The first statistical analysis pools all twenty-four votes on the three issues, including both successful and failed attempts to pass bills, motions to table and reconsider, and a variety of amendments. Here as throughout the book, votes are recoded so that a zero is a vote in favor of the soft-money (antigold, anticontraction) position, and a one is a vote in favor of the hard-money (progold, procontraction) position. Explanatory variables (except party, which is an indicator) are normalized so that coefficients can be compared, with each unit equal to a standard deviation. Most of the votes were close (for example, sixty-five to seventy against on the original Contraction Act, and eighty-three to fifty-three in favor on the eventual compromise Contraction Act). Most Democrats tended to support contraction and gold bonds (recall that representatives of the former Confederacy states, where there was much less support, were not yet back in Congress), but the Republican Party was generally divided more or less evenly among supporters and opponents. At times, as we will see, partisan politics played a key role in voting behavior. All standard errors are clustered at the congressional district level, as there are multiple observations (votes) for each congressional district.

Table 2.3 shows the results of a logistic regression that analyzes all the votes in this pool. Column 1 displays the effects of the basic explanatory variables: the party of the member of Congress along with the importance to the congressional district of manufacturing and farm production in output. Note that this is not total output, as we would use today—such data are not available—but the output used here—that is, all manufacturing and the selected farm products. The column also indicates the impact of wealth (described in the census as the "true value of real and personal estate"), because both intuition and much of the historical literature gives us reason to think that wealthier Americans, all else being equal, would tend to support the gold standard and more conservative monetary policies.

As can be seen, when we control for other factors, Republicans tended in general to be antigold (recall that the votes are coded so that negative coefficients indicate support for soft money, while positive co-

Table 2.3
Congressional voting on 1860s' monetary policy issues: All votes pooled

	(1) Vote	(2) Vote	(3) Vote	(4) Vote	(5) Vote	(6) Vote	(7) Vote
Vote Republican	-0.149	-0.191	-0.168	-0.194+	-0.183	-0.178	-0.205+
	(-1.31)	(-1.64)	(-1.48)	(-1.72)	(-1.59)	(-1.57)	(-1.82)
Wealth	0.0818*	0.107*	0.0690+	0.0442	0.0672+	0.0701+	0.0362
	(2.02)	(2.53)	(1.67)	(0.94)	(1.66)	(1.73)	(0.79)
Mfg output per capita	0.223**	0.139	0.379**	0.517**	0.131+	0.165*	0.426**
	(3.15)	(1.58)	(5.10)	(3.69)	(1.71)	(2.20)	(3.04)
Farm output per capita	0.0654	0.0608	0.0601	0.0602	0.0661		0.0611
	(1.03)	(0.91)	(0.98)	(1.00)	(1.05)		(1.02)
New England mfg		-0.0104		-0.384*			-0.291+
		(-0.08)		(-2.29)			(-1.72)
New England		0.490*		0.312			0.170
		(2.50)		(1.52)			(0.81)
Pennsylvania mfg			-0.515**	-0.647**			-0.589**
			(-5.35)	(-4.43)			(-4.17)
Pennsylvania			-0.0215	-0.0656			-0.0891
			(-0.12)	(-0.34)			(-0.48)
Proportion of farm output tradable					-0.207**		-0.145*
					(-3.24)		(-2.15)
Tradable farm output per capita						-0.163*	
						(-2.40)	
Nontradable farm output per capita						0.112+	
						(1.91)	
Constant	0.219*	0.181+	0.289**	0.346**	0.244*	0.242*	0.357**
	(2.31)	(1.82)	(2.90)	(3.10)	(2.55)	(2.54)	(3.30)
Observations	3103	3103	3103	3103	3103	3103	3103
Pseudo R^2	0.009	0.012	0.019	0.021	0.014	0.014	0.024

t statistics in parentheses
+ $p < 0.10$, * $p < 0.05$, ** $p < 0.01$

efficients suggest support for hard money). This effect is weak and rarely statistically significant, probably due to the divisions within the party, as mentioned. The role of party politics complicates the analysis of congressional voting, then as now, for there are obvious correlations between economic characteristics and policy preferences, on the one hand, and partisan affiliation, on the other—although in the case of the gold standard, both parties were divided. There is little one can do about this, however; partisanship as well as attitudes toward the gold standard were jointly determined by a combination of economic, social, political, and other factors.

Apart from Republicans, wealthier districts tended to support contraction and a return to the gold standard. So too did manufacturing districts. There is some indication that farming districts were also favorable to contraction, although these results are not statistically significant. Neither the farming nor manufacturing results are in line with my expectations, but the data allow for a more detailed look.

The data make it possible to explore the position of different sorts of manufacturers and farmers. In columns 2 through 4, I include terms that interact manufacturing output with location in New England and Pennsylvania, respectively, and then together. It should be remembered that these were two of the principal sites of manufacturing industries clearly competing with foreign products: textiles, iron, and steel. This leads me to expect that New England and Pennsylvania manufacturers would be more likely to support the depreciated dollar (i.e., to be opposed to contraction and gold). The results here show this quite plainly: the interaction terms for New England and Pennsylvania are negative. The results for New England are especially interesting: the region as a whole tended to be progold (in line with its general association with more mature commercial and financial centers), yet the region's manufacturing districts were more likely to be antigold.

Similar nuance can be inferred from more detailed data on farming. While farmers in general may have supported the Contraction Act, my approach anticipates recognizable differences among types of crops. I divide farm output into two categories. The first includes those farm goods that were heavily exported—wheat, cotton, tobacco, and rice—the producers of which would be expected to want a depreciated currency, and oppose contraction and a return to the gold standard. The second category is made up of farm goods that did not enter into world trade, such as orchard fruits and market vegetables; I expect these producers to be less concerned about the gold standard, and indeed largely indifferent to it. I then indicate what proportion of the farm output of the district was tradable. Column 5 in table 2.3 depicts the basic results (as in column 1) with an added variable indicating the proportion that each district's farm output made up of tradable crops. As can be seen, farm output per capita still tends to be associated with support for contraction, albeit not significantly, but the extent to which farming in the district was concentrated in tradable (i.e., export) crops is associated with *opposition* to contraction. The direction of the effects is greatly in line with my expectations. Representatives from the districts with more substantial tradable farm output tended to be more likely to vote against contraction.

Column 6 is another way to look at this relationship; it breaks farm output into tradable and nontradable in each district, per capita. The results are similar. Districts with large nontradable output tended to favor contraction and gold, all else being equal, while those with large tradable output were unfavorable. Column 7 combines all the relevant explanatory variables. As can be seen, although some variables lose statistical significance, the general picture is relatively obvious. Farmers of tradable (largely export) crops tended to oppose hard money, while the wealthy manufacturers and other farmers tended to support it; manufacturers in the import-competing regions of New England and Pennsylvania were more likely to side with export farmers and oppose hard money.

Table 2.4 looks at voting on this set of bills in the second way described above, categorizing congressional districts by the proportion of times their representatives voted in favor of hard-money positions. The OLS regression analysis presented in this table provides results similar to those in table 2.3.

We might ask how substantively important these considerations were. Table 2.5 uses models 5, 6, and 7 from table 2.3 to demonstrate the impact of a standard deviation increase in the principal variables. The impact of a standard deviation increase in each explanatory variable on the probability of voting for gold and hard money is demonstrated in table 2.5. The table shows the impact of the probability of voting for contraction (hard money) as each explanatory variable goes from one-half standard deviation below its mean to one-half standard deviation above its mean (holding all other explanatory variables constant at their means).

TABLE 2.4
Congressional voting on 1860s' monetary policy issues: Proportion of votes for hard money

	(1) Proportion votes for hard money	(2) Proportion votes for hard money	(3) Proportion votes for hard money	(4) Proportion votes for hard money	(5) Proportion votes for hard money	(6) Proportion votes for hard money	(7) Proportion votes for hard money
Republican	0.0897** (2.62)	0.0862* (2.45)	0.0831* (2.55)	0.0862** (2.64)	0.0816* (2.40)	0.0831* (2.46)	0.0822* (2.53)
Wealth	-0.0146 (-0.55)	-0.0144 (-0.52)	-0.0183 (-0.68)	-0.0304 (-1.11)	-0.0172 (-0.64)	-0.0170 (-0.63)	-0.0323 (-1.18)
Mfg output per capita	0.0383+ (1.81)	0.0392 (1.50)	0.0628** (2.96)	0.122** (4.02)	0.0235 (1.05)	0.0271 (1.27)	0.104** (3.36)
Farm output per capita	0.00238 (0.13)	0.00271 (0.14)	0.00190 (0.10)	0.00186 (0.10)	0.00431 (0.24)		0.00324 (0.19)
New England mfg		-0.0159 (-0.49)		-0.0977** (-2.68)			-0.0784* (-2.10)
New England		0.0328 (0.81)		-0.0123 (-0.29)			-0.0424 (-0.95)

TABLE 2.4 (*continued*)

	(1) Proportion votes for hard money	(2) Proportion votes for hard money	(3) Proportion votes for hard money	(4) Proportion votes for hard money	(5) Proportion votes for hard money	(6) Proportion votes for hard money	(7) Proportion votes for hard money
New England		0.0328 (0.81)		-0.0123 (-0.29)			-0.0424 (-0.95)
Pennsylvania mfg			-0.0735* (-2.58)	-0.131** (-3.61)			-0.118** (-3.31)
Pennsylvania			-0.0448 (-0.87)	-0.0739 (-1.40)			-0.0810 (-1.55)
Proportion of farm output tradable					-0.0365** (-2.68)		-0.0311* (-2.16)
Tradable farm output per capita						-0.0363** (-2.74)	
Nontradable farm output per capita						0.0139 (0.88)	
Constant	0.453** (16.30)	0.453** (15.84)	0.470** (17.01)	0.494** (18.36)	0.458** (16.65)	0.457** (16.79)	0.498** (19.11)
Observations	178	178	178	178	178	178	178
Adjusted R^2	0.081	0.072	0.113	0.135	0.103	0.107	0.148

t statistics in parentheses
$^+ p < 0.10$, $^* p < 0.05$, $^{**} p < 0.01$

TABLE 2.5
Substantive significance of factors affecting voting in the 1860s

Explanatory variable	Model 5	Model 6	Model 7
Republican	**−0.045**	**−0.045**	**−0.051**
Wealth	0.018	0.018	0.010
Mfg output per capita	**0.032**	**0.041**	**0.079**
Farm output per capita	0.017		0.015
Proportion of farm output tradable	**−0.052**		**−0.036**
Tradable farm output per capita		**−0.041**	
Nontradable farm output per capita		**0.028**	

Note: Substantive effects estimated with Clarify. For party, the results show the difference in the voting behavior of Republican as against Democratic members of Congress, holding all other variables constant at their means. For all other variables, the results show the change in the probability of voting for hard money associated with the variable going from one-half standard deviation below its mean to one-half standard deviation above its mean, holding all other variables constant at their means. All the results are drawn from models 5, 6, and 7 of table 2.3. The results that reach normal levels of statistical significance (in Clarify regressions) are indicated in boldface.

The indicator for party reveals that Republicans were only about 5 percent more likely to vote against contraction and gold. Party to some extent confounds other factors, as there is reason to believe that in many cases, the determinants of partisan affiliation were closely related to the determinants of attitudes toward the gold standard. In any case, the table demonstrates that a standard deviation increase in a district's manufacturing output increases the likelihood that its member of Congress will vote for hard money between 3 and 8 percent (the interaction terms indicate that manufacturing districts in New England and Pennsylvania pulled in the other direction). On the other hand, a standard deviation increase in the proportion of a district's farm output that is tradable *reduces* the likelihood that its representative will vote for contraction by between 3 and 5 percent.

Taken together, I believe that this statistical analysis provides general support for my argument. It should be remembered that data are a major problem, as is the interpretation of often-ambiguous and strategically complicated congressional voting. Nonetheless, it appears that the economic features of segments of the population had a generally systematic impact on the voting behavior of their representatives on monetary issues. Members of Congress specifically were more likely to vote for soft money if their constituency was less wealthy, and if more of their constituency's economic activities were in import-sensitive manufacturing (i.e., in New England and Pennsylvania) or farming, especially of export crops.

The 1870s

After 1869, macroeconomic conditions were relatively stable, and the monetary issue receded. But 1873 brought two crucial events: a "crime" and a panic. It also marked the beginning of an important long-term trend: the Great Depression, as it was called until the 1930s. The first event was the passage of the Coinage Act of 1873, signed into law in February 1873, which (as discussed above) effectively eliminated the monetary role of silver. The second was the outbreak of a global financial crisis, the Panic of 1873, which hit the United States late in the year and caused a deep recession. The longer-term trend, which was certainly not clear at the time, was that this marked the start of over twenty years of gradual decline in global prices—with, as noted, especially marked declines in the prices of agricultural products. The trend would be particularly significant in the 1890s.

The Panic of 1873 along with the difficult economic times that ensued had more immediate economic and political effects. Both houses of Congress began working on measures that would force the secretary of the treasury to expand the money supply and depreciate the currency. In early April 1874 the resulting legislation, popularly called the Inflation Bill, narrowly passed the Senate (29–24); a House version passed even more narrowly (129–116), while a somewhat more moderate compromise version passed more easily late in mid-April. Much to the shock of many, President Grant vetoed the Inflation Bill, and there were not enough votes to override the veto. Note in figure 2.3 that in the run-up to the Inflation Bill debates, the dollar depreciated to over $5.70/£, but after the presidential veto made it a dead letter, the currency appreciated significantly to almost $5.30/£.

Following the midterm elections of 1874, the battle over the Resumption Act heated up. It seemed possible that Congress would in fact refuse to support a return to gold. The dollar began to depreciate again, and stayed relatively weak for nearly three years as party, presidential, and interest group politics made the future of Resumption uncertain (see figure 2.3). It was not lost on investors that the original vote in favor of the Resumption Act was taken in January 1875 by a lame-duck Congress. It was widely known that the Republican leadership used a combination of threats and promises to elicit a party line vote in favor of returning to gold by 1879. Almost as soon as the new Congress convened, it embarked on successive attempts to repeal the Resumption Act. Yet all these efforts were either defeated in Congress, or vetoed by Grant or his Republican successor, Hayes (1877–81). As it became apparent that congressional hostility to the Resumption Act was not going to change the course of the country's return to gold, the dollar gradually appreciated up to the point where the gold standard was restored in January 1879.

The analysis here looks at seventeen votes on the Inflation Bill and Resumption Act, most of which had to do with its repeal or substantial amendment. All the anti–Resumption Act measures were ultimately defeated, either in Congress or by presidential veto, but they still provide interesting insights into the economic basis of voting on the return to gold.

Tables 2.6–2.8 analyze the principal House of Representatives votes on the Inflation Bill and the Resumption Act, including attempts to repeal it. The results are quite consistent across methods and generally in line with the results for the 1860s. Farmers of export (tradable) crops as well as New England and Pennsylvania manufacturers were more likely to favor soft money. Other manufacturers, farmers of nontradable products, and wealthier districts were supportive of the return to gold.

The most prominent change from the previous decade is that in this period, the issue had taken on a strong partisan dimension, as the Republican leadership rallied its members to support presidents Grant and Hayes as they brought the currency back to gold. This can be seen by the strong positive effect of party (i.e., Republican Party membership) in all the statistical analyses. While Republican members of Congress were weakly more likely to vote for soft money in the 1860s, in the 1874–77 period they were nearly 20 percent more likely to vote for hard money. Presumably the party leadership was able to whip members of Congress whose constituents were less concerned about the issue, although we cannot evaluate this with the available data. Still, the economic interest factors continue to operate more or less as before.

TABLE 2.6
Congressional voting on 1870s' monetary policy issues: All votes pooled

	(1) Vote	(2) Vote	(3) Vote	(4) Vote	(5) Vote	(6) Vote	(7) Vote
Vote Republican	0.809** (7.37)	0.763** (7.06)	0.815** (7.38)	0.769** (7.03)	0.789** (7.01)	0.790** (7.05)	0.758** (6.80)
Wealth	0.220** (3.06)	0.263** (3.54)	0.206** (2.73)	0.237** (3.05)	0.213** (2.95)	0.215** (2.97)	0.234** (3.04)
Mfg output per capita	0.589** (6.86)	0.425** (4.53)	0.723** (7.73)	0.602** (5.03)	0.513** (5.71)	0.539** (6.21)	0.537** (4.47)
Farm output per capita	0.221** (2.82)	0.187* (2.39)	0.219** (2.87)	0.193* (2.54)	0.214** (2.79)		0.189* (2.52)
New England mfg		-0.317** (-2.80)		-0.488** (-3.61)			-0.427** (-3.15)
New England		1.764** (9.74)		1.676** (9.07)			1.603** (8.43)
Pennsylvania mfg			-0.482** (-2.92)	-0.384* (-2.13)			-0.332+ (-1.85)

Pennsylvania			-0.326 (-1.45)	-0.218 (-0.96)			-0.256 (-1.12)
Proportion of farm output tradable					-0.168* (-2.13)		-0.104 (-1.36)
Tradable farm output per capita						0.00726 (0.09)	
Nontradable farm output per capita						0.233** (3.10)	
Constant	-0.725** (-10.34)	-0.810** (-11.20)	-0.660** (-8.85)	-0.734** (-8.86)	-0.729** (-10.64)	-0.727** (-10.52)	-0.738** (-9.29)
Observations	3665	3665	3665	3665	3665	3665	3665
Pseudo R^2	0.087	0.105	0.097	0.110	0.090	0.089	0.111

t statistics in parentheses

$^+ p < 0.10$, $^* p < 0.05$, $^{**} p < 0.01$

TABLE 2.7
Congressional voting on 1870s' monetary policy issues: Proportion of votes for hard money

	(1) Proportion of votes for hard money	(2) Proportion of votes for hard money	(3) Proportion of votes for hard money	(4) Proportion of votes for hard money	(5) Proportion of votes for hard money	(6) Proportion of votes for hard money	(7) Proportion of votes for hard money
Republican	-0.184** (-3.48)	-0.209** (-3.99)	-0.189** (-3.50)	-0.209** (-3.99)	-0.182** (-3.50)	-0.178** (-3.39)	-0.207** (-3.98)
Wealth	0.0264 (1.49)	0.0449* (2.39)	0.0239 (1.33)	0.0381+ (1.85)	0.0233 (1.33)	0.0246 (1.41)	0.0375+ (1.86)
Mfg output per capita	0.212** (6.12)	0.141** (3.55)	0.257** (6.60)	0.199** (3.29)	0.174** (4.60)	0.189** (5.17)	0.166** (2.60)
Farm output per capita	0.0743* (2.19)	0.0558+ (1.67)	0.0714* (2.13)	0.0562+ (1.71)	0.0703* (2.11)		0.0541+ (1.66)
New England mfg		-0.135* (-2.34)		-0.192** (-2.62)			-0.161* (-2.12)
New England		0.689** (10.71)		0.669** (9.74)			0.635** (8.96)

	(1)	(2)	(3)	(4)	(5)	(6)	(7)
Pennsylvania mfg			-0.223**	-0.179*			-0.153+
			(-3.42)	(-2.29)			(-1.92)
Pennsylvania			0.00755	0.0631			0.0465
			(0.07)	(0.61)			(0.45)
Proportion of farm output tradable					-0.0765**		-0.0457
					(-2.64)		(-1.53)
Tradable farm output per capita						-0.0107	
						(-0.31)	
Nontradable farm output per capita						0.0796*	
						(2.48)	
Constant	0.491**	0.457**	0.511**	0.476**	0.487**	0.486**	0.471**
	(11.74)	(10.56)	(11.50)	(9.68)	(11.85)	(11.74)	(9.79)
Observations	235	235	235	235	235	235	235
Adjusted R^2	0.193	0.315	0.233	0.329	0.214	0.207	0.334

t statistics in parentheses

+ $p < 0.10$, * $p < 0.05$, ** $p < 0.01$

TABLE 2.8
Substantive significance of factors affecting voting in the 1870s

Explanatory variable	Model 5	Model 6	Model 7
Republican	**0.190**	**0.190**	**0.183**
Wealth	**0.052**	**0.052**	**0.057**
Mfg output per capita	**0.123**	**0.129**	**0.113**
Farm output per capita	**0.051**		**0.046**
Proportion of farm output tradable	**−0.041**		**−0.025**
Tradable farm output per capita		0.001	
Nontradable farm output per capita		**0.056**	

Note: Substantive effects estimated with Clarify. For party, the results show the difference in the voting behavior of Republican as against Democratic members of Congress, holding all other variables constant at their means. For all other variables, the results show the change in the probability of voting for hard money associated with the variable going from one-half standard deviation below its mean to one-half standard deviation above its mean, holding all other variables constant at their means. All the results are drawn from models 5, 6, and 7 of table 2.6. The results that reach normal levels of statistical significance (in Clarify) are indicated in boldface.

Opposition to the gold standard was strongest among the farming regions producing export crops as well as in some New England and Pennsylvania manufacturing districts. Meanwhile, wealthier districts, along with the rest of manufacturing and farming, tended to support the return to gold. An interesting change is that manufacturing outside Pennsylvania and New England was more progold in the 1870s than in the 1860s. This may simply be due to the confounding effect of Republicans voting along party lines (most manufacturing districts were Republican), but it may also have to do with the fact that the now-higher levels of tariff protection made manufacturers uninterested in the antigold cause.

Conclusion

Both the narrative and statistical analyses presented above tend to support an interpretation of the politics of US currency policy in this period in which economic interests play a major role. In particular, they appear consistent with the idea that those most likely to benefit from a weak dollar—farmers producing tradable crops and manufacturers facing import competition—were strong supporters of either staying off the gold standard or going to a depreciated silver standard. There is no question that the data are of questionable quality, and the evaluations of the arguments are indirect. Nevertheless, the results seem consistent over a series of votes that took place over a period of about ten years. And they served as a precursor to an even more striking and much better-known US debate over the gold standard in the 1890s.

3

The United States: Silver Threats among the Gold, 1880–96

The United States was on the gold standard from 1879 until 1933, with a brief interruption during World War I. For almost all that time, US currency policy was politically controversial. The controversy became particularly heated during periods of economic distress, especially in the 1890s. In what is perhaps the most famous modern political conflict over exchange rate policy, the Populist movement launched a concerted attack on the gold standard, which led up to a presidential election fought largely over gold.

The 1890s' "battle of the standards" in the United States came at a crucial time in both global and US economic history. Internationally, this was the high point of the first era of globalization: the decades before 1914. World trade and finance had been growing rapidly since the 1870s, and the international gold standard was well established and expanding. The Populist assault on gold represented a stunning rejection of the central pillar of the classical world economy—one that attracted attention around the world.

In the US context, the rise of the Populist movement came at a similarly pivotal time, as the country had matured industrially while remaining predominantly agrarian. The battle of the standards was also a fight over whose vision of society would dominate: the big cities with their booming finance, commerce, and industries, or the countryside with its thriving cotton, tobacco, and wheat farms whose products dominated world markets. The conflict over the gold standard keenly reflected as well as powerfully affected the course of US political and economic development. It also provides a valuable setting in which to evaluate my argument about the distributional implications and political ramifications of exchange rate policy choices.

The Populist Assault on Gold

The course of conflict over the gold standard in the United States in the 1890s is perhaps the best-known episode in exchange rate politics in modern history. It is often examined in an isolated, US context, where what has impressed scholars and schoolchildren alike has been the mass mobilization of the Populists, the rise of their third party, and the vehemence of their "cross of gold" rhetoric. All these things are worthy of attention, but for our purposes, the character of the debate is interesting primarily as an example of political strife over currency policy.

The Populist attack on the gold standard was closely connected to the previous attempt to forestall a return to gold, which had failed by 1879. Nonetheless, agitation against the gold standard continued through the 1880s, albeit at a lower level of intensity than before. The country seemed firmly committed to gold, and economic conditions were reasonably good. As the global Great Depression of 1873–96 went on, though, prices of tradable goods continued to decline. In the early 1890s, farm prices fell particularly rapidly and far. Table 3.1 and figure 3.1 show the evolution of representative prices after 1893. Between 1893 and 1896, farm prices fell 22 percent while prices of building material, a classic nontradable good, fell by 7 percent. Many prices of manufactured goods fell along with farm prices, but in their case

TABLE 3.1
Representative prices, 1893–99

	Farm products	Metal products	Building material
1893	100	100	100
1894	88	86	96
1895	86	92	93
1896	78	92	93
1897	83	84	91
1898	88	86	96
1899	89	130	105

Source: Warren and Pearson 1935.

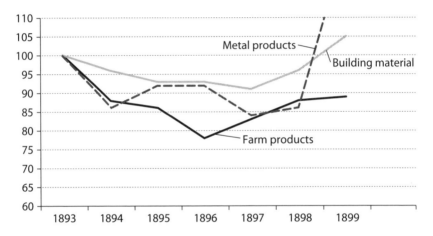

Figure 3.1 Evolution of representative prices, 1893–99. *Source*: Table 3.1.

productivity advances more than made up for price declines.[1] Table 3.2 shows how seriously productivity-adjusted agricultural prices were lagging behind prices. Agriculture was particularly depressed during the early 1890s, as indicated by the fact that between 1890 and 1896, production of farm equipment dropped 39 percent in constant-dollar terms, while output of industrial machinery and equipment rose 62 percent, and the total output rose 23 percent.[2] Traded goods prices

1 Between 1879 and 1889 (when census data are available), for example, labor productivity grew 5 percent in agriculture, and 46 percent in mining and manufacturing.
2 Calculated from Hoffman 1956, 143.

TABLE 3.2
Value added per gainful worker, 1869–99 (1879 = 100)

Sector	1869	1879	1889	1899
Agriculture	84	100	105	118
Manufacturing and mining	84	100	146	159
Construction	82	100	95	90

Source: Robert Gallman's (1960, 13–43) variant A is used for construction.

were falling dramatically relative to nontradables prices, and it did not escape the attention of farmers and others that devaluation would have reversed this trend.

The Issues

After 1879, the currency question in order was whether to *stay* on the fixed-rate gold standard, or leave it and adopt another monetary system. As had been true in the late 1870s, antigold sentiment in the 1890s generally took the form of support for movement to a silver standard.[3] As before, the demand for the free coinage of silver at a sixteen-to-one rate against gold implied a devaluation of the dollar against gold-backed currencies, significant increases in the money supply, and a floating exchange rate against gold. In theory, two other options were available. The country could have gone back to greenbacks, and many Populist monetary theorists supported this in principle as well as regarded silver as a compromise with miners and others who wanted a specie standard.[4] But it was a compromise that had been made, and seemed stable enough. The second theoretical option still available was international bimetallism, an internationally negotiated bimetallic system that would probably have involved a depreciation and refixing against gold. This last option, however, required the collaboration of other governments, which so far had not been forthcoming. In this case, the choice posed was between the unilateral adoption of a silver standard and continued adherence to the gold standard.

3 For its general contours, see Hicks 1931; Hollingsworth 1963; Hoffman 1956; Timberlake 1978; Friedman and Schwartz 1963, 89–134; Sundquist 1983, 134–69. As above, references are given only for specific quotations, facts, or controversial assertions.

4 See, for example, the observations of Ignatius Donnelly quoted in Hicks 1921, especially 126.

International Factors

The international gold standard was well established by 1890. Almost all of western Europe, the United States, Canada, and Australia were on gold, and attempts to change this—such as yet another international bimetallic conference called at the United States' instigation in November 1892—failed. Commitment to gold was hardly universal. The independent nations of Latin America and Asia, including Japan, were all on either silver or a fiat currency. So too was the world's largest nation, Russia. Even several important colonies—British India, the Dutch East Indies, and the Philippines—were on silver. From a global standpoint, the pattern of currency use was that industrial nations were on gold, while agrarian and mining nations were on silver or paper. The principal exceptions were Canada and Australia within the British Empire, and the United States. In this context, it was not unreasonable for Americans to consider adopting (again) the monetary system used by their main competitors in world markets.

In the open world economy of the late nineteenth century, the impact of a country's exchange rate regime on the ability of its producers to compete on world markets was a critical issue. Indeed, US Populists frequently drew comparisons between United States' commitment to gold and the silver or paper currencies of the countries with which US farmers and miners were competing. In the previous twenty years, in fact, foreign competitors had dramatically increased their pressure on US farmers—wheat farmers in particular. One 1896 pamphlet, with the subtitle *A Campaign Handbook for the Struggling Millions against the Gold-Hoarding Millionaires*, was well aware of the advantages that a depreciated silver currency (i.e., a gold premium) brought to other nations' producers:

> It is true that with gold at a premium, exchange between New York and London would fluctuate, that the pound sterling would buy exchange for more dollars just as the premium rose and for fewer dollars just as it fell, but this would no more lead to the cessation of foreign buying of our products than such a premium checks the purchase of wheat, etc., in the Argentinian, Indian and Russian markets by the British trader. In the face of a premium on gold, in fact stimulated by such premium, the exports of Russian and Argentinian wheat to Great Britain have grown very largely

of late years, and just as this premium on gold, this bounty on exports, stimulates the export of wheat and other products from such countries, a similar premium on gold in the United States would result in increased exports of our products.[5]

The Indian experience was the focus of much Populist attention. Indian agricultural products were said to be driving US products out of third markets, and this was ascribed to the depreciation of India's silver-based currency:

> It was not until after the demonetization of silver by the United States that any attempt was made to raise wheat in India. There was no money in it as long as silver was at par. The first shipment was made in 1874, and amounted to 95,000 bushels, from which it has risen to nearly 50,000,000, while our shipments have declined in the same time from about 100,000,000 to less than 50,000,000 bushels. It is not necessary that India should raise enough to supply the whole demand of Europe (although she could do it); sufficient to prevent the advance of the price beyond the cost of production is enough to ruin the American farmer. This it does, and not only fixes the price and shuts off part of that market, but fixes the price in the home market. This applies with just as much force, in proportion to the amount produced, to cotton, hemp, rice, corn, wool, hides, linseed, rape seed, mustard seed, peanuts, and numerous other products, as it does to wheat.[6]

US farmers flocked to the Populist campaign against gold in an international economic context in which other commodity-producing countries were using their depreciated silver or paper currencies to gain a competitive edge. Indeed, the wheat exports of Argentina, Russia, and India grew at an extremely rapid rate in the 1880s and 1890s. Some of this was due to the expansion of railroad networks and cheapening of overseas shipping, but some was also due to these nations' depreciated currencies. The Populists argued, in the words of one, "that the yellow man using the white metal, holds at his mercy the white man using the yellow metal."[7]

5   Stevans 1896, 165.
6   M. J. Farrell, quoted in Elliott 1889, 245.
7   Moreton Frewen, quoted in Jones 1964, 14.

Gold supporters also had their eyes firmly on the international context of their battle to protect the United States' commitment to gold. Although the international gold standard was well established and international financial flows were robust, there were constant concerns about both currencies and debtors. Financial difficulties in 1890 in Argentina (which was not on gold) nearly bankrupted one of the world's most important investment banks, Barings, and caused real concern on the London and other European markets. The leading US bankers and investors were well aware that skittish European capitalists could turn away from the United States should its financial and monetary conditions become questionable. Northeastern financial and commercial interests had strong incentives to safeguard the stability of the nation's currency.

The Interests

The configuration of interests was largely a continuation of what it had been in the earlier debates of the 1860s and 1870s. But as the nation's economy evolved over the decades, the anticipated distributional affects also changed. They remained, however, in line with our theoretical expectations. I leave aside nontradables producers, largely because the historical literature has little to say about them (unlike in the Greenback era, where railroad owners and small businesspeople were prominent).

As had been the case earlier, United States' international financial community was well aware of its position in the world financial order. The United States was the world's principal borrower, but its attractiveness to foreign investors depended on their perceptions of the country's creditworthiness. Hints of devaluations à la Latin America or other macroeconomic deviations were sure to drive capital away from the United States. By the 1890s, European investors were all too familiar with the financial difficulties of industrializing and semi-industrial nations. Twenty years of experience had reinforced the role of the gold standard in "certifying" financial reliability. A continued commitment to gold was seen as close to essential for ongoing US access to international capital markets. A new angle was the fact that by the 1890s, US investment abroad was significant. Many on Wall Street hoped that New York would soon be an international financial center, for which ironclad dedication to gold was a prerequisite. Merchants involved in foreign trade also remained strongly supportive of the gold standard because of the predictability it provided them as well as their customers and suppliers.

Farmers and miners were the core of the antigold alliance in the 1890s. Much of the industrial backing for silver and Greenbacks, so prominent in the 1860s and 1870s, had dissipated.

Industrialists generally were not sympathetic to the gold standard, yet by the 1890s they had ceased to be particularly active on currency policy. There were several reasons for this. The first was that their main concern was in securing tariff protection. They had been successful, especially with the McKinley Tariff of 1890. High tariffs made the exchange rate less relevant, as it effectively eliminated foreign competition.

Second, the ability of industry to obtain high tariffs depended to some extent on political compromises made with gold supporters. The agrarian Democrats who were the principal opponents of gold were also notoriously hostile to industrial protection. On the other hand, the northeastern free traders in finance and commerce were committed to gold. The result was an alliance, largely within the Republican Party, between midwestern industry and eastern commerce and finance in favor of high tariffs for the former along with the gold standard for the latter. This was something like a US version of Germany's marriage of iron and rye; in the US context, industrial protectionists acquiesced on the gold standard while financial gold bugs assented on protection. The link was embodied in Ohioan William McKinley, who designed the protectionist tariff of 1890. McKinley had long supported silver, but ran for president in 1896 on a Republican platform that was both protectionist and progold.

A third reason for the fading industrial attention to silver was the increasing international interests of some manufacturers. By the 1890s, portions of US industry were becoming more internationally oriented, following a trail that the New England textile manufacturers had started down earlier. Interest in foreign markets had grown, manufactured exports had expanded, and even foreign direct investment (FDI) was increasing.[8] Manufacturers with export markets might have wanted devaluation, and in fact much of the support for international bimetal-

---

8 For a survey, see Lake 1988.

lism came from those who favored an internationally negotiated devaluation of the dollar. The failure of this option meant that internationally oriented manufacturers had to choose between full participation in the gold standard and something akin to pariah status in international trade and payments; they chose the former. All things considered, industrialists were marginal to the battle of the standards, either because their opposition to gold had lessened, they had come to regard the currency question as secondary to the tariff, or they had cut deals that required them to abandon silver in return for tariffs.

The nation's agricultural producers, on the other hand, had, if anything, strengthened in their opposition to the gold standard. One source of this increased resolve was the continued decline in the relative price of farm products, as shown in table 3.1. The lower that farm prices went—and the more silver prices accompanied them—the greater would be the positive impact of switching from gold to silver.

A second development also encouraged agricultural interest in the currency question: the expansion of export-oriented farming over the course of the late nineteenth century. In the 1860s and 1870s, southern cotton was of overwhelming importance as a farm export. Cotton output grew rapidly in the late nineteenth century, as the cotton economy recovered from the Civil War, so that cotton farmers remained crucial and strongly engaged in the silver movement. Meanwhile, wheat farming expanded particularly quickly in the 1870s and 1880s as the Great Plains were opened to grain production, in large part because the railroad and steamship now allowed their output to be sold on world markets. As a result, between the early 1870s and early 1890s, the US acreage sown to wheat roughly doubled; wheat output also doubled, as did wheat exports. Given the decline in the price of wheat, the value of wheat exports increased by less (about 60 percent), but the significance of wheat to the US farm economy was far greater in the 1890s than it had been in the aftermath of the Civil War. (The acreage and output of oats and barley tripled over this time, but they were not such important crops.) The expansion of wheat production increased the number of farmers concerned about world market prices for their crops. At the same time, and largely for the same reasons (transportation improvements), the opening of the Latin American pampas, Canadian prairies, and other wheat-growing regions subjected US wheat producers to stiff international competition—most of it from countries that were not on the gold standard. In the 1860s, Argentina, Australia, Canada, and India had exported no wheat at all; by the 1890s, they were exporting more than one-third as much as the United States (and by 1910, they would be exporting nearly three times as much).[9]

In the words of T. B. Buchanan of Colorado,

> To add to the trials of American producers of cotton and breadstuffs there are not only low and constantly shrinking prices for these staples, but an absolute falling off in the export demand. These staple United States products are being more and more neglected by foreign consumers, while their production has been greatly stimulated in other parts of the world, and especially so in India....
>
> But why does England buy more wheat from India and less from us? This is the important question to the farmer of our great Northwest. One answer is, simply because the Englishman buys one commodity to be paid for at a future time in another commodity, while the one in which payment is to be made is constantly declining in price.... The Indian wheat is to be paid for in silver or its equivalent, the American in gold or its equivalent. There is no fixed relation of value between English and Indian money, while there is between English and United States money. This constitutes abundant reason why the Englishman should prefer to buy Indian wheat rather than American, if there were no others, and this reason will exist and be in full force so long as silver tends to lower and lower prices as compared with gold....
>
> The price—the silver price—which the Indian farmer gets for his wheat has remained substantially the same; while the price which the American farmer gets, being reckoned in gold, has grown less and less year by year, when the cost of his labor is the same.[10]

This refrain, relating the export difficulties of US primary producers to the country's commitment to the gold standard, was repeated in tract after anti-gold-standard tract.

---

9 Harley 1980.
10 Quoted in Elliott 1889, 168–71.

Devaluation appealed to farmers because it would reverse adverse price trends: it would make farm exports more competitive on world markets and raise the domestic price of exportable crops. Reflation and devaluation would have mitigated the crisis in agriculture, and soft-money interests were well aware of this.

US farmers remained at the forefront of attempts to depreciate the dollar. To be sure, interest was not universal. Dairy and produce farmers had little to gain from a depreciation, as their products were effectively not tradable across borders. But the focus of US farming was on cotton and tobacco in the South, and wheat in the Midwest and Great Plains; these farmers were heavily export oriented, strongly interested in how their crops were faring on world markets, and extremely hostile to the gold standard.

The mining districts of the Rocky Mountain West remained strong-holds of prosilver sentiment. The silver miners themselves, the principal mining interests of the region, had an obvious interest in policies to raise the dollar price of silver (i.e., lower the gold price of the dollar). Lead and copper miners, also critical in the West, had reasons similar to those of farmers to support a Silverite depreciation, which would raise the dollar price of their export products. It was also the case that the different minerals shared some interests, as they tended to be found together and so lead miners had silver interests. As before, the mining sector was numerically relatively small—only about 2 percent of the national labor force in 1890 versus 43 percent for agriculture—but it was concentrated in sparsely populated states in which miners were politically and economically important, and each of which had two senators.

The interest group configuration of the 1890s, then, was roughly similar to that of the controversy in 1865–79 over the return to gold. Two differences are worth noting. For one, the positions of the strongest supporters and opponents of gold—the international financial and farm sectors, respectively—had become more polarized and entrenched with the solidification of the gold standard along with the decline in commodity prices. This helped make the battles of the 1890s even more bitter than those of the 1870s. Second, the industrial sector was largely uninvolved in the debate, primarily due to its general satisfaction with high protection for manufactured goods. This illustrates the potential substitutability of trade protection for a depreciated currency—a consideration that recurs in many debates over exchange rate policy.

Politics and Policies

Silver sentiment erupted fiercely amid the agricultural depression that began in 1888. Republican William H. Harrison beat Grover Cleveland in the 1888 election in part because Harrison promised support for silver against Cleveland's New York gold standard orthodoxy. Harrison made good on his promise with the 1890 Sherman Silver Purchase Act, which doubled the amount of silver purchased by the Treasury under the 1878 Bland-Allison Act. The bill was too mild to satisfy antigold interests, but strong enough to cause fear in financial markets that the dollar would be devalued. These worries grew after the 1892 elections gave the Democrats, who had run on a Silverite platform, control of the presidency and both houses of Congress for the first time since the 1850s. The Republicans had been unable to straddle the money issue and were voted out of office. In the meantime, the new People's (Populist) Party was scoring electoral successes throughout the West.

The Democrats got their chance in 1892. Nevertheless, Cleveland was a "gold Democrat" close to Wall Street, and when the Panic of 1893 hit the country's financial market, he along with other hard-money supporters blamed it on uncertainty about the country's dedication to gold. Cleveland, in defiance of his party's platform, prevailed on Congress to repeal the silver purchase clause of the Sherman Act. He allied with gold Republicans and used patronage to bludgeon key Democrats into submission. Some of the strongest attacks on the administration came from silver Republicans, for whom the threat to withhold patronage was idle. One noted that "the administration with its petty spoils and patronage, has been able to make . . . many converts [from free silver]." Another quoted a letter to Cleveland: "It has been openly proclaimed . . . that the congressman or senator of Democratic faith who would not act with the administration in opposition to the expressed sentiments of the platform on which you and they were elected would be ignored in the distribution of patronage. . . . Those nearest to you . . . have taken the ground that federal patronage would be made the club to beat back the tide of popular sentiment."[11]

To the disgust of Silverites on both sides of the aisle, Cleveland was able to cobble together a bipartisan hard-money coalition. The silver

---

11 Quoted in Timberlake 1978, 39.

Democrats looked on in dismay. After Cleveland rejected all attempts to conciliate with his own party members, one asked plaintively, "What does this prove when a Democratic president and secretary of the treasury refuse to agree with six-sevenths of the Democratic senators ... upon a compromise measure, and prefer to leave the administration banner in the hands of Republicans and Democrats jointly to placing it in the hands of Democrats alone?"[12] Whatever it proved, it foretold the end of the gold Democrats. The Democrats lost the 1894 midterm elections—in the view of the Silverite majority within the party, due to the party's betrayal of its currency platform—and free silver supporters took definitive control of the Democratic Party.

With US adherence to the gold standard under threat, the Treasury faced frequent runs on its gold reserve. The Treasury was able to maintain the commitment to gold because of a series of loans from US and international bankers—what would now be considered international "bailouts"; the most famous of these loans was the Belmont-Morgan syndicate agreement of 1895.[13] These financial ties served to reinforce the Treasury's position and help it overcome both economic and political pressure on the gold standard.

Meanwhile, the Populists moved to pick up the voters that the Democrats appeared poised to lose. In 1890, the Farmers' Alliance movement scored electoral successes in a number of western states. The People's Party was formed in 1892 by the Southern and Western Alliances, along with labor groups; the Populists got over a million votes for president, and the party sent hundreds of legislators to state houses and Congress.

Money came first in the Populist pantheon. The 1892 Omaha platform, on which the Populist presidential candidate won more than a million votes, thundered:

> The national power to create money is appropriated to enrich bondholders; a vast public debt, payable in legal tender currency, has been funded into gold-bearing bonds.... Silver, which has been accepted as coin since the dawn of history, has been demonetized to add to the purchasing power of gold ... and the supply of currency is purposely abridged to fatten usurers, bankrupt en-

12 Ibid., 41.
13 See, for example, Garber and Grilli 1986.

terprise, and enslave industry. A vast conspiracy against mankind has been organized on two continents, and it is rapidly taking possession of the world.

The platform went on to begin its demands with:

First, *Money*. We demand a national currency, safe, sound, and flexible, issued by the general government only, a full legal tender for all debts, public and private. . . .

(a) We demand free and unlimited coinage of silver and gold at the present legal ratio of sixteen to one.
(b) We demand that the amount of circulating medium be speedily increased to not less than fifty dollars per capita.[14]

Populist currency policies called for a silver standard, with the dollar fluctuating against gold, and sufficient issuance of paper money (backed by silver) to ensure that the dollar depreciated while prices rose. Other measures included the requirement that paper dollars be valid in all transactions (against the widespread use of gold clauses), low-interest government loans, a postal savings system, and the abolition of nationally chartered banks; all went in the direction of depreciating the dollar and raising prices—"price stability," in the context of continuing price declines.

In the words of Populist senator William Allen of Nebraska, "We believe it possible so to regulate the issue of money as to make it of approximately the same value at all times." Popular Populist orator Mary Elizabeth Lease, who advised farmers to "raise less corn and more Hell," was more inflammatory: "Wall Street owns the country. . . . Money rules, and our Vice President is a London banker. . . . We want money, land, and transportation."[15]

As the Populists gained strength and the movement for free silver swept the country, the Democrats risked surrendering much of their base to a powerful third party and instead swung over to unequivocal support for free silver. At the 1896 Democratic National Convention in Chicago, a young congressman from Nebraska, William Jennings Bryan, galvanized the delegates and country with a stirring call to arms.

14 For the platform, see Hicks 1931, 439–44.
15 Quoted in ibid., 316–17, 160, respectively.

Bryan dismissed the pleading of the party's financial leaders: "You come to us and tell us that the great cities are in favor of the gold standard; we reply that the great cities rest upon our broad and fertile prairies. Burn down your cities and leave our farms, and your cities will spring up again as if by magic; but destroy our farms and the grass will grow in the streets of every city in the country." Speaking for the party's majority, Bryan challenged gold backers at home and abroad: "You shall not press down upon the brow of labor this crown of thorns, you shall not crucify mankind upon a cross of gold."

Bryan became the joint Democratic-Populist candidate for president in 1896, and made the centrality of the currency question to his candidacy clear in his acceptance speech at the convention:

> The farmers are opposed to the gold standard because they have felt its effects. Since they sell at wholesale and buy at retail they have lost more than they have gained by falling prices, and, besides this, they have found that certain fixed charges have not fallen at all.
>
> Taxes have not been perceptibly decreased, although it requires more of farm products now than formerly to secure the money with which to pay taxes. Debts have not fallen. . . . Railroad rates have not been reduced to keep pace with falling prices, and besides these items there are many more.[16]

The 1896 election was fought largely over the money question, which split both parties. Bryan lost the support of the gold Democrats. The Republican candidate, McKinley, endorsed gold, despite his long-standing support for a moderate silver position, because it had become apparent that this was crucial to the eastern business community and related electoral support. McKinley lost the support of silver Republicans, but gained millions of dollars in business contributions to ensure the political victory of gold.[17] Bryan's campaign had many of the features of a popular crusade, with rolling mass meetings and incendiary rhetoric. The Republicans, on the other hand, relied for the first time on major corporate campaign contributions; McKinley's campaign man-

16 Quoted in Stevans 1896, 224.
17 How many millions is not clear. The formal audit showed $3.5 million, with $3 million from New York; the actual figure could have been twice or three times this amount (Croly 1912, 220).

ager and handler "assessed" eastern banks and corporations at 0.25 percent of their capital.[18]

International financial markets watched the campaign closely. Not only was the exchange rate policy of the world's largest debtor important, but US deviation from the gold standard also could have had a broader impact on other nations' decisions about whether to start using or stay on gold. Articles in the London *Times* give a flavor of how European financial markets saw the US attack on gold:

> New York and Chicago will do everything they can to maintain the national credit and therefore to promote friendly relations abroad. Bankers, financiers, merchants, and every class with great interests at stake are for conciliation. . . .
>
> [On the other hand, one] of these Silver Senators was told the other day that free coinage would at once put the country on a silver basis. "That is what I want," he answered. "But it would destroy our foreign trade." "That, also, is what I want; this country can produce everything it needs." (January 25, 1896, 5)

> The Democratic party, the oldest political organization in this country, has been captured by the Silverites, and if to-day fulfills the promise of yesterday the Silverites stand ready to divide the spoil with the Populists. The party is henceforth to be governed, as Bismarck said the world could not be governed, from below. There has been an upheaval of the political crust, and strange creatures have come forth. The issue is no longer between Silver and Gold only, but between society and a very crude form of Socialism. . . .
>
> Throughout all that you hear the note of that spirit of communistic revolution which seems to have taken possession of the Democratic party. It is not finance, but financial freebooting, which the Silverites erect into a policy.
>
> If the rank Socialism of their platform went by itself it might prove mischievous enough, but it is made worse by Sectionalism in a flagrant form. . . . The South and West do not mean to divide the Republic. They mean to dominate it. (July 9, 1896, 5)

---

18 On the details of these two episodes—the Republican commitment to gold and reliance on corporate contributions—see Croly 1912, 192–204, 209–27.

He [McKinley] spoke yesterday at his home in Canton, and drew a striking comparison, not new, but new in his mouth, between the present contest and that of the Civil War. He says: "Then it was a struggle to preserve the Government of the United States; now it is a struggle to preserve the financial honour of the Government of the United States. . . ." That is a long step in the political education of Mr. M'Kinley, and he will presently take others. He perceives that the logic of events has made him the champion of the financial honour of the country. (July 13, 1896, 7)

While the rhetoric was undoubtedly overblown, the articles capture some of the financial markets' sense that the gold standard was essential to the continuance of the existing international monetary and financial order. The articles also indicate how polarized debate had become by the 1890s, so that the gold standard was something of a dividing line between two great camps both in the United States and internationally. And they reinforce the sense in which the battle of the standards was in some ways a much broader contest over the future of the US political economy.

The narrow defeat of Bryan in 1896 sealed the fate of silver, and in any event antigold sentiment dampened over the next few years as economic conditions improved and prices began to rise. In 1900, Congress passed the Gold Standard Act, Bryan was defeated a second time, and the country's commitment to the gold standard was firm. Indeed, as commodity prices rose internationally after 1896, gold became less politically contentious everywhere. Countries flocked to the gold standard, including semi-industrial and agrarian countries that had previously avoided it—Japan and Russia in 1897, Argentina and India in 1899, Austria-Hungary in 1902, Mexico in 1905, Brazil in 1906, and Thailand in 1908. By 1908, China and Persia were the only countries of any import not on gold.

During the 1890s, the battle over the gold standard was refought in the United States, initiated this time by those who wanted to take the country off gold rather than those who wanted to put it on gold. The result was nonetheless similar. Those opposed to the gold standard were defeated, although the country was probably close to evenly divided on the matter. In both instances, the progold executive used its position to override or manipulate the more antigold Congress. And many of the analytic conclusions drawn in the previous chapter, about the Greenback era, also apply to the Populist period:

- The principal interest group division followed the expected lines. It pitted the international financial and commercial sectors, on the one hand, against farmers and miners, on the other.
- Relative price movements continued to have a substantial impact on the politics of exchange rates. Just as the worldwide decline in commodity prices after 1873 excited opposition to the gold standard, the reversal of this downward trend after 1896 dampened opposition.
- Divisions continued to cut across the two established parties, as they were more sectoral and sectional than partisan. Frustration with the two parties actually led to a particularly successful third-party movement.
- Extremely high trade barriers on manufactured imports tended to neutralize industrialists' general antipathy for gold and a relatively appreciated dollar.

Again, the narrative of this period is in line with the explanatory approach presented here. Before moving on to a more systematic evaluation of statistical evidence regarding the events in questions, it is relevant to consider existing interpretations of them. The Populist era has received much attention from scholars, but rarely from the perspective used here.

Existing Interpretations

Populism has attracted a great deal of scholarly interest. The prevailing approaches present the "clash of the standards" as pitting debtors against creditors over the nominal price level. The story of Populism is typically told in terms of beleaguered farm debtors who wanted reflation to raise the overall price level and reduce the real burden of their debts. The distinction between this view and mine is of some broader interest. The debt-driven view suggests that the Populist demands with respect to monetary policy in this period were primarily concerned about the overall price level, as in typical closed-economy circumstances, while I assert that Populist concerns were instead about relative prices, especially the relative price of tradables, as we would expect in an open economy.

There is no doubt that many US farmers were in distress in the late nineteenth century. Work by new economic historians in the 1950s and 1960s, it is true, found little deterioration in farmers' terms of trade over the late nineteenth century; nor did risk-adjusted interest rates or railroad rates appear particularly outlandish.[19] More recent analyses, however, have confirmed that many farmers were subject to great volatility in income, in many areas there was a significant deterioration in farmers' terms of trade for several years at a time, and these agrarian difficulties were roughly correlated (both over time and across place) with patterns of support for Populism (and pro-Populist Democrats).[20]

These studies explain farm discontent in the Populist era, but they leave unanswered why agrarian demands focused so heavily as they did, and in the ways that they did, on monetary issues. Indeed, from the standpoint of the standard story, there is a puzzling weakness of evidence for a relationship between farm indebtedness and farm protest. While some studies found such a correlation among farm communities, most have been less confident that indebtedness was a good predictor of support for Populism.[21] The most careful study of voting for Populist candidates in the literature, on county patterns in Kansas in the 1890s, discovered that controlling for other economic characteristics, the value of mortgages was actually associated with *lower* levels of Populist support. In contrast, farm occupation and the variability of farm yields were positively correlated with Populist votes, and wealth (whether in banks or land) and farm income were negatively correlated with Populist support. Once these factors (and several others) are included in a multivariate analysis, debt levels enter negatively, if at all.[22]

---

19 For a summary of the findings, and an example of the perplexed reaction they evinced from economic historians, see Lee and Passell 1979, 292–301.

20 Stock 1984; Bowman 1965; Bowman and Keehn 1974; McGuire 1981.

21 For some indicators of a general correlation, see Stock 1984; Nugent 1966. For more specific evidence from state-level studies, see, for example, Miller 1925; Farmer 1924; Barnhart 1925. Most of these studies, however, do not adequately distinguish between the other side of the pincer movement: adverse price trends. They tend simply to assume that if indebted farmers were in difficulty, it was due to excessive debt levels rather than particularly negative price movements.

22 Williams 1981. For the relevant table, see ibid., 244. For the mention of mortgages (which are not included in the table), see ibid., 249.

Indeed, while Populist rhetoric did complain of farm debt, it tended to focus on other issues. First and foremost was the apparent tendency for farm prices to decline more than those of other goods. Associated with this was the concern about the prices of specific inputs, such as railroad transportation (alleged to be artificially expensive due to monopolistic practices) and farm implements (purported to be artificially expensive due to protective tariffs). For example, one survey of Kansas farmers in 1893 found that 65 percent attributed farm distress to low prices, 15 percent to drought, 11 percent to "money scarcity" and "interest rates" combined, 5 percent to railroads, and the rest to scattered other factors.[23]

It is also the case that other heavily indebted groups of the national population were not drawn to the Populist cause. Urban residential mortgages were the fastest-growing segment of the loan market during the Populist period, but middle-class homeowners in the big cities are widely believed to have been hostile to Populist monetary schemes.[24] So too were many manufacturing and commercial groups large net debtors, yet their attitude toward easy money tended to be one of lukewarm support at best, and opposition at worst. Of course, these groups may have expected the debt-reducing effects of Populist monetary policies to help them less than other effects hurt, but this simply pushes the problem back to trying to specify more clearly the anticipated impact of populist policies on different groups, and the relationship between these expected effects and the groups' political positions.

If farmers were concerned primarily about the overall nominal price level, the strength of their insistence on going to a depreciated silver standard is hard to understand. Certainly there would have been some rise in the overall price level, so that any nominal contracts—such as farm mortgages—would have been less burdensome. But inflation typically affects the relative prices of goods and services in addition to the aggregate price level. If it had raised the price of farmers' inputs—such as farm implements, fertilizer, and transportation—more than the price of their output, farmers might have been made worse off. Either Populist thinkers expected no relative price effects of their monetary policies—which is unlikely given the substantial relative price move-

23 Farmer 1924, 426.
24 On the urban mortgage market, see Snowden 1988.

ments of the greenback period—or they anticipated that the prices would have been favorable to farmers.

In addition, most farm mortgages were short term. One survey of representative counties found that mortgages in the west-north central and south central states, where Populist support was strongest, averaged 3.8 and 2.7 years in maturity, respectively.[25] The lag between political action, policy implementation, and price effects, short maturities of farm mortgages, and inevitable readjustment of new loans to new monetary conditions would all have reduced the ability of free silver to provide relief to indebted farmers.[26]

Certainly farm debt was a major concern of US farmers in the late nineteenth century, and raising the nominal price level would have supplied some debt relief. Still, the depth and breadth of Populist monetary sentiment, and specific characteristics of Populist monetary proposals, are hard to square with a story based entirely on a concern for the overall price level—as would be the case in a closed-economy analyses of the politics of monetary policy. But the depth and character of the movement against gold—for a depreciated currency—is consistent with my overall argument about the expected distributional effects of a weak-currency policy: it was most strongly supported by the producers of exportable commodities.

The confusion of standard economic explanations of the period has led some historians to contend that Populism had important, even predominant noneconomic components. These include the idea that farm protest was aimed at the process of the commercialization of agriculture rather than at particular economic conditions.[27] Especially influential have been assertions by Lawrence Goodwyn and others that Populism was largely a cultural attempt by farmers to fashion a new social order.[28]

While noneconomic factors played a key part in US politics in the late nineteenth century, it is hard to believe that Populist economic demands were purely a smoke screen for cultural conflict. The Populists worked out elaborate monetary proposals and flooded the country with

25 Snowden 1987, 675.
26 For a summary, see Rockoff 1990, 752–53.
27 Mayhew 1972.
28 Goodwyn 1976; see also McNall 1988. An interpretation of Goodwyn's argument is complicated by his rather bizarre sectarianism in defining "true" Populism, but I believe the core of his reasoning is clear.

pamphlets about the implications of their economic policies. A clearer understanding of the economic bases of the Populist phenomenon, though, requires rethinking the economic impact of soft money.

I adduce statistical evidence below that tends to support my argument. But it is worthwhile to consider some more qualitative indications that Americans were not oblivious to the sorts of considerations I discuss. My claim does not necessarily imply that political actors had a full understanding of the economics of these issues or organized themselves precisely along the lines these economic effects might suggest. Certainly US farmers wanted relief from debt, and certainly soft money would have offered some relief. At the same time, this does not appear to have been the whole story.

Many Populist complaints concentrated on how price trends were affecting agricultural products particularly adversely. The focus was usually on declining nominal or relative prices for primary products, and the remedies proposed had to do with reversing this trend. Of course, this would have alleviated some of the pressure on debtors, but typically debts were mentioned, if at all, as one among many problems caused by deflation.

A quaint example of this is found in the most famous Populist propaganda tract of the 1890s, *Coin's Financial School.* The fictitious protagonist of this popular pamphlet, after discussing the impact of deflation on debtors, went on to treat other prices. He imagined a farmer going forth to "see if he could buy as much of this world's goods with 50 cents as he formerly could with a dollar."

> We will suppose, before starting, he goes to pay his taxes. He will find that his 50-cent wheat will not pay as much as his $1.40 wheat did in 1873. He will find his taxes just as much, and it will take all of twice as much wheat to pay them as in 1873.
>
> While passing out of the Court House suppose he meets a county official and should ask him what salary was paid to his office in 1873 and now. The answer would be the same number of dollars now as in 1873. The same is true of city, state, and national officers, also with the army, navy, and official abroad. . . . He starts for the depot and to get there he takes a street-car. He finds the fare the same as in 1873. He gets on a Pullman car to find the cost the same as in 1873. He registers at a first-class hotel. He finds the cost about the same as in 1873. He sends a telegram,

and finds it costs the same as in 1873. He gets a shave with the same result. He buys tea and coffee, with the same result. . . . He finds interest, except in cities on first-class loans, about as high as in 1873. Should he now meet the man who told him that his 50-cent wheat would buy as much of the world's goods as it ever did, it might result seriously for the other fellow.[29]

Every price comparison mentioned here is with a nontraded good or service: government, transportation, lodging, communications, a shave, restaurant food, and financial services. This is probably not coincidental, for comparison with manufactured goods prices would almost certainly have shown (as in table 3.1) a relative trend in favor of farm prices.

Populist monetary policies were indeed usually framed as policies to help primary producers in ways analogous to trade protection's support for manufacturers. Nevadan Thomas Fitch, a Republican concerned to influence his colleagues in the party of protection, was explicit in addressing the first National Silver Convention in 1889:

> Protection is not a great moral principle in whose behalf men can be expected to sacrifice their personal interests. It is a coalition in which results should be mutual, and thus far the wheat and silver States have not received their share. In all Nevada there is neither a spindle nor a loom, and the prairies of the Dakotas stretch for hundreds of miles unlit by furnace fire. How can Massachusetts expect that the people of the Northwest will continue to vote for a high protective tariff to sustain New England factories when both political parties in Massachusetts openly avow hostility to the great exporting industries of the Northwest? . . .
>
> Free coinage would, as you know, not only restore silver to its former value, but it would, as has been shown here, add 35 per cent to the present prices of wheat, of cotton, and of farm produce, and it would increase the wages of the laborer and add to his opportunities for obtaining employment.[30]

---

29 Harvey (1894) 1963, 213–14. The book probably sold about a million copies when it was first published.

30 Quoted in Elliott 1889, 222–23.

It is not surprising, even in light of the traditional focus on debt, that Populists highlighted the relationship of free silver to primary product prices. After all, increasing primary prices would reduce debt burdens, and of course that was one of its attractions. Yet the Populists were also explicit about the other relative price effects of going off gold. Prominent among these were impacts directly related to foreign trade. In the words of one Populist orator,

> A premium on gold will tend to increase our exports by causing a higher rate of foreign exchange—that is to say, by yielding a larger net return in dollars on the sale of bills of exchange drawn against goods exported. A premium will tend to diminish our imports by increasing the cost of bills of exchange with which to pay for goods imported.
>
> The tendency of increasing our exports and decreasing our imports will be, first, to set our spindles running, swell the number of paid operatives, [and] increase their wages, thereby adding to the number and paying capacity of consumers, and thus enlarge our home market for all home products and manufactures, with prosperity in general as the result assured.[31]

It was common indeed for Populists to maintain that going off gold would stimulate exports and reduce imports. The principal objection that gold supporters raised to this line of reasoning was that the volatility of a silver-backed dollar against gold-backed currencies would depress trade. To this, Populist thinkers insisted that the price effects would dominate the impact of increased exchange rate uncertainty—as perhaps it would have for the goods of interest to them.

It seems apparent from this that it is hardly farfetched, nor does it do violence to the qualitative evidence, to assert that the Populists' monetary proposals were concerned to ensure what we would call today a real depreciation of the dollar, and they wanted to benefit from the distributional effects of this depreciation. This is not to say that the Populists or anyone else had a clear sense of the differential price effects of a real appreciation, only that they had a general understanding of contemporary price trends. After all, Americans had experienced fif-

31 William P. St. John, quoted in Stevans 1896, 266.

teen years of a floating, depreciated currency during the Greenback era (which most Populist monetary thinkers had analyzed closely, and anyone older than about thirty-five in 1890 remembered). They had also, by 1896, endured nearly ten years of a real appreciation of the gold dollar. It is not surprising that there was general awareness of the broad contours of the relative price trends that the country had been experiencing and those likely to result from refloating the dollar against gold.

The Political Economy of Gold and Silver: A Statistical Analysis

Chapter 2 included in-depth analyses of congressional voting on monetary bills in an earlier era, in which the main political issue was whether and how to return to the gold standard. That concern was alive for a long time, from 1865 until 1879, and underwent many twists and turns. In contrast, the 1890s' Populist episode was concentrated in the four years up to the 1896 presidential election. This is not to claim that the issue ended in 1896—it remained a topic of controversy through the 1930s—or that there was no complexity to the matter. Nevertheless, compared to the highly varied topics of the 1860s and 1870s—which ranged from forcing the Treasury to issue more currency, to recognizing the gold value of bonds, to returning to gold—the issue in the 1890s was straightforward. Should the country remain on the gold standard at the existing exchange rate (\$4.86/£, in sterling) or embrace a silver standard that would have meant a substantial depreciation?

In previous work, I have examined voting on a series of monetary measures in both the House of Representatives and Senate.[32] The measures used in the House are listed and their contours outlined in the box "A Brief Description of Congressional Voting on Six Monetary Measures, 1892–95." The lineup on these bills is clear, as indicated in part by the fact that the Populist members of Congress were always unanimous in their voting. All the votes were close, and all were extremely visible to the public.

---

32 Frieden 1997. This work uses the more limited data available at the time. It also includes an analysis of Senate votes on these monetary issues.

A Brief Description
of Congressional Voting
on Six Monetary Measures, 1892–95

Table Free Coinage Bill. To table a Free Coinage Bill (HR 4426), March 24, 1892. Failed, 148–149. Democrats 81–130; Republicans 67–11; Populists 0–8. Administration (Republican) was in favor. A negative vote is soft money.

Free Coinage Bill. Resolution to consider a Free Coinage Bill (S 51), July 13, 1892. Failed, 136–154. Democrats 121–94; Republicans 10–60; Populists 7–0. Administration (Republican) was opposed. A positive vote is soft money.

Bland Amendment. An amendment to set the mint prices of silver and gold at a ratio of sixteen to one (HR1 Amendment), August 28, 1893. Failed, 125–226. Democrats 97–115; Republicans 15–110; Populists 8–0. Administration (Democratic) was opposed. A positive vote is soft money.

Repeal Sherman Act. To repeal the Purchase Clause of the Sherman Act (HR 1), November 1, 1893. Passed, 194–94. Democrats 123–72; Republicans 71–17; Populists 0–5. Administration (Democratic) was in favor. A negative vote is soft money.

Free silver override. To override the president's veto of the Silver Seignorage Bill (HR 4956), April 4, 1894. Passed, 144–114, but this was insufficient to override the veto. Democrats 119–59; Republicans 18–55; Populists 7–0. Administration (Democratic) was opposed, needless to say. (The original bill had passed, 168–129, on March 1, 1994, with Democrats 144–15, Republicans 14–114, and Populists/Silverites 10–0.) A positive vote is soft money.

Gold bonds authorization. To authorize gold bonds (HR 8705), February 7, 1895. Failed, 135–162. Democrats 89–95; Republicans 46–58; Populists 0–9. Administration (Democratic) was in favor. A negative vote is soft money.

129

In all cases, the issue at stake was relatively simple: Should the United States maintain its commitment to the gold standard? In every instance, the soft-money vote would have taken the United States off gold, either directly or indirectly. The only minor distinctions are about the repeal of the Sherman Act and authorization of gold bonds. In the first situation, it is theoretically conceivable that the country could have stayed on gold even if the Sherman Act, which committed the federal government to buy large amounts of silver with paper currency, had not been repealed. As the paper currency was redeemable in either gold or silver, and as the price of silver was declining rapidly against gold, it is almost certain that the Treasury would eventually have run out of gold and been driven off the gold standard. In the second circumstance, the issuance of gold bonds did not *require* the country to stay on gold, but the two questions were so closely tied together by the 1890s that it was effectively a referendum on the monetary standard itself.

In what follows, I discuss a statistical analysis of voting in the House of Representatives on these six important legislative decisions about the gold standard between 1892 and 1895. As in chapter 2, I look at congressional roll call votes in two different, complementary ways. The first is by pooling all votes by all members of Congress on the six measures, so that each roll call vote is an observation. The second is by turning to each congressional district and calculating the proportion of the six votes (or however many the member voted on) cast in favor of the hard-money position. In this case I can use a third method, examining only those members of Congress whose votes on these six measures were consistent—that is, they always voted either for the soft- or hard-money position. There were too many votes, and too few such stable voters, to carry out this analysis for the 1860s and 1870s.

Substantially more detailed and relevant economic data are available for the 1890s than for those in the 1860s and 1870s. This is in part because the 1890 census was much more "modern" in its conception and execution—for example, most output was reported in dollar terms rather than in volume. It is also because the great contemporary interest in these matters led the Census Bureau to explore such matters as indebtedness in the census itself. As a result, the 1890 census contains information about levels of mortgage and other indebtedness—more than was contained in many subsequent censuses. This allows me to assess quite explicitly the assertion that opposition to the gold standard

TABLE 3.3
Congressional voting on six major monetary measures, 1892–95: All votes pooled

	(1) Vote	(2) Vote	(3) Vote	(4) Vote
Republican	1.280** (5.14)	1.220** (5.13)	1.291** (5.20)	1.246** (5.26)
Debt per capita	1.155** (5.09)		1.178** (5.31)	
Mfg output per capita	0.437 (1.36)	1.275** (4.32)	0.450 (1.39)	1.436** (5.17)
Farm output per capita	−1.085** (−4.72)	−0.154 (−1.23)		
Proportion of farm output tradable	−0.0908 (−0.58)	−0.556** (−3.62)		
Debt		0.0992 (0.90)		0.0649 (0.64)
Tradable farm output per capita			−0.842** (−4.67)	−0.496** (−2.91)
Nontradable farm output per capita			−0.970** (−4.38)	0.0224 (0.19)
Constant	0.187 (1.16)	0.330* (2.00)	0.164 (1.01)	0.321⁺ (1.95)
Observations	1479	1479	1479	1479
Pseudo R^2	0.345	0.307	0.345	0.302

t statistics in parentheses
⁺ $p < 0.10$, * $p < 0.05$, ** $p < 0.01$

was motivated primarily by a desire to allow for inflation that would reduce the burden of nominal debts—a contention that is different from, although not entirely inconsistent with, my argument that the principal goal was to engineer a real depreciation of the dollar.

Tables 3.3–3.6 present the analysis. In table 3.3, a number of things are readily apparent. The Republicans tended now to be much more monolithically progold—in the midst of the cementing of the coalition between protectionist midwestern industry and progold eastern commerce and finance, under the auspices of the Republican Party of the

McKinley era. Also reflective of this coalition was the fact that the manufacturing districts tended to be progold, although this variable loses significance in some of the fuller analyses. Recall that US manufacturing had by this time procured nearly prohibitive tariff protection, so that the real exchange rate was largely irrelevant to its ability to compete with imports.

Farming districts were clearly antigold. Looking in more detail, while the results are a bit ambiguous, it appears that opposition to gold was particularly strong in districts producing tradable (i.e., export) crops, which I define as cotton, wheat, and tobacco. Crucially for the debt-based story, in virtually every instance the greater the indebtedness of residents of a district, the more likely the district's representative was to vote *in favor* of gold. In other words, not only were heavily indebted districts not pro-Populist (antigold), they were quite decidedly progold. As indicated above, much of the narrative evidence actually indicates that the more heavily indebted segments of the population—middle-class homeowners and prosperous farmers outside of export crops, for example—were either uninterested in the fight against gold or hostile to it.

Tables 3.4 and 3.5, which analyze the proportion of progold votes and those whose voting behavior was consistent, tell much the same story. Table 3.6 uses the results from table 3.3 to demonstrate the substantive importance of the various factors. While manufacturing output per person was often statistically significant, it typically had only a small impact. Republicans were about 25 percent more likely to vote for gold than Democrats, and debt had a similarly substantial effect—a standard deviation increase in a district's debt per capita raised the probability that the member of Congress would vote in favor of gold by about 25 percent. A standard deviation increase in farm output per person had a similar but opposite impact. The evidence for any substantial difference between districts with primarily tradable and nontradable farm output is mixed. These results are consistent across a wide variety of specifications and robust to the inclusion of a large number of other variables that are not of especial interest to the analysis here.

There are several important inferences, in my view, to be drawn from this analysis. First, concern about nominal debts cannot have been a major motive force for opposition to the gold standard: those districts carrying the largest debt levels were typically strongly progold. Second,

Table 3.4

Congressional voting on six major monetary measures, 1892–95: Proportion of voting in favor of hard money

	(1) Votes (proportion hard)	(2) Votes (proportion hard)	(3) Votes (proportion hard)	(4) Votes (proportion hard)
Republican	0.169** (4.54)	0.165** (4.19)	0.175** (4.62)	0.170** (4.23)
Debt per capita	0.193** (7.87)		0.203** (8.36)	
Mfg output per capita	0.0128 (0.46)	0.114** (4.16)	0.0180 (0.60)	0.158** (6.00)
Farm output per capita	−0.161** (−5.98)	−0.0205 (−0.91)		
Proportion of farm output tradable	−0.0660** (−2.72)	−0.156** (−6.23)		
Debt		0.00205 (0.10)		−0.00474 (−0.24)
Tradable farm output per capita			−0.171** (−7.30)	−0.125** (−4.73)
Nontradable farm output per capita			−0.133** (−4.79)	0.0319 (1.47)
Constant	0.518** (25.96)	0.530** (24.79)	0.513** (25.50)	0.529** (24.60)
Observations	299	299	299	299
Adjusted R^2	0.516	0.434	0.517	0.424

t statistics in parentheses
$^{+} p < 0.10, ^{*} p < 0.05, ^{**} p < 0.01$

while there was an apparent partisan cast to the voting—Republicans were heavily progold—there were also sharp divisions along economic lines, particularly between agricultural and manufacturing districts. And finally, there is some evidence that districts specializing in export (i.e., tradable) crops were especially likely to be antigold.

These results support the general view that we can understand the politics of the gold standard in this period as dividing those who would

TABLE 3.5
Congressional voting on six major monetary measures, 1892–95: All stable votes

	(1) Voted consistently for hard money	(2) Voted consistently for hard money	(3) Voted consistently for hard money	(4) Voted consistently for hard money
Republican	2.335** (2.94)	2.277** (3.64)	2.368** (2.92)	2.339** (3.59)
Debt per capita	2.325** (3.07)		2.392** (3.02)	
Mfg output per capita	0.492 (0.24)	2.260⁺ (1.69)	0.494 (0.24)	2.600* (2.03)
Farm output per capita	−2.356** (−2.63)	−0.259 (−0.88)		
Proportion of farm output tradable	−0.133 (−0.24)	−1.007* (−2.39)		
Debt		−0.107 (−0.44)		−0.158 (−0.67)
Tradable farm output per capita			−1.811** (−2.58)	−0.915* (−2.21)
Nontradable farm output per capita			−2.169* (−2.26)	0.147 (0.48)
Constant	0.440 (0.38)	0.793 (0.94)	0.420 (0.36)	0.846 (1.02)
Observations	179	179	179	179
Pseudo R^2	0.656	0.593	0.657	0.591

t statistics in parentheses
⁺ $p < 0.10$, * $p < 0.05$, ** $p < 0.01$

have benefited from a real depreciation of the dollar from those who valued the commercial and financial stability as well as predictability of the gold standard. This reinforces the evidence drawn from the qualitative historical analysis above and is consistent with findings from the earlier period of US debates over the gold standard.

TABLE 3.6
Substantive significance of factors affecting congressional voting on six major monetary measures

Explanatory variable	Impact of explanatory variables on voting for gold and hard money			
	Model 1	*Model 2*	*Model 3*	*Model 4*
Republican	**+0.254**	**+0.237**	**+0.255**	**+0.243**
Debt per capita	**+0.261**		**+0.265**	
Manufacturing output per capita	+0.091	**+0.023**	+0.097	**+0.015**
Farm output per capita	**−0.236**	+0.267		
Proportion of farm output tradable	−0.021	**−0.033**		
Debt		−0.124		+0.301
Tradable farm output per capita			**−0.190**	**−0.111**
Nontradable farm output per capita			**−0.208**	−0.005

Note: A vote in favor of staying on gold is considered support for hard money, and is indicated by a 1, so that a positive result indicates support for hard money. For party, the results show the difference in the voting behavior of Republican as against Democratic members of Congress, holding all other variables constant at their means. For all other variables, the results show the change in the probability of voting for a return to gold associated with the variable going from one-half standard deviation below its mean to one-half standard deviation above its mean, holding all other variables constant at their means. All the results are drawn from models 1, 2, 3, and 4 of table 3.3. The results that reach normal levels of statistical significance are indicated in boldface.

Currency Politics and the Gold Standard

The gold standard was the longest-lasting and arguably most important international exchange rate regime in history. It was central to the organization of the world economy from the 1870s through the 1920s. It successes are associated with the generally positive features of the integrated world economy of that era: rapid economic growth, substantial convergence among countries, and relative macroeconomic stability. On the other hand, the gold standard is often blamed for the most spectacular economic catastrophe of modern times: the Great Depression of the 1930s.[33] This makes understanding the international and domestic political economy of the gold standard of both historical and theoretical interest. I return to this issue in chapter 7 below.[34]

The United States saw perhaps the most acrimonious and enduring battles over the gold standard in the world during the late nineteenth century. Analyzing the US divisions over gold provides insights into the broader international monetary struggles going on at roughly the same time, both within and among countries. This analysis is also informative about the general contours of conflicts over currency policy more generally.

I now turn to another hotly contested episode in modern currency politics: the thirty-year process that culminated in the creation of the euro. As with the gold standard, the fight was over the creation and maintenance of a fixed exchange rate system, although in this case it was at the regional level, applying only to (some of) the members of the European Union. Just as Americans clashed continually between the 1860s and 1890s over whether and how they should tie themselves to a fixed exchange rate system, so did Europeans debate a similar effort between the 1960s and 1990s. The contexts were different, but the issues and divisions are worthy of comparison.

33 Eichengreen 1992.
34 It is covered in great detail in Eichengreen 1992 and related writings by him; I have addressed it in Frieden 1993.

4

European Monetary Integration: From Bretton Woods to the Euro and Beyond

A hundred years after the United States was divided by political conflict over the global monetary order, the European Union was consumed by debates over the creation of a regional monetary regime. The US debates resulted in the triumph of the gold standard, and the European ones culminated in the EMU with the adoption of a single currency, the euro, managed by the common European Central Bank.

Just as the US struggle over gold implicated the broader nature of the US economy and its relation to the world economy, the European struggle over monetary integration implicated the very nature and future of the European political economy. And just as the US battle of the standards brought into play the full range of actors in US society, so did the European battle for the euro bring into play the full range of European socioeconomic and political players.

Both the US and European debates ended in general victory for supporters of a fixed exchange rate—gold and the euro, respectively—and the cause of economic integration, both with the rest of the world and internally. In the case of Europe, however, there was a great deal of variation in whether, when, and how countries adhered to the new currency. The United States, as one nation, had to adopt a common standard, but the many countries of Europe could choose to join the process of monetary unification early, late, or never. As of 2014, three of the initiating fifteen member states still had not adopted the euro; the pace of its adoption was varying tremendously among the next thirteen member states; and the dozen or so other countries contemplating EU membership also had a wide variety of currency policies. More generally, over the course of the thirty years during which EU members developed and implemented proposals for monetary integration, national policies toward these proposals varied greatly. On top of all this, when the Great Recession that began in 2007 hit the eurozone, the region entered into its gravest economic and political crisis since World War II—much of it revolving around the politics of the common currency.

In this chapter, I analyze the process of European monetary integration with the same tools used in the US context. Exciting as the more recent euro crisis is, I concentrate on the decades that led up to the creation of the common currency. This is because this period is one in which, as in the gold standard era, national governments had to decide on their currency policy, and, again as in the gold standard period, there were major domestic political conflicts over this choice. The battles over exchange rate policy in Europe since the early 1970s were at the center of the broader process of European integration. The eventual adoption of the euro was perhaps the crowning achievement of prointegration forces, and both the process and result reflect the central realities of contemporary Europe's political economy.

The analysis of European monetary politics is complicated by several factors. First, the European debates began as the reigning international monetary order—the Bretton Woods system of currencies fixed to the US dollar and the dollar fixed to gold—fell apart and continued in the absence of any established monetary regime. This means that there was never any question of linking European currencies to an established standard, so that the only possible regime choice available involved creating an intra-European monetary regime.[1] Second, European exchange rate arrangements were discussed in the context of the creation and expansion of a continental economic union. Not only were the economies of western Europe tightly tied together in the European Union, they also had ambitious plans to deepen their economic ties and expand them to new members of the union.[2] Currency proposals were often seen in light of how they might speed or slow the integration of the region's goods as well as financial markets. Third, while there were major domestic political battles over monetary integration, the lines between domestic and intra-European politics were frequently blurry. It is not unreasonable to explore the domestic politics of currency policy in the late nineteenth-century United States without paying too much attention to interstate negotiations, yet this would be a grave error within the European experience.

While emphasizing the domestic political economy of European currency policy does violence to a more rounded analysis of the course of European monetary integration, it suits my purpose well. While I attempt to provide an accurate picture of the broader setting, as elsewhere in this book my principal goal is to tease out the distributional implications of currency choice and see the extent to which they affected the debates and policy outcomes.

In particular, and in accord with my general argument, I examine how exposure to exchange rate risk, tradability, and pass-through affected (and continue to affect) the exchange rate policy preferences of socioeconomic actors in Europe. As in other settings, I expect those more exposed to exchange rate volatility to be in favor of a fixed-rate system—hence the series of measures leading up to and including the achievement of the EMU along with the adoption of the common currency. On the other hand, I expect those whose output is more tradable, and where pass-through is more complete, to be particularly wary of fixing the exchange rate and thereby giving up the option of depreciating the currency to improve their competitive position. In the European context, I anticipate the financial sector and intra-European direct investors to favor fixing rates. I also expect exporters of specialized

---

1 This, of course, rules out a re-creation of an *international* regime, which seems reasonable as the United States showed no interest in participating in such an initiative.
2 The regional union went through several name changes, but I use only the most recent—the European Union—here.

manufactures (i.e., with low levels of pass-through) to be more concerned about currency predictability than about competitiveness. Conversely, I presume that producers of tradable goods susceptible to substantial price competition (i.e., with high levels of pass-through) will be opposed to fixing exchange rates.

Although the specifics of the European context and limits of data availability make rigorous empirical evaluation of these expectations difficult, I provide evidence in their favor. I first present a narrative of the course of European monetary integration, attempting to show how these distributional factors affected the course of the process. I then develop a statistical analysis of the crucial period between 1973 and 1995, when the essential national decisions that led to the creation of the euro were considered and made. Unlike in the US case, I have no detailed data to investigate the domestic politics of the process, so I rely on a more aggregate cross-national analysis. This analysis tends to support my argument. Countries with higher levels of manufactured exports to the eurozone's core (Germany and Benelux) were associated with more fixed exchange rates against the DM. But countries facing a deterioration of their trade balance—that is, more import and export competition—were less likely to fix. More specifically, the results are consistent with expectations that exporters of sophisticated manufactures and cross-border investors will support stable exchange rates, while import and export competers will favor depreciation.

I start with a survey of existing analyses of the path to the EMU and then summarize the course of the process of European monetary integration. I go on to offer an empirical evaluation of potential sources of variation among countries, and over time in their policies toward fixing exchange rates and eventually creating a common currency, focusing on the period between 1973 and the beginning of the final movement toward the EMU in 1995. As an extension, I briefly look at the eurozone crisis that began in 2008.

Analyzing European Monetary Politics

The varied progress and nature of European currency arrangements has brought forth much analysis. Most scholarly explanations, however, have *not* focused on the sorts of distributional factors emphasized here. Typically, they have stressed two considerations: the degree to which

Europe could be considered an OCA, and the desire of Europeans for low levels of inflation. While these may well have played a role, I believe that they are at best incomplete explanations for the course of events.[3]

One influential set of explanations underscores criteria associated with the theory of OCAs (see the introduction and chapter 1).[4] OCA theory specifies circumstances under which it is optimal for a nation to give up its exchange rate autonomy.[5] This is the case where exchange rate policy would otherwise be superfluous, either because it would be ineffective or because it could better be carried out by a bloc of national monetary authorities than alone. High levels of factor mobility among countries make individual national currency policies by any one of them ineffective, while production structures that imply correlated exogenous shocks makes such policies unnecessary. In other words, the more mobile factors are across countries and the more similar their susceptibility to external shocks, the more desirable is a monetary union.

The OCA approach is unlikely to explain much of European currency policy. Before the EMU, there was too little labor mobility among European countries and too little correlation among exogenous shocks to justify the level of interest in currency unification. Europe was not an OCA, and even the "hard core" of the EMS may not have been one at the time of its establishment.[6] Of course, on both dimensions there is variation among EU member states, so that some might be more appropriate members of a currency union than others. In this light, the

---

3 For a parallel to the European literature discussed here, see Bernhard, Broz, and Clark 2002. For an authoritative survey of the process, see Gros and Thygesen 1999. For the essential source on the early years of monetary integration, through 1993, see James 2012. On the British experience, see Duckenfield 2006. On the political economy of the German position, see Kinderman 2008.

4 For early classics, see Mundell 1961; McKinnon 1963; Kenen 1969. For more recent surveys, see Masson and Taylor 1993; Tavlas 1994.

5 Although the theory is about currency unions, it applies—albeit perhaps less stringently—to fixed-rate systems. Matthew Canzoneri and Carol Ann Rogers (1990) discuss optimal-taxation-based (seignorage) evaluations of currency union, but these seem unlikely to have been empirically of particular importance.

6 Capital is more mobile than labor, but its relevance to adjustment is not so clear, and capital controls were common until the late 1980s. For two representative and influential studies, see De Grauwe and Vanhaverbeke 1993; Bayoumi and Eichengreen 1993. Jeffrey Frankel and Andrew Rose (1998) present the intriguing possibility that if "unsuitable" countries form a currency union, they might evolve to be more suited over time, as their factor markets become more integrated and their production structures more similar.

OCA criteria may have had differential effects on different countries that are worth considering.

A second set of arguments focuses on the possibility that European countries chose a fixed-rate system—in particular, currencies pegged to the DM—in order to "import" German anti-inflationary credibility.[7] Various rationales have been proposed as to why a currency peg might itself be more credible than simply committing to lower inflation.[8] Along these lines, it is commonly asserted that European exchange rate arrangements served as a nominal anchor for credibility-enhancing purposes.[9]

Certainly this could not explain German support for monetary integration, which is why some scholars focus on geopolitical instead of economic policy grounds to account for German policy.[10] It is also irrelevant to the important cases of Austria, Belgium/Luxembourg, Denmark, and the Netherlands, all of which were low-inflation countries that stood only to lose monetary credibility from linking their currencies to those of high-inflation countries. But there are undoubtedly European countries for which an attraction to the currency peg and single currency was Germany's link to monetary policy credibility.

Both of these approaches emphasize the domestic monetary policy effects of currency policies. In a way, they are analogous to the spotlight on the nominal price level in the analysis of the US politics of the gold standard. Many interpretations stress the expected impact of gold or silver on US inflation; mine points to the impact on the real exchange rate and its volatility. So too do many interpretations of the EMU emphasize its anticipated impact on domestic inflation; mine, again, un-

7 Giavazzi and Pagano 1989; Weber 1991.
8 Most plausible are that the exchange rate is much more visible to market operators than is monetary policy, and the possibility that deviating from a peg imposes more costs on policymakers because of its impact on both inflation and cross-border relative prices. J. Lawrence Broz (2002) presents one version of the contention, and some evidence about its applicability. It must be said that the reasoning's logic is not fully worked out: it is hard to see why a stated commitment to a currency target is more credible than a stated commitment to a domestic monetary target. Indeed, Michele Fratianni and Jürgen von Hagen (1991) argue against any substantial independent effect, but the evidence is hard to evaluate.
9 Gian Maria Milesi-Ferretti (1995), however, discusses how policymakers may have partisan electoral incentives not to tie their hands, inasmuch as precommitment strategies might reduce the electoral disadvantages of potential opponents. If, for example, left-wing parties have a bad inflationary reputation, anything that reduces a government's ability to inflate reduces the electoral disadvantage of the Left.
10 Garrett 2001

142

derscores the impact on the real exchange rate and its volatility. In what follows, I attempt to evaluate the explanatory power of the different approaches.

My argument in the European context, as elsewhere, emphasizes the real effects of currency policy on cross-border trade and investment. Currency unions are, in my presentation, simply a special case of fixed exchange rate regimes. Nonetheless, the process of European monetary integration has led to interest in the more specific properties of currency unions themselves. For example, recent research tends to show that sharing a currency has a substantial impact on cross-border trade. One study found that currency unification tripled trade among union members.[11] This helps refocus attention on the ways in which currency policies can affect the environment for international trade and investment, and reinforces the plausibility of explanations of currency policy that center on its impact on a country's trade and financial ties.

As presented in chapter 1, the trade-off between exchange rate stability and the freedom to vary the currency's value tends to pit two broad groups against one another, based on how highly they value the two conflicting goals. On the one hand, exchange rate volatility principally affects those with substantial cross-border contractual interests. Foreign investors, lenders, and borrowers dislike the unpredictability associated with substantial fluctuations in currency values, which are often not amenable to hedging at longer time horizons. In addition, exporters of goods with limited pass-through are typically harmed by volatility. I expect those with cross-border economic interests to have been more oriented toward fixing the value of the national currency. On the other hand, both import-competing and exporting firms are helped by depreciation. I expect opposition to fixing exchange rates thus to have come especially from import-competing and exporting sectors. Conversely, the less threatening is import and export market competition to national producers, the less likely these producers are to oppose fixing the exchange rate.

As noted in chapter 1, manufactured exporters can be torn in confusing ways by this trade-off, especially in Europe. In general, exporters favor maintaining the exchange rate as an active policy instrument. Yet the impact of the exchange rate's level is mitigated in the case of industries with little pass-through; an appreciation does not cause an analo-

11 Rose 2000.

gous rise in the (foreign-currency) price of exports, nor does a depreciation significantly increase (domestic-currency) export prices. In these
instances, currency volatility can be quite costly. Exporters of specialized, product-differentiated manufactured goods—typically some of
the most important European exporters—therefore are less likely to
want a weak exchange rate and more likely to value currency stability.
This masks much nuance and complexity, of course. There are firms for
which the trade-off between reduced currency volatility and the loss of
exchange rate autonomy is not clear, either because both or neither is
important. And I have ignored the interests of nontradable producers,
such as public sector employees and small businesses, which usually
favor maintaining monetary policy autonomy rather than sacrificing it
to stabilize currency values that have little direct impact on them.

An added complication is that as the member states moved toward
the euro, preferences over national policy began to mix with expectations about the euro. There is evidence, for instance, that some German
export-oriented manufacturers welcomed the euro because they anticipated that it would be weaker than the purely German DM.[12]

The principal goal of this chapter, then, is to identify the distributional effects and political lineup relevant to the making of European
exchange rate policy. Specifically, I hold that the main supporters of
fixing European exchange rates were firms and industries with major
cross-border investments, markets, or other business interests, while
the primary opponents were producers of standardized import-
competing and export products. I expect the support of the former for
fixing exchange rates to be relatively constant, while the opposition of
the latter should increase at times of a real appreciation and associated
competitive difficulties for national producers.[13] My focus on special
interest considerations is not meant to deny the potential significance

12 For detail on German exchange rate politics, see Kinderman 2008.
13 Again, all this ignores much detail. One of the more interesting features of the run-up to the
EMU was that import competers in the likely core increasingly came to insist on including the
periphery—especially Italy and Spain—in order to eliminate the possibility of such competitive depreciations as those of 1992–93. Perhaps most striking in this regard is the position of
import-competing French industries, which went from opponents of the EMS in the early
1980s to strong supporters of a broad EMU by the mid-1990s. In the former period, EMS
membership ruled out a French devaluation and led to a real appreciation; in the latter period,
Italian and Spanish nonmembership in the EMU would have allowed them to depreciate
against the franc, again causing a real appreciation of the French currency. The result was that
potentially affected firms switched from opposition to French membership in the EMS to
strong support for the inclusion of the entire European Union in the EMU.

of other factors. It is to demonstrate instead that the political economy of European monetary integration can be analyzed in a much broader context, as part of the political economy of exchange rate policy more generally.

The Course of European Monetary Integration, 1969–99: From Qualified Failure to Skepticism to Qualified Success

Discussions within the European Union over the possibility of stabilizing exchange rates began only a few months after the signing of the Treaty of Rome, which created the earliest incarnation of the European Union.[14] As fissures appeared in the Bretton Woods system, these talks accelerated, culminating in the 1969 Werner Report. This report recommended the beginning of a process of monetary union among EU members. Within a few weeks of its adoption, however, the Werner Report's recommendations were overtaken by the collapse of Bretton Woods.

In the confused months after the August 1971 US decision to go off gold, EU member states resolved to hold their currencies within a 2.25 percent band against each other and allow this band to move within a 4.5 percent band against the US dollar. This arrangement was known as the "snake in the tunnel," as EU currencies would wriggle within a circumscribed range vis-à-vis the dollar. In addition to the six member states, Great Britain, Ireland, and Denmark joined the snake on May 1, 1972, to prepare for their entry into the union eight months later. However, Britain and Ireland left the snake in June 1972; the Danes left shortly thereafter, but rejoined in October.

The collapse of attempts to salvage an international fixed-rate monetary regime in 1973 ended the tunnel aspects of the snake. From then on, the European Union's goal was to achieve a joint float of member currencies against the dollar, without targeting how they would move relative to the dollar. In other words, the only consideration from 1973 onward was intra-EU exchange rates.

14 On early monetary plans and developments, see Tsoukalis 1977, especially 51–111; Ypersele 1985, 31–45.

Even this more limited goal was difficult to achieve.[15] As already indicated, Britain and Ireland left the snake within weeks of joining, and in February 1973 Italy followed suit. In addition, throughout 1973 only a series of parity changes allowed the system to hold together, and even then France chose to exit in January 1974. The French returned in July 1975, only to leave for good eight months later.

Within three years of the European Union's founding, then, the only members still in the snake were Germany, the Benelux countries, and Denmark. Even within this narrowed arrangement, realignments were frequent, typically to devalue the Danish krone and/or revalue the DM. Although by 1978 the European Union began moving toward the EMS, nothing in the prior snake experience gave much cause for hope that all nine EU members could fix their exchange rates in any meaningful way.

It is not hard to explain in a discursive way why four EU members (Germany and the Benelux countries) were able to maintain fixed exchange rates among themselves, while five others (Denmark, Britain, Ireland, France, and Italy) in varying degrees were not (I attempt a more systematic explanation below). The ease with which the Germany-Benelux link held is largely due to the fact that monetary and financial conditions in the Benelux countries were so tied to those in Germany. As for Denmark, despite the formal link to the snake, the krone was so frequently devalued against the unit of account that the ties were hardly binding. In addition, Danish membership in the snake was facilitated by the fact that two Scandinavian countries with which Denmark was closely connected economically and politically were also members: Norway from May 1972 to December 1978, and Sweden from March 1973 to August 1977.

As for those incapable of staying in the snake, Britain and Ireland were new EU members, Britain's Labour government was in a state of economic policy turmoil, and North Sea oil complicated matters still further. Ireland's close economic links to Britain made it difficult to break from the pound, and indeed the Irish had tied their currency to sterling at a one-to-one, no-margins parity since independence.

As for France and Italy, since the late 1960s they had experienced consistently higher inflation than Germany, and during the 1970s they

15 Tsoukalis 1977, 112–68; Ludlow 1982, 1–36; Coffey 1987, 6–16. For a useful chronology of the snake, see Coffey 1987, 123–25.

showed little real interest in monetary union, preoccupied as they were with domestic macroeconomic difficulties. Their attempt to commit to monetary integration was consistently blocked by domestic political opposition to the measures necessary to make this commitment possible. Due to the importance of these two countries, it is useful to discuss their problems in more detail.[16]

Italy went through a series of payment crises in the mid-1970s, all related to chronic inflation.[17] In 1974, consumer price inflation approached 25 percent, with a public sector borrowing requirement of 7.9 percent of the gross domestic product (GDP). The government signed a stand-by agreement during that year with the International Monetary Fund (IMF), but it met with only moderate success. Although inflation declined to 11 percent in 1975, Italy plunged into its most serious postwar recession (the GDP declined by 3.6 percent), and the public sector borrowing requirement rose to 11.4 percent of the GDP. Under union pressure, the employers' association agreed to a wage indexation scheme (the *scala mobile*, or escalator) that embedded past inflation in wages and thus production costs. In this context, the exchange rate was allowed to depreciate continually to maintain competitiveness.

A new IMF program in 1977 again attempted to restrain demand. The government tried in vain to get the trade unions and business-people to renegotiate the scala mobile as well as reduce indexation, finally decreeing a loosening of the mechanism. Inflation bottomed out at 11.6 percent in 1978, but the public sector borrowing requirement was 14.3 percent of the GDP in that year and stayed above 10 percent of the GDP through 1980, by which time the consumer price index was again rising at 21 percent a year. The country appeared to be in a vicious circle of budget deficits, inflation, indexed wage increases, and continual lira depreciation. It was hardly surprising that Italy showed no particular interest, other than verbal, in monetary union through the 1970s; no informed observer regarded a commitment to a stable lira as credible.

France was doing only slightly better.[18] When Valéry Giscard d'Estaing became president in 1974, consumer price inflation was run-

---

16 For even more detail, see Frieden 1994b.

17 On this period, see Fazio 1979; Caranza and Fazio 1983. For a more analytic survey, see Guerrieri and Padoan 1989.

18 For two good surveys, see Oudiz and Sterdyniak 1985; Lauber 1983. See also Besnard and Redon 1985, 178–98.

ning at nearly 14 percent. With the franc out of the snake, the government of Jacques Chirac first tried monetary stringency, which reduced inflation a couple of percentage points but brought growth to a halt. In 1975, Chirac attempted to stimulate the economy with a fiscal policy that was relatively lax by French standards (with a public sector borrowing requirement of about 3 percent of the GDP, compared to the traditional near-balanced one). France rejoined the snake in July 1975, but by early 1976 unemployment was still high even as the current account deficit was growing. In March 1976, after the Left did well in regional elections, Chirac took the franc out of the snake; a few months later, Giscard dismissed Chirac and appointed Raymond Barre to the premiership.

For almost five years after his appointment, Prime Minister Barre implemented austerity programs. Yet inflation was stubbornly high at nearly 11 percent for the period, unemployment rose continually even as real wages stagnated, and the current account remained in deficit. The government apparently attempted to shadow other European currencies, but domestic conditions drove it to continual franc depreciation to maintain competitiveness.[19] By 1980 inflation was still 13.5 percent, unemployment was at 6.3 percent (triple the 1973 levels), and five years of austerity seemed to have accomplished little except for paving the way for a Socialist electoral victory in March 1981. In this context, French assurances about the desirability of monetary union were no more plausible than those of Italy.

The experience of the 1970s held out few hopes for success in the 1980s. The union's two major high-inflation countries, France and Italy, had been unable to fix their exchange rates with other EU members. Resistance to austerity measures along with pressures from tradables producers to maintain international price competitiveness led to continual rounds of franc and lira depreciations against the DM.

Nonetheless, renewed discussions of EU monetary union began to gather momentum in October 1977, when Roy Jenkins, president of the European Commission, made a prominent public appeal for monetary integration. In April 1978, French president Giscard and German chancellor Helmut Schmidt proposed a new EMS, and the European Council approved it in December 1978. Its implementation was delayed by wrangling over implications for the Common Agricultural

---

19 This is at least what Gilles Oudiz and Henri Sterdyniak (1985, 32–35) argue.

Policy, but in March 1979 the EMS and its exchange rate mechanism (ERM) went into effect. All EU members except the United Kingdom affiliated with the EMS and its ERM, which allowed a 2.25 percent band among currencies (6 percent for the lira).[20]

The prevailing opinion at the time was that French and Italian inflation rates were too high and intractable, and the French and Italian desires to sustain a relatively weak currency were too strong, to allow the EMS to operate as planned. Indeed, in the first four years of its operation there were seven realignments of EMS currency values. During this period, DM revaluations as well as lira and franc devaluations reduced the DM value of the two problem currencies by 27 and 25 percent, respectively—hardly a sign of commitment to fixed rates.

Over the following four years between April 1983 and January 1987, however, there were only four more realignments, generally smaller than previous changes. Over the second four years, the lira and franc were brought down 13 and 9 percent against the mark, respectively. After 1983, in fact, exchange rate variability within the EMS declined substantially while monetary policies converged on virtually every dimension.[21] From January 1987 until September 1992, there were no realignments within the ERM, while Spain, the United Kingdom, and Portugal joined the mechanism, and Finland, Sweden, and Norway explicitly linked their currencies to the European currency unit.

Perhaps most important in this process was the unexpected turnaround in French policy in the early 1980s. In this case, a newly elected Socialist government was torn between its expansionary macroeconomic policies and commitment to the EMS. Eventually, in 1983, the Mitterrand government chose to try to do what was necessary to stabilize the franc. This decision was perhaps the most significant of the entire Mitterrand presidency, which lasted from 1981 until 1995. It tore the Socialist Party apart, and profoundly affected the course of both French and European politics.[22]

20 Peter Ludlow (1982) is especially detailed on the negotiations and early operation of the EMS. See also Ypersele 1985, 71–95; Ungerer 1983. For excellent surveys of the EMS experience more generally, see Giavazzi and Giovannini 1989; Fratianni and von Hagen 1991; Goodman 1992.

21 The relative parity changes are calculated from "Policy Coordination in the European Monetary System" (1988, 19). For information on exchange rate variability, see ibid., 20–34.

22 In addition to Frieden 1994b, see especially Sachs and Wyplosz 1986; Cameron 1992; Favier and Martin-Roland 1990; Bauchard 1986; July 1986.

Ireland undertook an almost equally dramatic decision to break its millennial currency tie to the pound sterling—and, by extension, to the United Kingdom—and throw its lot in with the German-dominated Continent.

In the aftermath of the French and Irish decisions, and somewhat less dramatic changes in Denmark and Italy, European integration more generally picked up speed. Over the course of 1985 and 1986, EU members discussed and adopted the Single European Act, which called for the full mobility of goods, capital, and people within the union by January 1, 1993.[23] From then on, national barriers began falling. Most capital controls were gone by 1991, and the prospect of a unified market for goods defined much of the economic and political activity of the European Union in the run-up to 1993. As economic integration advanced and the EMS appeared stable, EU members devised plans for full monetary union and incorporated them into the 1991 Maastricht Treaty.

Indeed, there was an increasing sense that if the single market were to survive, monetary integration might be essential.[24] Member states that had eschewed all trade barriers could hardly be expected to welcome attempts by other member states to promote exports and reduce imports by depreciating their currencies. Once again, the potential substitutability of trade and exchange rate policies came to the fore: if the European Union was to be a single market, it needed a single exchange rate. Otherwise there would be powerful incentives to engage in competitive depreciations, which could reliably be expected to give rise to strong protectionist pressures in response—thus calling into question the very nature of the single market itself.

Even as plans for forward movement toward a full currency union gathered speed in 1992, a major currency crisis called even the less ambitious EMS into question.[25] Problems began with German unification, which led the Bundesbank to fear inflation and raise interest rates. The resultant European recession put EMS member governments under substantial political pressure to pursue more expansionary policies, including both looser monetary policy and a more competitive exchange rate. The only ways to do so were either to leave the ERM or to convince the Bundesbank to loosen its monetary policy and allow

23 For two analyses, see Sandholtz and Zysman 1989; Moravcsik 1991.
24 For a detailed analysis of the relationship, see Eichengreen 1996.
25 For an excellent survey, see Eichengreen and Wyplosz 1993.

the DM to depreciate. The Bundesbank would not budge, thereby handing national governments the difficult choice of either following Germany into even more recessionary policies or breaking the link to the ERM.

This threw the crisis back into the realm of domestic politics. A rise in British interest rates to defend sterling, for example, would have been passed on by mortgage lenders, and many within the ruling Conservative Party worried about the objections of property owners.[26] For its part, the Italian government might have enacted drastic fiscal measures to make its commitment to lower inflation more credible, but in the midst of a deep political crisis this was difficult to achieve over the objections of public employees and others who feared that their positions would be threatened. The German authorities might have loosened monetary policy save for the Bundesbank's traditional concern about inflation, reinforced by strong anti-inflationary constituencies in the German body politic.

The growing political conflict over European integration as a whole also exacerbated the problems. In the aftermath of the June 1992 failure of the first Danish referendum on the Maastricht Treaty and with the results of a September 1992 French referendum in doubt, serious questions were raised about the future of the Maastricht process. The prospect of delinking the EMU from European integration more generally—a prospect that was eventually realized—served to weaken the credibility of EMS members' commitments to the system.

In any event, in September 1992 the British and Italian governments took their currencies out of the ERM, and then allowed them to float. The currencies of Spain, Portugal, and Ireland were devalued during the subsequent months, although they remained in the mechanism. In summer 1993, with the system again under attack on currency markets, the remaining ERM members agreed to widen fluctuation bands to 15 percent (the Dutch guilder remained in a 2.25 percent band). Many felt that the impetus for monetary integration had faded. Still, over the following several years, the ERM was stable and eventually momentum for the EMU was rebuilt after the currency crises faded. Although Denmark and the United Kingdom negotiated the right to "opt out" of the EMU and Sweden has been able to avoid membership,

26 For a much more detailed analysis of the political economy of the British position, see Eglene 2011.

eventual membership in the eurozone was required of all other EU member states.

Eleven EU member states—Austria, Belgium, Finland, France, Germany, Ireland, Italy, Luxembourg, the Netherlands, Portugal, and Spain—started the final steps toward a single currency in 1999. Greece joined in 2000, and these twelve finalized full currency union in 2002. Since then, the euro has gained seven more adherents (Cyprus, Estonia, Latvia, Lithuania, Malta, Slovakia, and Slovenia) among EU member states. Some others have unilaterally adopted or pegged their currency to the euro. And the eurozone has confronted a major financial and sovereign debt crisis. All this gives us substantial raw material for analysis.

Analyzing European Currency Policy: Variables of Interest

Different member states of the European Union joined the snake or ERM at different times, and had differing degrees of success in holding to their fixed-rate commitments. I take advantage of the variation in the pace and nature of these policy commitments to evaluate explanations of European monetary integration specifically, and currency policy more generally. Attempts to hold to fixed exchange rates were more successful at some times than at others in Europe.[27] In addition, EU members had highly varied experiences within the snake and EMS. This means that there is meaningful variation both over time and among countries.

A simple policy choice to be explained is the degree of fixity of the nominal exchange rate to the DM. This definition of the thing to be explained, which might be questionable in other historical and regional

---

27 For simplicity, I consider the target zones of the snake and ERM equivalent to a fixed-rate system. This raises two problems. First, target zones imply fixing within a much broader range than is usually associated with fixed rates. The general policy problem is roughly similar, however, especially when—as has been the case—currencies have often reached the limits of their bands. Second, the acceptable bands were substantially widened in the aftermath of the 1992–93 crises, so that this first point may be less valid recently. Yet with the exception of the Irish pound, most currencies that stayed within the wider-band ERM kept roughly inside to their previous narrow band, and the Irish pound *appreciated* (as sterling rose), which represents a less troubling policy problem than the more common pressure to depreciate.

contexts, is justifiable in post-1973 Europe. First, exchange rate stability was a publicly stated goal of all EU members. Second, it was clear early on that such stability implied fixing against the DM. Third, the attention of all relevant actors—policymakers, observers, and economic agents—was on nominal exchange rates.[28]

Dependent Variables

The statistical analyses use two simple measures of trends in national currency values against the DM. The first is the annual rate of nominal depreciation, which directly measures the general trend of the currency against the DM anchor (all European currencies declined relative to the DM over the period, so there were no appreciating currencies). The second measure is the annual coefficient of variation of monthly exchange rates. This gauges shorter-term volatility within each year rather than the trend of the currency's value.

Table 4.1 shows these two measures of the stability of European currencies against the DM. The table includes the thirteen pre-EMU currencies of the European Union other than the DM (Luxembourg shared a currency with Belgium), plus that of Norway.[29] The table is divided among three groups: hard-currency countries are those that were always members of both the snake and ERM, soft-currency countries are those that were not reliable members of either, and intermediate countries are those that were members of the ERM but not the snake. The four countries that were not in the European Union before 1995 (one of which, Norway, remains a nonmember) are shown at the bottom.

The easiest way to measure the relationship between exchange rates is the rate of change in their nominal values—in this case, the average annual rate of depreciation against the DM, as presented in section A of table 4.1. This has the advantage of transparency of interpretation,

---

28 I put it this way to avoid the stronger claim that nominal and real exchange rates were tightly linked in the period, even though there is substantial evidence for this in almost all European countries.

29 There might be an argument for including Iceland and Switzerland, except that neither has expressed real commitment to *European* currency stability. Iceland has had relatively high and variable inflation, and Switzerland's international financial role makes purely European considerations somewhat less relevant.

TABLE 4.1
European currencies during the snake and EMS

A. Average annual percentage depreciation of nominal exchange rates against the DM, select periods

	1973–78	1979–83	1984–89	1990–94
Hard currencies				
Netherlands	1.14	0.77	0.01	−0.13
Belgium	2.36	4.24	1.01	−0.48
Denmark	4.59	4.37	1.71	0.16
Intermediate currencies				
France	6.53	5.02	2.31	0.01
Ireland	12.90	3.02	3.49	1.96
Soft currencies				
United Kingdom	12.90	0.89	6.68	2.57
Italy	17.28	5.26	4.08	6.21
Spain	12.35	6.54	3.51	5.16
Greece	13.24	13.02	18.75	10.23
Portugal	20.83	14.16	10.64	2.88
Non-EU members				
Austria	0.12	−0.71	−0.12	0.19
Norway	4.92	1.08	6.61	2.29
Finland	8.83	−0.32	3.06	6.83
Sweden	8.41	3.83	5.35	6.18
Average	9.03	4.37	4.79	3.15

B. Coefficients of variation of nominal exchange rates against the DM

	1973–78	1979–83	1984–89	1990–94
Hard currencies				
Netherlands	2.15	1.18	0.31	0.43
Belgium	2.80	9.84	1.55	1.17
Denmark	7.20	7.99	2.85	1.57
Intermediate currencies				
France	11.00	10.74	4.59	1.00
Ireland	20.47	6.75	7.02	4.83
Soft currencies				
United Kingdom	20.47	7.43	10.91	8.11
Italy	24.02	10.64	6.63	12.56
Spain	23.14	16.31	7.38	11.65
Greece	18.43	18.98	26.54	14.66
Portugal	35.65	21.75	17.57	7.31
Non-EU members				
Austria	1.63	1.48	0.23	0.23
Norway	8.28	4.89	11.40	5.00
Finland	14.24	5.63	6.06	16.08
Sweden	12.54	12.20	8.23	13.00
Average	14.43	9.70	7.95	6.97

though it does not indicate potential currency *volatility*. For this purpose, the coefficient of variation of national currencies against the DM is presented in section B of table 4.1.[30] The two measures produce similar classifications of countries and country-years, and when they are used in statistical analysis they give rise to virtually identical results. The differences are also interesting, as they pick up (inasmuch as they differ) differences between determinants of broad currency policy and shorter-term policy toward volatility.

Explanatory Variables

Attempts to evaluate arguments based on the distributional effects of exchange rate policies are hampered by the general unobservability of special interest politics. In this chapter, I use two variables that can be interpreted as affecting policy by way of their differentiated and distributionally relevant effects on particularistic groups. The first strives to pick up the interests of manufacturers with significant intra-European export interests, given that they are more sensitive to exchange rate risk. The second tries to capture the interests of those tradables producers facing significant import and export competition. Neither is unproblematic, but there are no readily available superior alternatives. The two variables are as follows:

Exports to the German currency bloc. As discussed above, I anticipate that producers of specialized manufactured products will be concerned to keep exchange rates stable. Of course, this is countered by a concern for the level of the real exchange rate. Keeping this in mind, manufacturers with limited pass-through, where pricing to market is common, tend to want to reduce currency risk. This should be of special importance in European monetary politics to the extent that manufactured exports to Germany are significant. Here I use exports to the DM bloc, defined as Germany plus Benelux. The higher the share of manufac-

---

30 The coefficient of variation is the standard deviation divided by the mean; in the case of table 4.1, currency values are taken at monthly intervals, so that the volatility being measured is monthly over the time periods in question, which are of five or six years. For the statistical analyses, the value is the volatility of monthly exchange rates over each country-year. This picks up both overall declines against the DM and general volatility, so that differences between the two dependent variables are presumably ascribable to different determinants of volatility itself (as opposed to depreciation).

tured exports to the DM zone as a share of the GDP, the more support I expect for stabilizing the currency with the DM. The use of the DM bloc as the relevant region is unimportant: overall manufactured exports to Germany alone or to the broad European Union as a share of the GDP are highly correlated with this, and their use yields nearly identical results. Variable name: *manufactured exports to DM zone as percent of the GDP (–)*. Expected sign: negative. (A negative sign implies that a higher value of the variable is associated with less devaluation and less volatility. All variables are described in detail in the appendix to chapter 4.)

Import competition. On the other hand, some of the most significant pressures to depreciate (or not join the snake or ERM) came from producers that stood to lose from their government's forgoing the ability to change the exchange rate to affect competitiveness. There is no ready way to measure tradability and its interaction with pass-through, or even more broadly concern about competitive pressures, but one reasonable proxy is the rate of change in import and export competition. That is, where a country's producers are experiencing a surge in imports or drop in exports, they are more likely to be interested in a depreciation and less supportive of fixing the exchange rate. This implies that a deterioration in the trade balance should increase support for depreciation and reduce support for a fixed rate. This is analogous to the common observation that increased import competition tends to increase protectionist pressures (and pressure for depreciation) from affected industries.[31]

In using this measure, for important reasons I control for the state of the current account. It would not be surprising if large current account deficits were to be associated with depreciations, for they put direct currency-market pressure on the exchange rate. What I use here is the impact of changes in the trade balance *controlling for the state of the current account*. This measure can only plausibly be picking up particular sensitivity to trade relations: the state of imports and exports. In other words, this variable is *not* simply the economic impact of a trade

---

31 It has analogous weaknesses. In fact, if producers can gain from a depreciation or trade protection, they should support these no matter how much import competition they face (even in the absence of import competition). Nonetheless, the virtually universal observation is that support for protection/depreciation is strongly affected by import competition. A variety of explanations for this have been proposed, but serious consideration of these is well beyond the scope of this study.

deficit, for a trade deficit that does not lead to a current account deficit does *not* put pressure on the currency in foreign exchange markets. It thus seems reasonable to regard it as an indicator of the position of national import and export competers.[32] The greater the deterioration in the trade balance (again, controlling for the current account balance), the greater the pressures to depreciate. Here I use the change from the previous year in the trade balance as a share of the GDP, so that a positive (negative) number is an improvement (deterioration). Variable name: *Change in trade balance as percent of the GDP (–).* Expected sign: negative.

The two proxies for private interests I use here are not particularly close to what we want to measure: the political behavior of private interests in their attempts to affect public policy. Nor do they cover all the private interests I argue should matter, especially those of cross-border investors. Better proxies, however, are difficult even to identify, let alone obtain data on. The extent of intra-European trade is probably a reasonable approximation of the importance of stabilizing exchange rates for the commercial sector and export-oriented producers. But this ignores the interests of cross-border financial and investing interests—for the simple reason that data on them is essentially unavailable for the period in question. One might imagine that FDI among European countries would be easy to obtain. In fact, unfortunately, this measure is only available for a few countries before the early 1980s, and even then with much error. When the statistical analysis is performed with FDI data, over half the observations have to be omitted, and the omitted countries are biased toward southern Europe. It is thus not clear that these results (which are not reported here but tend to be similar to those for manufactured exports) are valid. FDI measures are in any case correlated (correlation coefficient of 0.54) with the manufactured export figures. It is, by the same token, extremely difficult to come up with reasonable proxies for private sector concern about the ability to use the exchange rate to affect competitiveness. The strategy used here—

---

32 Of course, the trade balance picks up exports as well, and this is also a measure of pressures from exporters for a competitive depreciation. In a sense, the inclusion of overall levels of exports in the previous measure, and consideration of changes in net imports in this measure, provide a contrast between a structural or secular trend in manufactured exports, on the one hand, and year-to-year surges in net imports, on the other. It seems legitimate to presume, at least as a first cut, that these are reasonable proxies for specialized exporting and import/export-competing interests, respectively.

to look at increased net imports as an indicator of how much competition producers face—has many flaws, but seems better than the available alternatives. All in all, the two measures used are plausible, if imperfect, indicators of important private sector interests in currency policy. In the absence of other indicators that might be used, they constitute a reasonable first cut.

Alternative Explanatory Variables

As mentioned above, the principal alternative perspective emphasizes currency pegs as anti-inflationary commitment mechanisms; some attention is still paid to OCA theory. The variables I use to evaluate these arguments are as follows.

Credibility concerns. It is hard to imagine any clean measure of the demand for anti-inflationary credibility. High inflation certainly implies a greater need for credibility, but it also implies a higher cost of achieving it. In addition, high inflation leads quite directly to currency depreciation when the authorities are not using the exchange rate as an anti-inflationary commitment device, which invalidates any simple expectation that high inflation should be generally associated with currency stability. What we would really like is something that reflects government need for or use of currency policy for credibility purposes, but there is no easy way of assessing this. Here I use a series of measures that all could plausibly be associated with government desires to enhance anti-inflationary credibility. None is a direct measure of the demand for credibility, but all are potentially related to it.

Inasmuch as the independence of the central bank is associated with lower inflation, this should reduce the government's need for the anti-inflationary credibility that a currency peg is purported to provide and thus the likelihood of such a currency link. A more dependent central bank, in contrast, should increase the demand for credibility and hence the likelihood of a currency peg. The measure used is the standard one created by a group of scholars in an influential study.[33] Variable name: *central bank independence (+)*. Expected sign: positive.

To the extent that the Left is more inflation prone than the Right, we expect the Left to have a greater need for the sort of commitment technology that a currency link is expected to supply. So the further to

33 Cukierman, Webb, and Neyapti 1992.

158

the Left is a government, the more likely it is to choose the DM currency peg. The variable used here measures the partisan (Left-Right) nature of the cabinet in power; parties are coded on a widely accepted scale and weighted according to their importance in the cabinet. In this scale, lower numbers are more to the Left. (Alternate measures of the legislative center of gravity or government's ideology, which use similar scales, yield nearly identical results.) Variable name: *cabinet center of gravity (+)*. Expected sign: positive.

It is a commonplace of macroeconomic political economy that less stable and/or more fragmented governments are particularly in need of monetary policy credibility. So the more unstable and fragmented are governments, the more likely they should be to choose the DM link. I use two measures, which are not closely related in institutional terms. The first is the share of all legislative seats held by the governing coalition, which indicates roughly the security of the government in office. (A measure that uses the share of all votes gives the same results.) The bigger this seat share, the more stable the government, the less likely it is to need the currency as a commitment mechanism, and the less likely is a peg. The second measure is the number of parties in government, which gives a rough sense of the government's stability; more parties in government should increase the need for credibility and therefore the propensity to link to the DM.[34] Variable names: *Percent of seats held by government parties; number of government parties (+; −)*. Expected signs: positive; negative.

None of these variables is, as noted, a direct measure of the demand for credibility. But there is almost certainly no such direct measure, and all the variables employed here have been used to evaluate credibility-based arguments in other studies. They do seem plausible proxies for a government's desire to use exchange rate policy for anti-inflationary credibility purposes.

Similarity of economic structure. In the OCA framework, the more similar are national economies, the less they need independent mon-

---

34 This last measure has major problems. The number of parties in government is the direct result of the electoral system, and will generally increase with proportionality or district magnitude. And inasmuch as we know that small open economies are generally much more likely to have the "purest" proportional representation schemes, this measure may well be closely related to openness. In fact, the correlation between the number of parties in government and manufactured exports to the European Union as a share of the GDP is 0.18, so that the relationship is present but not particularly strong.

etary policies. Here I use the correlation of a nation's industrial structure with that of Germany, which should indicate how different the exogenous shocks affecting the two countries are likely to be. Other related measures might be used. The correlation of a nation's trade structure with that of Germany has attractions (as it is more directly related to pressures on the exchange rate), but it risks endogeneity given that trade structure is much more likely to be affected by exchange rate policy than overall industrial structure. In any case, the two measures are highly correlated and give nearly identical results. Other measures of the OCA criteria tend to give rise to similar categorizations of countries.[35] In the case of the measure of industrial structure, the greater the correlation with Germany, the more likely the country is, by the OCA criteria, to maintain a fixed exchange rate with the DM. Variable name: *industrial correlation with Germany (-)*. Expected sign: negative.

Control Variables

It is important to control for other factors that could be expected to affect exchange rate movements. Foremost among these are the macroeconomic conditions; these and a couple other common explanations of currency movements are included as controls.

Macroeconomic conditions. Developments in national macroeconomic performance affect the propensity of a currency to depreciate. While the arguments for depreciation in each of these instances are not unproblematic, generally speaking, especially difficult years should be associated with a weaker currency.

Recessions may increase the propensity of monetary authorities to use depreciation to stimulate the economy. This depends on the trade-off between the income and substitution effects of a depreciation, but the consensus is that depreciations can be stimulative in the short run. Variable name: *lagged growth rate of GDP (-)*. Expected sign: negative (i.e., the stronger the GDP growth, the less depreciation).

Unemployment can be expected to be significant for the same reason as the overall rate of economic growth. Variable name: *lagged unemployment (+)*. Expected sign: positive.

35 See, for example, Gros 1996.

The weaker a country's current account, the more downward pressure there will be on its currency and the likelier a depreciation. Note that this is the more or less purely economic effect mentioned above, for which I control to assess the independent impact of trends in imports and exports. Variable name: *lagged current account balance as percent of the GDP (−)*. Expected sign: negative.

The difference between movements in the country's terms of trade and those of Germany should affect the currency. The more the country's terms of trade deteriorate relative to Germany, the harder it should be to sustain a fixed exchange rate. A positive number here means that the terms of trade improved in the year relative to Germany's, while a negative number means they deteriorated. This implies that increases in the measure should make it easier to sustain the currency peg, and vice versa. Variable name: *difference in terms of trade relative to Germany (−)*. Expected sign: negative.

As can be seen from the variable names, all these are lagged one year except for the terms of trade figure. This is because policy can be expected to respond to such macroeconomic trends only with something of a delay, except for the terms of trade, which is a price-based measure and thus should have nearly immediate effect. In any case, using simultaneous (lagged, in the case of the terms of trade) data makes no difference to the results. The current account is expressed as a percentage of the GDP, unemployment is a share of the labor force, the GDP growth is a rate of (real) change, and the terms of trade are also a rate of change; all are expressed in percentage points.

Other controls. Three other control variables are included, as they are commonly mentioned in the literature.

Of course this is endogenous, but many believe that membership in the snake and EMS as international (regional) institutions may have had a substantial independent impact on government behavior. This is a dummy variable that takes the value 1 if the country was a member of one of the two ERMs, and 0 otherwise. Variable name: *member of the snake or ERM (−)*. Expected sign: negative.

In the spirit of the political business cycle, governments may be expected to manipulate the currency in the run-up to an election. What in fact they do depends on the relative desirability of the stimulative effect of depreciation and the income effect of an appreciation. Nevertheless, the traditional view of inflation and depreciation as similar in source and effect would lead us to expect elections to be associated with depreciations. The measure here—which has its problems, but is probably adequate for the present purposes—is simply whether an election occurred in the year in question. Variable name: *election (+)*. Expected sign: positive.

Controls on capital movements should facilitate the maintenance of a fixed exchange rate. Of course, countries whose exchange rates face market skepticism for other reasons—such as macroeconomic fundamentals or political instability—are more likely to impose capital controls in the first place, so it may not be clear what to expect. Yet in general, it seems reasonable to expect countries with capital controls to be less likely to depreciate, all else being equal. The measure used is a composite created by Dennis Quinn and drawn from the IMF's categorization of restrictions on capital movements. Variable name: *capital controls (−)*. Expected sign: negative.

Table 4.2 presents simple descriptive statistics, showing the evolution of the means of all dependent and explanatory variables over the course of the period, divided into four subperiods (snake, early EMS, late EMS, and EMU). Table 4.3 presents a correlation matrix, which demonstrates several important things. First, the two dependent variables are closely related (0.82 correlation). Second, several alternate measures of similar factors are closely related—for example, exports to the DM zone are highly correlated (0.91) with exports to the European Union more broadly. Third, where available the correlation between FDI and exports among the same countries is relatively high (0.50 to 0.53). Fourth, there are few correlations of note among explanatory variables—none above 0.5, and most substantially below that. This is of particular importance because it would be reasonable to worry about the collinearity of many of the macroeconomic and monetary variables. It is reassuring to know that these problems are minimal.

Analyzing European Monetary Politics: A Statistical Assessment

The statistical analysis uses the two measures in table 4.1 as dependent variables. The annual depreciation rate is a better indicator of broad trends of currency policy; the volatility measure picks up both overall depreciations and intrayear currency fluctuations. In any case, the two

TABLE 4.2
Average of all countries across periods

	1973–78	1979–83	1984–89	1990–94
Average depreciation versus DM	9.034	4.963	4.227	3.147
Coefficient of variation versus DM	0.033	0.027	0.019	0.019
Industrial correlation	0.723	0.745	0.750	0.685
Lagged GDP growth	3.671	2.240	2.731	1.651
Lagged unemployment (as % of labor force)	3.969	6.681	9.170	8.810
Lagged current account as a % of the GDP	−1.917	−2.446	−0.762	−0.196
Difference in terms of trade	0.198	1.833	−0.820	0.078
Membership of the snake or ERM	0.356	0.420	0.435	0.536
Central bank independence (0–1; 1 most independent)	0.340	0.344	0.345	0.345
Capital controls (0–15; 15 most controls)	6.030	5.150	4.244	2.207
Cabinet center of gravity (1–5; 5 most right wing)	2.788	2.934	3.017	2.873
Election	0.286	0.357	0.298	0.271
Number of government parties	2.035	1.832	2.100	2.255
Percent of seats held by government parties	47.628	48.546	49.578	53.252
Manufacturing exports to DM zone as a % of the GDP	3.479	3.801	4.504	5.063
Manufacturing exports to European Community as a % of the GDP	9.155	9.771	11.649	12.042
Trade balance change as a share of the GDP (lagged)	0.039	0.153	0.142	0.548

TABLE 4.3
Correlations among principal variables

	Depre-ciate	Cov	GDP growth	Un-employ	Curr acct	Diff toft	Indus corr	Snake/ EMS	Cabinet cg
Depreciate	1.00								
COV	0.82	1.00							
GDP growth	-0.19	-0.15	1.00						
Unemploy	-0.08	-0.15	-0.02	1.00					
Curr acct	-0.20	-0.21	0.11	-0.00	1.00				
Diff toft	-0.37	-0.22	0.13	-0.04	-0.04	1.00			
Indust corr	-0.20	-0.30	-0.00	0.43	0.16	-0.08	1.00		
Snake/EMS	-0.15	-0.40	-0.00	0.47	0.02	-0.04	0.47	1.00	
Cabinet cg	0.07	0.06	-0.07	0.38	-0.11	-0.08	0.14	0.21	1.00
Election	0.06	0.03	-0.02	0.03	-0.03	0.01	0.02	0.04	0.04
Gov seats	0.03	-0.04	0.10	0.07	0.04	-0.06	0.02	-0.01	0.05
Gov parties	-0.09	-0.08	-0.01	-0.04	-0.04	-0.01	-0.01	0.16	-0.04
CBI	0.06	-0.12	-0.01	-0.11	-0.18	-0.09	-0.12	-0.05	0.07
Cap ctrls	0.33	0.26	0.09	-0.17	-0.35	0.03	-0.37	-0.22	-0.11
Mfg exp-DM	-0.21	-0.39	-0.04	0.09	0.21	-0.10	0.48	0.38	-0.03
Mfg exp-EC	-0.20	-0.33	-0.01	0.17	0.05	-0.08	0.42	0.39	-0.00
FDI-DM	-0.22	-0.32	0.03	0.08	0.40	-0.03	0.36	0.40	-0.02
FDI-EC	-0.17	-0.26	0.06	0.21	0.30	-0.02	0.27	0.43	0.07
Tr bal chg	-0.18	-0.22	-0.38	0.09	-0.41	0.17	-0.01	0.15	0.08
Inflation	0.23	0.28	-0.14	0.08	-0.35	0.04	0.03	-0.05	0.08

are strongly correlated and yield similar results; where results differ this in itself is interesting, as I discuss below. I look at all current European Union members except Germany, the anchor country, and Luxembourg, which shared a currency with Belgium. I also include Norway, as it often attempted to stabilize its currency against the DM and there would have been little ex ante justification for excluding it at the outset of the sample. The time period runs from the beginning of 1973 to the end of 1994, with annual observations. I stop the examination in 1995 because at that point the European Union was clearly in the run-up to the EMU, whose dynamic was quite different from that of the attempts to fix exchange rates that had come before. The explanatory variables are as described above and in more detail in the appendix to this chapter. The regressions using these panel data are all corrected for serial autocorrelation and heteroskedasticity, and panel corrected standard errors are presented.

	Gov seats	Gov parties	CBI	Cap ctrls	Mfg exp-DM	Mfg exp-EC	FDI-DM	FDI-EC	Tr bal chg	Inflation
Election										
1.00										
-0.07	1.00									
0.02	0.28	1.00								
0.04	-0.02	-0.11	1.00							
-0.02	0.06	-0.16	0.04	1.00						
0.04	0.23	0.05	0.03	-0.21	1.00					
0.06	0.13	0.12	-0.08	-0.14	0.91	1.00				
-0.03	0.24	-0.13	-0.11	-0.46	0.53	0.37	1.00			
-0.00	0.28	0.02	-0.11	-0.45	0.56	0.50	0.83	1.00		
0.01	-0.14	0.00	-0.00	0.01	0.10	0.22	-0.04	0.05	1.00	
-0.04	-0.21	-0.12	-0.22	0.41	-0.40	-0.27	-0.51	-0.43	0.16	1.00

The results can be seen in tables 4.4 and 4.5. The first column of each table presents the full model, with all the variables discussed above. The second model reanalyzes the data, dropping the explanatory variables that do not come close to statistical significance. In the third model, variables from the second model that now fail to reach statistical significance are dropped.

It can readily be seen that the results are quite stable across specifications, as are the coefficients. Starting with table 4.4, in which the left-hand-side variable is the annual depreciation rate, six explanatory variables are significant in all three models; only two other variables even come close to reaching significance in one or two specifications.

The three principal macroeconomic control variables are clearly important. The state of the current account, GDP growth, and terms of trade (relative to Germany's) all have the expected signs, and obviously had a powerful impact on exchange rates.

TABLE 4.4
Results (dependent variable = average depreciation rate)

	(1)	(2)	(3)
Constant	3.660	3.305**	3.633**
	(3.703)	(1.409)	(1.372)
Lagged growth rate of the GDP	−0.742**	−0.647**	−0.672**
	(0.208)	(0.203)	(0.203)
Lagged unemployment	0.029	NA	NA
	(0.111)		
Lagged current account balance as percent of the GDP	−0.258	−0.393**	−0.394**
	(0.177)	(0.180)	(0.179)
Difference in the terms of trade relative to Germany	−0.424**	−0.391**	−0.378**
	(0.092)	(0.093)	(0.093)
Industrial correlation with Germany	−2.823	NA	NA
	(4.172)		
Member of the snake or ERM	−0.986	−1.549	−1.486
	(1.115)	(0.957)	(0.950)
Cabinet center of gravity	0.660	NA	NA
	(0.675)		
Election	1.258	1.233	NA
	(0.897)	(0.911)	
Percent of seats held by government parties	0.042	NA	NA
	(0.040)		
Number of government parties	−0.379	NA	NA
	(0.374)		
Central bank independence	−3.184	NA	NA
	(2.602)		
Capital controls	0.951**	1.066**	1.084**
	(0.260)	(0.240)	(0.239)
Manufacturing exports to the DM zone as a percent of the GDP	−0.289**	−0.257**	−0.255**
	(0.147)	(0.126)	(0.125)
Change in the trade balance as a percent of the GDP	−0.740**	−0.541**	−0.547**
	(0.248)	(0.247)	(0.247)
N	278	313	313

Standard errors appear in parentheses under the coefficients.
* draws attention to coefficients significant at or above the 10 percent level
** draws attention to coefficients significant at or above the 5 percent level

TABLE 4.5
Results (dependent variable = coefficient of variation)

	(1)	(2)	(3)
Constant	2.628**	2.334**	2.304**
	(1.052)	(0.755)	(0.767)
Lagged growth rate of the GDP	-0.121**	-0.107**	-0.112**
	(0.055)	(0.054)	(0.052)
Lagged unemployment	-0.011	NA	NA
	(0.031)		
Lagged current account as a percent of the GDP	-0.077	-0.110**	-0.118**
	(0.052)	(0.051)	(0.051)
Difference in the terms of trade relative to Germany	-0.044*	-0.027	NA
	(0.025)	(0.025)	
Industrial correlation with Germany	0.278	NA	NA
	(1.189)		
Member of the snake or ERM	-1.060**	-1.103**	-1.077**
	(0.306)	(0.260)	(0.266)
Cabinet center of gravity	0.473**	0.498**	0.516**
	(0.186)	(0.182)	(0.183)
Election	0.269	NA	NA
	0.225)		
Percent of seats held by government parties	0.002	NA	NA
	(0.012)		
Number of government parties	-0.081	NA	NA
	(0.102)		
Central bank independence	-2.730**	-2.427**	-2.567**
	(0.765)	(0.784)	(0.777)
Capital controls	0.100	0.144**	0.139**
	(0.073)	(0.068)	(0.069)
Manufacturing exports to the DM zone as a percent of the GDP	-0.145**	-0.136**	-0.130**
	(0.040)	(0.032)	(0.033)
Change in the trade balance as a percent of the GDP	-0.188**	-0.144**	-0.149**
	(0.067)	(0.065)	(0.064)
N	278	305	312

Standard errors appear in parentheses under the coefficients.
* draws attention to coefficients significant at or above the 10 percent level
** draws attention to coefficients significant at or above the 5 percent level

The variables meant as proxies for private interest concern about exchange rate risk and price competitiveness are statistically significant as well as in the expected direction. First, the larger the country's manufactured exports to the DM zone as a share of the GDP, the less likely it was to depreciate. In other words, countries more commercially integrated with Germany were more likely to fix their currencies against that of Germany. This finding is consistent with the idea that export-oriented manufacturers (with low pass-through) and multinational firms whose interests tend to track those of manufactured exporters value currency stability. Second, deterioration in the trade balance (controlling for the current account balance), such as would be caused by an import surge, is strongly associated with depreciation. To put it another way, the more net import competition a country faces, the less likely the country is to fix its currency against the DM. This finding is consistent with the idea that the import and export competers concerned about increased foreign competition press for a depreciation, and, more generally, the argument that currency policy was made taking into account its anticipated impact on trade and investment.

The proxies used here to attempt to capture such purely monetary considerations as anti-inflationary credibility or OCA motivations for currency pegs were not significant in any specification. None of the measures associated with credibility concerns had any impact on the propensity to hold to a currency peg: neither the partisan composition of government, the two measures of general government strength or stability (the government's share of all seats and the number of parties in government), or central bank independence. The correlation of national industrial structures with Germany's, the proxy for the OCA status, is not significant.

The other factors considered yielded mixed results at best. There is some evidence that membership in the snake or ERM was associated with more stability against the DM, as expected, but this variable does not reach statistical significance.[36] There is little support for the notion that governments were more prone to depreciate in election years, as the results are not statistically significant. One variable is clearly significant, but in the opposite direction to that usually anticipated. Capital controls, far from helping to sustain the exchange rate against the

---

36 The snake/ERM variable is mildly correlated (0.39) with manufactured exports, however, so that there may be some problems of collinearity.

DM, are associated with more depreciation. There is an apparent problem of simultaneity here, though, as countries facing attacks on their currencies are more likely to impose capital controls.

Table 4.5 presents the results of the same sort of regression analysis using the coefficient of variation of the nominal exchange rate as the dependent variable.[37] The results for the private interest variables and macroeconomic controls are essentially as before: more manufactured exports to the DM zone, improvements in the trade balance, faster GDP growth, and a stronger current account are all associated with reduced volatility. Evolution in the terms of trade is significant in only one specification. Most of the other variables are as before: elections along with government strength and stability are insignificant; the capital controls variable is significant in a direction opposite to that expected. So far the results are essentially the same as in the previous specification.

There are three differences between these results and those having to do with the depreciation rate; these differences have mixed implications for credibility-related perspectives. The partisan composition of government matters in the way generally anticipated by credibility-based arguments: the more left wing the government, the less volatile the currency. But central bank independence does not: it is associated with less short-term volatility. In addition, snake/EMS membership is also associated with less volatility. The results imply that these three factors are not strong enough to affect longer-term trends in currency values—the depreciation rate—but they do reduce currency volatility. Left-wing governments do use a currency peg more than right-wing ones for short-term purposes; an independent central bank can stabilize the exchange rate in the short run more effectively than a dependent one, and membership in the snake or EMS increased the national ability to stabilize currencies. Again, it should be noted that these variables reduce short-term *volatility*, but not the propensity to depreciate itself, and they do not unambiguously support the OCA or credibility-based arguments.

The substantive interpretation of most of the coefficients in the regressions is relatively straightforward. Those having to do with the average annual depreciation rate are easier to interpret than the coeffi-

---

37 In the regression, unlike in table 4.1, the relevant time period is a year, so this is the standard deviation of a currency's value (measured monthly) over its annual mean value.

cient of variation. Looking at column 3 of table 4.4, the variables expressed as percentage points (of the GDP or rates of change) are easily understood. One percentage point improvements in the GDP growth rate, current account as a share of the GDP, and terms of trade relative to Germany are associated with 0.672, 0.394, and 0.378 percentage point reductions, respectively, in the currency's annual depreciation rate against the DM. Similarly, a 1 percentage point increase in manufactured exports to the DM zone as a share of the GDP and a 1 percentage point improvement in the trade balance are associated with respective 0.255 and 0.547 percentage point reductions in the rate of depreciation. These are all quite appreciable numbers.

Increasing capital controls by one point on a fifteen-point scale leads to an increase in the depreciation rate of 1.084 percent. This means little in and of itself; one way of seeing it is that a three-point difference, roughly equivalent to that between Norway and Greece, increases the depreciation rate by 3.252 percent a year.

The impact of explanatory variables on the coefficient of variation cannot be assessed so directly. A sense of their importance can be seen in how a one standard deviation change in explanatory variables (holding all others at their means) affects the volatility measure. By this measure, for example, a one standard deviation increase in the lagged GDP growth rate or lagged current account is associated with a reduction in the coefficient of variation of 11.7 and 16.3 percent, respectively. An increase of one standard deviation in manufactured exports to the DM zone or trade balance leads to respective 17.1 and 14.1 percent reductions in volatility, while such an increase in central bank independence is associated with a 15.1 percent decline in the coefficient of variation. On the other hand, one standard deviation's move to the right of the cabinet center of gravity or increase in capital controls are associated with, respectively, 13.6 and 14.8 percent increases in volatility.

The principal results reported here are quite robust. Removing outliers—the Netherlands and Austria on one end, and Greece and Portugal on the other—leaves the results essentially intact. This does reduce the significance of a couple of variables, which is not surprising as it involves removing nearly one-third of all observations, but the major explanatory variables remain important. When countries are omitted one by one, the results are undisturbed. Adding year-fixed effects only strengthens the results; adding country-fixed effects has little impact, although (not surprisingly) it reduces the size of some coefficients.

Many versions of the empirical models were assessed, with no impact on the principal results—those pertaining to the proxies for sectoral considerations. Manufactured exports to the European Union as a whole (as opposed to only to the DM bloc) gives essentially identical results. Inclusion of the fiscal deficit (lagged or simultaneous) serves to make most other variables more significant and their coefficients larger.[38] The fiscal deficit is itself significant and associated with more depreciation.

The results can be summarized as follows:

- The evidence is consistent with the argument that producers more exposed to currency risk prefer a fixed currency, while tradables producers concerned with price competitiveness prefer flexibility. Specifically, the more important were manufactured exports to the DM zone (Germany and Benelux)—which we associate with specialized exporters with little pass-through—the slower the depreciation rate and less volatile the currency. On the other hand, an increase in net import competition, controlling for the current account, increased the depreciation rate and volatility significantly.
- Macroeconomic control variables all had the expected effects. Such fundamentals as the current account balance, GDP growth, and terms of trade relative to the anchor country all reduced the depreciation rate as well as currency volatility substantially.
- Variables intended to capture inclinations to fix currencies to gain anti-inflationary credibility were almost never significant. The only exception was that left-wing parties were more likely to hold the currency stable in the short run, but there was no partisan difference in depreciation rates. A measure of suitability for membership in an OCA was never significant. To be sure, the difficulty of measuring the demand for anti-inflationary credibility implies that this evidence is not definitive. Nonetheless, while credibility motivations cannot be excluded, it is difficult to see support for them here.

38 Not surprisingly, it does make the current account insignificant; it also makes central bank independence significant (but again, not in the direction anticipated by credibility-based accounts). Using HP-filtered cyclic components for the GDP growth rates made no difference to the results.

The results are in line with my expectations about the role of private interests. A greater importance of manufactured exports to Germany and its close partners was associated with a more fixed exchange rate; increases in net import competition spurred depreciation. These two results provide a rough evaluation of the impact of private distributional interests—in the event, of exporters of complex manufactures and import competers—on exchange rate policy.

After EMU: Expansion and Crisis

The creation of the euro was only one point on a longer trajectory. The eventual goal is for nearly all members of the European Union—save for those allowed to opt out—to adopt the common currency. This presents newer members of the European Union and those countries planning to join the European Union with the challenge of adopting appropriate currency policies. These countries, largely in central and eastern Europe, have in fact pursued a wide variety of different exchange rate policies. Some have been eager to join the euro, and several already have (Slovenia in 2007, Cyprus and Malta in 2008, Slovakia in 2009, Estonia in 2011, Latvia in 2014, and Lithuania in 2015). In preparation, a range of countries have adopted policies that link their currencies to the euro more or less rigidly. Other countries seem in no rush to join the eurozone or even fix their currencies to the euro. This is an interesting question, which I have addressed (with David Leblang and Neven Valev) with tools similar to those used here and with results very much in line with the assertion presented here.[39] Over the next decade, countries both inside and outside the eurozone will need to determine their policy toward adoption of or linkage to the euro.

Eurozone member states have faced more immediate problems, however. The first few years of the euro were serene, but once the Great Recession began in 2007, conditions became much more difficult—and some observers even expected the eurozone to break up. Although a full analysis of the euro crisis, in all its various stages, is well beyond the scope of this book, it is worth describing the crisis and how its course reflects the factors of interest to this analysis.

39 Frieden, Leblang, and Valev 2010.

At the time of the euro's introduction, it was clear to most observers that there were at least three key issues that had not yet been resolved. All three contributed to the crisis as it unfolded.

The first problem that the EMU, like any currency union, faced was the underlying differences in macroeconomic conditions among the member states. By the early 2000s, there was a sharp divergence between the relatively slow-growing northern European countries and more rapidly growing southern European economies. Germany and Spain, both the most important instances, are exemplary. In the simplest terms, the German economy was stagnant while Spain's was growing quickly. And this fast growth meant that while inflation was at or near zero in Germany, prices were rising somewhat more rapidly in Spain. Between 1998 and 2007, German inflation averaged just 1.5 percent a year, while in Spain it averaged 3.2 percent. This may seem a small difference, but compounded over nearly a decade, it led to a substantial divergence in prices.

At the same time, a decade of wage restraint and austerity following German unification had made the country's manufacturing sector extremely competitive, as Germany returned to its traditional export-oriented position. Spain, by contrast, was booming, and wages were rising steadily. So between 1998 and 2007, unit labor costs in Germany actually fell by 3.9 percent even as in Spain they rose by 30.4 percent.[40] These trends are shown in table 4.6 and figures 4.1 and 4.2, which demonstrate the evolution of unit labor costs and the real exchange rate in Germany and Spain as well as the other peripheral eurozone countries—Greece, Ireland, Italy, and Portugal. (Because the nominal exchange rate was of course the same throughout the eurozone, the real exchange rate in this case is simply calculated by weighting relative unit labor costs by the importance of other markets to the home country.)

For most of this period, the European Central Bank's main interest rate was around 3 percent. This meant that real interest rates in Germany were about 2 percent, while they were slightly negative in Spain. More generally, given the difference in price and income trends in the two countries, it made it extremely attractive for Spaniards to borrow. Meanwhile, Germany's traditionally high savings rate was being raised

40 Data from Eurostat, http://epp.eurostat.ec.europa.eu/tgm/table.do?tab=table&init=1&plugin =0&language=en&pcode=tsdec330 (accessed March 6, 2013).

TABLE 4.6
Unit labor costs, real effective exchange rates, and current account balances for
Germany and peripheral Eurozone countries, 1998–2012

A. Unit labor costs

	Germany	Spain	Ireland	Italy	Portugal	Greece
1998	100	100	100	100	100	100
1999	100.9	102.0	101.7	101.4	102.9	104.2
2000	101.0	104.7	111.5	100.9	107.6	105.7
2001	100.9	107.9	117.1	103.9	111.4	105.7
2002	101.2	111.2	119.5	107.5	114.8	115.4
2003	102.0	114.5	126.7	112.1	118.8	116.7
2004	101.1	117.5	132.0	113.7	119.8	118.2
2005	100.0	121.7	139.4	116.7	124.2	122.4
2006	97.6	125.5	144.8	118.6	125.0	121.9
2007	96.1	130.5	149.7	120.7	126.0	124.8
2008	98.1	137.6	157.0	125.4	129.8	124.2
2009	104.7	139.3	146.6	130.9	133.0	137.5
2010	102.7	136.5	136.6	130.3	131.2	138.5
2011	104.0	133.8	132.6	131.2	130.0	134.5

B. Real effective exchange rate

	Germany	Spain	Ireland	Italy	Portugal	Greece
1998	100.0	100.0	100	100	100	100
1999	97.3	98.9	96.2	97.8	99.8	101.6
2000	91.1	96.4	90.5	92.2	99.4	94.9
2001	89.4	97.7	94.1	93.2	101.2	92.2
2002	89.6	99.7	95.8	96.5	103.2	101.4
2003	81.7	104.7	105.3	104.5	108.6	104.7
2004	82.0	107.6	111.4	107.7	109.5	107.5
2005	79.4	109.2	114.9	107.8	111.4	108.1
2006	76.8	111.7	117.8	109.2	110.8	105.9
2007	75.7	115.8	123.5	110.4	110.8	106.8
2008	75.6	120.4	132.1	113.2	112.0	109.2
2009	78.2	119.0	124.0	115.2	112.6	113.1
2010	74.8	114.2	112.3	111.6	109.6	101.0
2011	74.9	111.6	107.8	111.5	108.4	107.9

C. Current account balance as share of the GDP

	Germany	Spain	Ireland	Italy	Portugal	Greece
1998	−1	−1	1	2	−7	NA
1999	−1	−3	0	1	−9	NA
2000	−2	−4	0	−1	−10	−8
2001	0	−4	−1	0	−10	−7

TABLE 4.6 (*continued*)

	Germany	Spain	Ireland	Italy	Portugal	Greece
2002	2	−3	−1	−1	−8	−7
2003	2	−4	0	−1	−6	−7
2004	5	−5	−1	−1	−8	−6
2005	5	−7	−3	−2	−10	−8
2006	6	−9	−4	−3	−11	−11
2007	7	−10	−5	−2	−10	−14
2008	6	−10	−6	−3	−13	−15
2009	6	−5	−2	−2	−11	−11
2010	6	−4	1	−4	−11	−10
2011	6	−4	1	−3	−7	−10
2012	7	−1	5	−1	−2	NA

Source: Eurostat, http://epp.eurostat.ec.europa.eu/tgm/table.do?tab=table&init=1&plugin=0&language=en&pcode=tsdec330 (accessed March 6, 2013).

further as its population aged and trade surpluses built up. The result was a massive flow of funds from northern Europe to the eurozone periphery. As capital flowed from the surplus countries of northern Europe to the deficit countries of the eurozone periphery, it reinforced the macroeconomic divergence. The debt-financed consumption boom raised wages and prices, and increased the difference between the two regions. One indication of the divergence was the trends in the various countries' real effective exchange rates (REER): between 1998 and 2008, Germany's declined by nearly 25 percent, even as the Spanish real exchange rate—that is, taking into account local labor costs and the structure of its exports—appreciated by over 20 percent (see table 4.6, sections A and B, and figure 4.2). So the attempt to devise a common monetary policy for different regions of the eurozone led to an imbalanced pattern of capital flows and growth.

This was reflected almost immediately in the current account deficits of the northern and peripheral European countries—the lenders and borrowers. As the periphery boomed, capital flooded in from northern Europe, and allowed massive trade and current account deficits to develop. Section C of table 4.6 and figure 4.3 show the extent of the macroeconomic imbalances. In 1998, both Spain and Germany had small current account deficits of about 1 percent of the GDP; Italy and Ireland were running surpluses. By 2008, Germany's current account surplus was 6 percent of the GDP; Spain, Ireland, and Italy had deficits

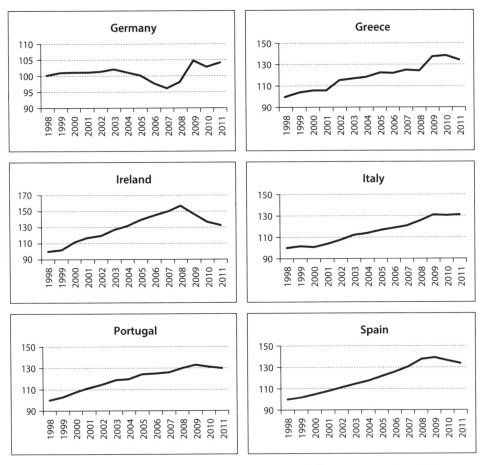

Figure 4.1 Unit labor costs for Germany and peripheral European countries, 1998–2011

of 10, 6, and 3 percent, respectively. Simply put, Germany's surplus was going to finance the eurozone periphery's deficits.[41]

The second major problem was that the creation of the eurozone led quickly to a tightly integrated eurozone-wide financial market,

41 It should be noted that, contrary to popular impressions, the vast majority of these loans went to private borrowers. Greece and to a lesser degree Portugal were the only peripheral countries whose governments ran major budget deficits in this period. Spain's enormous deficits went almost entirely to the private financial sector to be lent to the country's booming housing market.

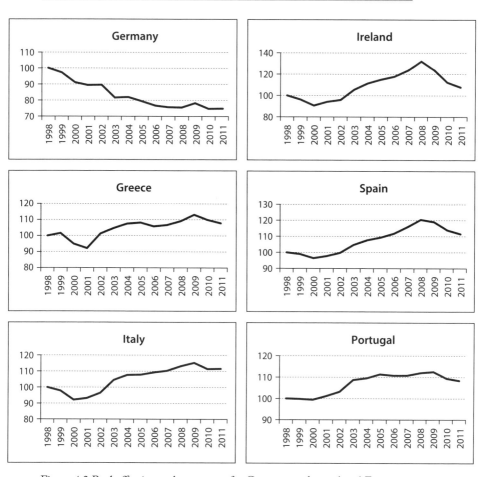

Figure 4.2 Real effective exchange rates for Germany and peripheral European countries, 1998–2011

while bank regulation remained decentralized and in the hands of national authorities. This allowed banks to take advantage of regulatory differences to seek out higher-yield and higher-risk loans, and also created great uncertainty as to who would ultimately be responsible for any banking problems that might arise.

A third problem was that many market participants anticipated that if indeed financial difficulties did arise in one of the eurozone member states, the other member states would be forced to bail it out. This expectation was widespread, despite attempts by eurozone and na-

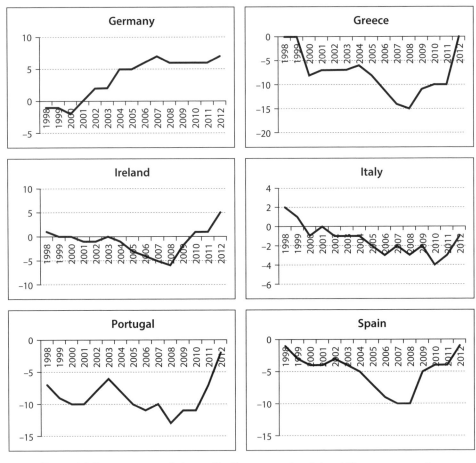

Figure 4.3 Current account balances for Germany and peripheral European countries, 1998–2012
Source (figures 4.1–4.3): Tables 4.6–4.8, adapted from Eurostat, http://epp.eurostat .ec.europa.eu/tgm/table.do?tab=table&init=1&plugin=0&language=en&pcode =tsdec330 (accessed March 6, 2013).

tional authorities to insist that there would be no bailout. International and regional experience told market operators otherwise: a major financial meltdown in one country could threaten the entire eurozone and would force other countries to step in. Inasmuch as there were expectations of a bailout, market participants did not have to worry about the risks associated with weaknesses in an individual country's finances. These expectations led spreads on sovereign borrowing by all eurozone

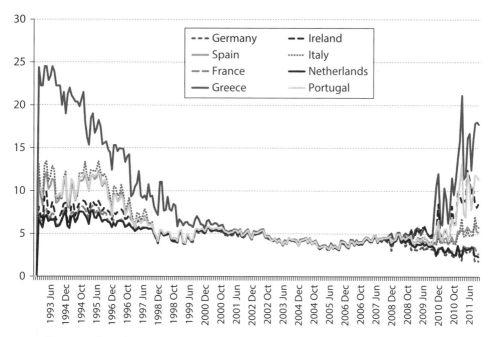

Figure 4.4 Spreads on eurozone sovereign debt, 1993–2011. *Source*: Chinn and Frieden 2012.

countries to decline precipitously when the euro was introduced. As figure 4.4 indicates, for almost ten years every government of the eurozone could borrow at interest rates roughly equal to those charged to Germany. This, of course, encouraged sovereign borrowing in the eurozone periphery. Not all countries took advantage of this—Spain and Ireland, for example, did little public borrowing—but some, led by Greece, did.

In any event, these three problems came together to bring the eurozone close to collapse. The massive capital flows from the North to the periphery led to a boom and then a bubble in the periphery. As the crisis broke in 2007–8, this bubble also burst. Financial institutions throughout the eurozone turned out to be holding trillions of euros worth of questionable assets. This was true of investors in the creditor (northern) countries and financial institutions in the debtor (peripheral) countries, as much of the lending was intermediated through local banks. Peripheral governments found themselves compelled to bail out their illiquid or insolvent banks, at extraordinary expense.

The result was a eurozone debt crisis, in which peripheral countries owed debts that they could not service to northern European creditors. While the many-faceted components of this crisis are fascinating and worthy of discussion, for our purposes—that is, with relevance to currency policy—what is particularly noteworthy is that to a great degree the source of the problem was the inability of individual eurozone governments to control their exchange rate. If, as had happened in 1992–93, peripheral governments had been able to devalue, recovery from the crisis would almost certainly have been more rapid—to the benefit of both debtors and creditors. But in the absence of this option, the crisis dragged on for years.

The eventual resolution of the eurozone debt crisis demonstrated, as did the general course of European monetary integration, that the OCA and other related considerations were effectively irrelevant to the process. The creation and defense of the euro were the result of complex political forces—influenced, to be sure, by the economic environment. While a complete analysis of the political economy of the euro crisis is beyond the scope of this chapter, the kinds of factors discussed in explaining monetary integration were clearly at work. Those in the periphery who were anxious to encourage continued economic integration were willing to subject their economies to severe austerity measures in order to maintain membership in the eurozone. Opponents in the uncompetitive, nontradables (especially public) sector attempted to halt or revise the course of the adjustment, and sometimes to encourage an exit from the euro, but were outgunned.

The origins and course of the eurozone crisis demonstrate that a wide variety of factors influence the process of European monetary integration. Monetary integration generally and the EMU more recently have been central to the broader course of European integration. Interstate bargaining and domestic political considerations that go far beyond purely monetary concerns have profoundly affected them. Perhaps the most important nonmonetary consideration is the widely held view that membership in the eurozone is a prerequisite to having a full-fledged voice in the future of the European Union in general. As the eurozone has become something of the hard core of the European Union, there is a broad perception that countries that are not in the eurozone will be excluded from decision making on a variety of other issues. For groups within and across countries that have strong views on European issues, membership in the eurozone may be crucial for reasons that have little to do with currency matters. In many of the troubled eurozone debtors—including some countries on the European periphery that were not in the eurozone at the time—there was a popular view that exclusion from the eurozone would lead to the loss of EU funds. So there is little question that the sorts of distributional factors discussed here are only part of the full story of European monetary integration.

Nonetheless, any account of the process that led to the euro's creation—and its management after its introduction—should take the political economy factors explored here into consideration. There were significant differences within EU member states over policy toward the snake, EMS, and EMU. The economic interests of groups in society played a prominent part in creating these differences, and therefore in the process of monetary integration more widely.

In the context of our broader analysis of the politics of exchange rate policy, it is especially relevant that some of the same factors that have been significant in other times and places were important in Europe as well. Those economic actors with important cross-border economic interests, concerned to sustain or deepen economic integration, were particularly favorable to fixed exchange rates and eventually to a common currency. Those groups worried about import and export competition, and about the loss of monetary policy independence to both affect domestic conditions and the real exchange rate, were especially wary of both fixing rates and the euro. This is, of course, reminiscent of the political economy of the gold standard in the United States, and it indicates the validity of my argument regarding the general sources of policy preferences in the politics of exchange rate policy.

From the Snake to the Euro and Beyond

Exchange rate policy has been central to European integration since its beginning. In some ways the politics of exchange rates within the European Union epitomizes the stark realities faced by national political economies in open economies. The EU member states faced the trilemma in its simplest form: given that they had decided on financial integration, they either had to give up their monetary autonomy or allow their exchange rates to fluctuate against one another. The latter choice might fundamentally have threatened the single European market: How could some member states allow others to use depreciated currencies to gain a competitive edge? Still, the former choice—for a common currency—required a massive series of political battles that are almost certainly not yet over, and drew into the conflict every aspect of the national and regional political economies.

Appendix: Definition and Sources of Explanatory Variables

Cabinet Center of Gravity

Party composition of the cabinet, weighted by ideological scores using a scale constructed by Geoffrey Garrett.

Data through 1991 provided by Geoff Garrett; updated using *European Journal of Political Research* (EJPR 28: 277–89, 1995; EJPR 26: 241–46, 1994; EJPR 24: 419–23, 1993; miscellaneous from EJPR 1991 and 1992).

Capital Controls

A measure of capital controls constructed by Dennis Quinn (1997). His fifteen-point scale measures "openness"; it is inverted here so that a higher number means more capital controls.
Data obtained from the author.

Central Bank Independence

An index of central bank independence, running from 0 (least independent) to 1 (most independent).
Data from Cukierman, Webb, and Neyapti 1992.

Change in the Trade Balance as a Percent of the GDP

Change in the trade balance from the previous year, in percentage terms.

Constructed from data for trade balance and the GDP in IMF, *International Financial Statistics Yearbook*, various years.

Difference in the Terms of Trade Relative to Germany

Percentage point change in the terms of trade over the previous year, relative to Germany's. An increase in this figure signifies an improvement in Germany's terms of trade relative to the country in question.

Data from IMF, *International Financial Statistics Yearbook*, 1996.

Election

Number of elections per year (usually 1 or 0).

Data obtained from Mackie and Rose 1991; *National Elections*, various years; *European Journal of Political Research* (EJPR 28: 277–89, 1995; EJPR 26: 241–46, 1994; EJPR 24: 419–23, 1993; miscellaneous from EJPR 1974–88).

Industrial Correlation with Germany

Correlation coefficient comparing the percent contribution to the GDP of each ISIC 1-digit and 2-digit category for manufacturing (ISIC code 3). Because industrial structure changes slowly, the correlation coefficient is calculated for 1970, 1980, and 1990 only.

Data from the Organisation for Economic Co-operation and Development (OECD), *Industrial Structure Statistics*, various years. Where data were missing from the OECD statistics, data were taken from the United Nations, *Yearbook of Industrial Statistics*, various years.

Lagged Current Account as a Percent of the GDP

Current account balance as a percentage of the GDP, lagged one year.

Data from OECD, *Economic Outlook*, various years.

Lagged Growth Rate of the GDP

Growth rate of the GDP, lagged one year.
Data for 1971–79 figures from *Economic Survey of Europe*, 1984–85; for 1980–93, from the OECD, Historical Studies: 1960–93.

Lagged Unemployment

Percentage of the labor force unemployed, lagged one year.
Data from OECD Main Economic Indicators, Historical Studies: Prices, Labor, and Wages, 1962–91; OECD, *Economic Outlook*, 1995 (vol. 58); OECD Main Economic Indicators, Historical Studies: 1960–79; *Economic Survey of Europe*, 1984–85.

Manufactured Exports to the DM Zone as a Percent of the GDP

Value of manufactured (SITC codes 6–8) exports to the Germany, Belgium, Luxembourg, and the Netherlands as a percentage of the GDP.
Data supplied by the United Nations, *Yearbook of International Trade Statistics*, various years.

Member of the Snake or ERM

Dichotomous variable = 1, if country is a member of either the snake or ERM, and 0, if not.
Data obtained from the *BIS Annual Reports*, various years.

Number of Parties in Government

Number of parties in government.
Constructed in Powell and Whitten 1993; updated using *European Journal of Political Research*, various years.

Percent of Seats Held by Government Parties

Percentage of legislative seats won by the government parties in the election at time t, where t denotes the current observation.

Constructed in Powell and Whitten 1993; updated using *European Journal of Political Research*, various years.

Latin American Currency Policy, 1970–2010

The countries of Latin America have experienced virtually every sort of currency policy known to humanity. Indeed, some individual Latin American nations have themselves gone through many different regimes. The region has been a hotbed of macroeconomic instability since its independence from Spain and Portugal in the 1820s, when it was responsible for the first large flurry of developing country debt and, soon after, the first wave of developing country defaults. Latin America's varied experiences with the gold standard and its alternatives were widely followed in the late nineteenth and early twentieth centuries. Over the past thirty years, Latin America has accounted for some of the most spectacular modern currency crises as well as many experiments in exchange rate policy, including the adoption of the US dollar by several countries in the region. All this makes Latin America a promising subject for the investigation of the political economy of exchange rate policy.

Currency policy has also been central to the economics and politics of Latin America. From the gold standard era to the present, the region's nations have faced major decisions about what exchange rate policies to adopt in light of the international economic context. And there have been nearly continual, often highly conflictual domestic struggles over currency policy. The policies adopted have frequently both clearly reflected and powerfully affected the very nature of the nation's political economy.

In this chapter and the next, I apply my general theoretical approach to recent Latin American experiences. Focusing on distributional cleavages within these societies, I analyze both the choice of exchange rate regime and policies toward the level of the exchange rate. My goal is to demonstrate the regularities and significance of special interest and electoral pressures on the making of currency policy in Latin America.

In addition to the centrality of Latin American governments' choices of exchange rate regimes and policies, the specific incidence of currency crises has had a particularly crucial role in the political and economic history of Latin America. The region's countries have indeed experienced similar exchange rate crises over the past three decades— Mexico in 1982 and 1994, Brazil in 1998–99, and Argentina in 2000–2002, among them. This suggests either a remarkable inability to learn from recent catastrophes or enduring sets of political economy constraints on policymaking (or both). By the same token, some countries have avoided disaster or mitigated it, and the sources of these more successful policies are worth trying to understand.

Here and in the next chapter, I look at the Latin American currency experience since the collapse of the Bretton Woods monetary order in the early 1970s. This chapter presents an overview of the region's experience. It starts with a reminder of my analytic expectations, especially as relevant to Latin America, and then goes on to give a historical background to the region's experience and provide a narrative analysis of regional currency policy developments, emphasizing special interest and electoral factors. It then provides a more systematic analysis, with a series of statistical evaluations of the sources of regional exchange rate policies. Chapter 6 looks more specifically at currency crises in Latin America, first describing them, and then attempting to explain the different patterns over time and across country.

Analytic Expectations

Exchange rate policies are important to Latin America, and political factors are critical to the determination of these policies. Ample case study accounts indicate the role of policies and politics, as do several more general cross-country studies.[1] I hope to enrich the country-specific literature by bringing to bear a systematic set of predictions about the political cleavages likely to be found in Latin America to the context of the general approach presented in this book.

Both the exchange rate regime—especially whether to fix against the US dollar—and its level have been central topics of political debate in Latin America for decades. Many governments have pegged their currencies to the US dollar, and some have even adopted it ("dollarized"). Others have chosen to float the currency, with or without policies to affect its level and volatility. Most countries have moved back and forth among these regimes—not always smoothly. At the same time, the level of the real exchange rate has been the topic of many policy, political, and scholarly debates. Bouts of appreciation have typically proved difficult to unwind and have often preceded currency crises. There is a striking contrast, in fact, between habitually "overvalued" Latin American currencies and habitually "undervalued" East Asian currencies; some observers regard the East Asian pattern as more conducive to economic development.[2] These and related issues are common topics of political and economic analysis, yet the academic study of the *political economy* of exchange rate policy in Latin America is sparse.

In this chapter, I apply the general theory presented in chapter 1 to the Latin American experience. Several preliminary points are worth making about the Latin American context for exchange rate policy. First, for many regional producers, limited pass-through of exports is unlikely to be a major consideration. The region largely exports goods for which pass-through is quite high: primary products (coffee, oil,

---

1 For an important example, see Roett and Wise 2000. For classic treatments of the general issues, see Klein and Marion 1997; Klein and Shambaugh 2008. For a set of case studies and a statistical overview, see Frieden and Stein 2001.

2 For a prominent recent example, see Rodrik 2008. Jeffrey Sachs (1985) noted early on the crucial importance of exchange rate policy to the differential response of Latin America and East Asia to the early 1980s' debt crisis, and proposed a political economy explanation of the differences.

copper, etc.) and relatively simple manufactures (footwear, luggage, steel, etc.). Given its status as middle income, the region does export some more complex manufactured goods; Brazil, for instance, is one of the world's leading exporters of regional jet aircraft. As a result, locally based exporters' interests may be conflicted between the desire for a depreciated currency and countervailing concerns for currency stability. I expect the demand for depreciation to be stronger than in Europe, however, as more of the region's exports are commodities or standard-ized manufactures.

Second, in contrast to the United States on the gold standard and Europe more recently, Latin American governments have no clear "tar-get" for their currency policy. There is no gold standard to link to and no EMU to which to aspire. There is, in other words, no established currency goal toward which governments might strive—other than their own national priorities. By the same token, there is no benchmark against which currency policy performance can be measured akin to the ability to stay on gold or accede to the euro. This observation can be tempered in the case of Mexico and the small, open economies in and around the Caribbean basin—such as those in the English-speaking Caribbean—many of which have a natural pull toward the US dollar. But especially in the case of the countries of South America, trade and investment ties are diversified enough among North America, Europe, and Asia that there is no natural currency anchor.

Third, during the period under examination most Latin American economies went through a dramatic transformation from being gener-ally closed to generally open—with important implications for ex-change rate policy. Before the 1980s, Latin American economies typi-cally pursued a policy of protectionist industrialization. Over the course of the 1980s, much of Latin America moved toward openness to inter-national trade. Most of them also permitted substantially free cross-border financial flows over the subsequent years. This transformation allows us to compare the politics of currency policy in countries as they move from closed to open economies. I expect the exchange rate pref-erences of manufacturers, for example, to be fundamentally different when prohibitive trade barriers protect them than when they are ex-posed to international competition.

Fourth, the 1980s also saw significant political transformations in the region. Before the early 1980s, most of the region's countries were under authoritarian regimes of one sort or another. Almost all the region was democratic by the 1990s. This political transition almost certainly increased the susceptibility of policymakers to mass political pressures, including electoral pressures.

Keeping in mind these regional particularities—and a host of similarly relevant national ones—my approach has obvious implications for the politics of exchange rate policy in Latin America. The two clearest expectations are as follows:

- I expect groups with substantial cross-border economic interests to support a fixed exchange rate. This includes the local financial and commercial sectors, multinational corporate affiliates, and those that have accumulated (or anticipate accumulating) foreign-currency debts. In the context of Latin America, with its substantial foreign debts, this last group (foreign-currency debtors) is likely to be particularly prominent.
- I expect the tradables sectors to generally support a depreciated exchange rate; given Latin America's typically higher inflation rate than that of the United States, this implies that they will also support a floating currency. This includes exporters and import competers, especially in manufacturing and agriculture—and is contingent on the producers in question not having substantial trade protection.

Two other expectations are consistent with my arguments about the political economy of exchange rates, although they are not directly related to interest group pressures:

- Given many of the region's countries' histories of high inflation, the anti-inflationary impact of a fixed rate may be important at times. Politicians may be able to gain political support by beating back inflation, for which a fixed rate can be useful. Yet this should not eliminate the political costs of a real appreciation when an inflationary economy is pegged to the dollar.
- Inasmuch as the region has been largely democratic since the early 1980s and many elections have been hotly contested, there may be electoral cycles in exchange rates—especially to encourage or maintain an appreciated currency in the run-up to an election, so as to boost local purchasing power.

To summarize, the distributional factors emphasized in chapter 1 imply that internationally oriented sectors will be more supportive of a fixed currency (and indifferent to or supportive of an appreciated one), while tradables sectors will be more favorable to a depreciated exchange rate (and by extension, a flexible one). Electoral factors, which I have not emphasized up to now, play a greater role in Latin America, for reasons I will explore, and imply a pattern of real appreciation before an election and a delayed depreciation afterward. Before assessing the empirical evidence, I provide historical background to situate the region's policy problems and some illustrations drawn from regional experience. Both the discursive and statistical analyses attempt to sketch out general trends from a region that is in fact quite varied. I will treat in somewhat more detail a few national experiences, but this is meant to be a superficial survey rather than a detailed analysis.

Historical Background

Throughout the gold standard era, Latin American nations were primary commodity exporters. Like other such countries, they stayed on or went off gold during the 1873–96 Great Depression of commodity prices. The region's primary export producers (cattle ranchers and wheat farmers in Argentina, coffee growers in Brazil, and miners in Mexico), like their US counterparts, had powerful reasons to want a depreciated currency. Unlike US primary export producers, the Latin Americans typically dominated their political economies and were almost always successful at keeping the currency weak—normally on silver or paper—so long as commodity prices were falling. There were periodic attempts by local financial leaders, often in concert with European bankers, to guide governments back toward gold, but with little effect. It was not until after commodity prices started rising in 1896 that Latin American governments were willing and able to switch to gold. With commodity prices rising, this normally meant locking in a depreciated exchange rate—again desirable for the primary producers.

During the 1920s, the region experienced a commodity boom and substantial inflow of capital, both foreign loans and direct investment by US multinational corporations. Buoyant commodity prices lessened the export producers' concerns, and many of the region's nations attempted to return to gold. When commodity prices began to slide in

1928, however, Latin American countries started to leave gold, and the movement accelerated in the first years of the Great Depression of the 1930s. As world commodity and financial markets collapsed, the region's economies turned inward; virtually all the region's nations went off gold and defaulted on their foreign debts. Latin American countries had been forced inward by the unsettled conditions caused by World War I between 1914 and the early 1920s, but this time the crisis was much more severe and lasted much longer.[3]

Unfavorable international circumstances between 1914 and the early 1950s had both economic and political effects. Global conditions drove Latin America toward its own economic devices; they also fatally weakened the exporting sectors and strengthened those producing for the domestic market. This was reflected in a shift toward governments whose political base was urban, proindustrial, nationalistic, and usually included the working class as well as urban business and middle-class groups. Both economic and political factors came together, so that even after the early 1950s, when world trade revived and most of the defaults had been settled, Latin American governments continued and purposely deepened their inward economic focus. These governments imposed substantial trade barriers in an effort to promote industrial development—a policy known as import-substituting industrialization (ISI). Governments typically also increased the public sector's direct involvement in the economy, especially in infrastructure provision, utilities, and basic industrial production.

One of the defining characteristics of ISI in Latin America was the appreciated real exchange rates, coupled with high levels of trade protection for the favored manufacturing sector. This was the era of the Bretton Woods international monetary order, in which an adjustable peg to the US dollar was the norm. Latin American nations followed suit, with fixed rates that they adjusted from time to time. Given the region's chronically high inflation, the result was normally a substantially appreciated real exchange rate. The strong real exchange rate was very much in keeping with the more general distributional effects of ISI to turn the terms of trade against the region's traditional producers of primary products for export—farmers and miners, especially—and in favor of urban industry. For it was precisely the former primary-producing groups that had been displaced politically over the course of

---

3 For the classic discussions, see Díaz Alejandro 1982, 1983.

the 1930s and 1940s as political power shifted toward the new modern business community, middle classes, and labor movements. Manufacturers were largely indifferent to the real appreciation because prohibitive protection made the exchange rate irrelevant to import competition; many may have actively supported the strong-currency policy, as it meant that raw materials, spare parts, and capital were artificially inexpensive. In fact, an appreciated real exchange rate was generally seen as a straightforward concomitant of the inward-oriented ISI policies that prevailed between 1950 and 1980. The political economy of this currency policy was manifest: politically dominant groups were not harmed and even may have preferred an appreciated currency.

By the late 1960s, most Latin American countries had high trade barriers, large public sectors, and capital and exchange controls. Policy was dominated by the influence of urban industrial groups. Their currencies were typically on adjustable pegs to the US dollar and were often appreciated (overvalued) in real terms. Trade and exchange rate policies, and in some cases other regulatory policies, imparted a strong antiexport bias to the ISI regimes of the era. This contributed to periodic payments crises that were the main policy challenge of the time. But around 1970, conditions began to change in critical ways for Latin America.

Modern Latin American Exchange Rate Policies and Politics

The early 1970s saw several significant international and regional developments relevant to Latin American macroeconomic policy. Even after the Bretton Woods system collapsed, many Latin American currencies remained pegged or otherwise linked to the US dollar. Yet the ten or more years after the end of Bretton Woods were a time of great monetary turmoil generally, as most industrialized countries experienced high inflation and volatile exchange rates. The lack of a clear international monetary anchor left currency conditions unsettled in most of the developing world, and Latin America was no exception.

Even as the Bretton Woods international monetary order fell apart, international capital markets opened to Latin America for the first time in forty years. Starting in the late 1960s, governments, banks, and private sector borrowers now had access to foreign-currency loans, and began borrowing enthusiastically. Among many other things, this meant that some Latin American nations experienced quite a substantial capital inflow with important macroeconomic effects. It also meant the rise of a new interest group: foreign-currency debtors (including many governments).

Latin America was, like the rest of the world, also affected by large increases in primary product prices starting around 1970. At first, in the early 1970s, this applied across the board to many Latin American exports—copper and coffee, for example. The bigger story was the enormous increase in oil prices after 1973. For crucial oil producers such as Mexico and Venezuela, this led to a big resource inflow with implications for currency policy. For most Latin American nations, which were net oil importers, the oil shocks increased pressure on the balance of payments and also increased the incentive to borrow abroad to finance oil imports.

Amid all this turmoil, exchange rate policy became a key political battleground in the debates over how to deal with the fact that the region's chosen policy package of ISI was in trouble. The antiexport bias contributed to chronic payments crises, expansionary macroeconomic policies led to high inflation, and income distribution seemed to be deteriorating. Discussions of ways out of the difficulties were common. The spectrum of views ran from those who wanted governments to dismantle protection as well as intervention and fight inflation aggressively, to those who supported a redoubling of protectionist industrial policy.

One prominent perspective gave currency policy a central role in helping weaken or dismantle ISI. The approach, associated (at least in the popular mind) with economists from the University of Chicago, was made up of supporters of what was sometimes called "global monetarism." This was the view that in conditions of high inflation, a fixed exchange rate (or at least one that lagged behind inflation) would force prices downward. This "monetary approach to the balance of payments" argued that the resultant real appreciation would put enough downward pressure on prices to restrain inflation. It would also put substantial pressure on the inefficient ISI industries that, as supporters believed, were a major obstacle to more market-oriented reforms.

In any case, over the course of the 1970s most Latin American countries stuck to the previous adjustable pegs. They did so as they experienced substantial resource inflows due to increased oil revenues, foreign borrowing, or both. The resource inflows led to domestic expansion and a real appreciation of the exchange rate. This in turn only encouraged further borrowing given that dollars were cheap.[4] Complaints from tradables producers—especially manufacturers—led to ever higher protectionist barriers to counteract the impact of the real appreciation. Between the mid-1970s and early 1980s, the currencies of Argentina, Mexico, and Venezuela appreciated by 33, 20, and 18 percent, respectively, in real terms.[5]

There were variations in exchange rate policy.[6] Brazil generally managed a continual depreciation of the cruzeiro, which avoided too large a real appreciation and sometimes led to real depreciation. In part this was because Brazilian inflation was high enough that any lag of the nominal exchange rate would have led to a massive real appreciation in a matter of weeks. But this was not the only story; inflation was roughly as high in some other South American countries (such as Argentina). Another, perhaps more important factor was the political influence of export-oriented manufacturers who were concerned about the real exchange rate. The result was an exchange rate policy whose priority was keeping the real exchange rate relatively weak. Colombia, too, with its powerful coffee producers, tended to avoid too much of a real appreciation.

At the other extreme were the southern cone nations of Argentina and Chile, in which the "Chicago boys'" currency policy was implemented. From 1976 in Chile and 1978 in Argentina, the exchange rate was managed so as to try to reduce inflation. Invoking global monetarism, policymakers lagged the nominal depreciation rate behind inflation. They did so with a preannounced table (or *tablita*) that committed the authorities to devalue the currency by less than the previous period's inflation. This meant forcing a real appreciation, which the two governments argued would help tame inflation by restraining price increases by domestic producers. The policy went together with a big reduction in trade barriers along with a removal of most capital and ex-

---

4 The process fueled reasonable concern about the moral hazard that could result from private actors borrowing abroad when dollars were cheap, and then demanding a bailout after the inevitable depreciation on the grounds that the government had implicitly committed to maintain the exchange rate level.

5 For a summary of the experience, see Frieden 1991, chapter 3.

6 For many of these experiences in more detail, see Frieden and Stein 2001.

change controls. The result was a massive real appreciation, by 25 percent in Chile and 33 percent in Argentina. In contrast with Brazil, the chosen exchange rate policy reflected the fact that the concerns of tradable producers, especially manufacturers, were largely unheard or disregarded. This policy orientation was consistent with the southern cone military dictatorships' antipathy to the concerns of industry, for they thought of powerful industrial labor unions as one of their main political problems. While the Chilean and Argentine regimes did not consciously attempt to deindustrialize, they were largely indifferent to the impact on the industrial sector of their crusades against leftist populism.[7]

The commodity boom, oil shocks, and foreign borrowing of the 1970s and early 1980s were associated with growing government budget deficits and inflation rates. In 1982, the region's monetary and financial policies imploded in a debilitating debt crisis, followed by an upsurge of high inflation and even hyperinflation coupled with a descent into the most serious economic crisis in the region's modern history.[8] The 1980s were a watershed in Latin American economic policy, as the 1930s had been before them.

The crisis of the 1980s led to various combinations of economic depression, macroeconomic instability, political turmoil, and hyperinflation. Almost everywhere, the result was a sea change in economic policy, away from ISI, fiscal deficits, and inflation, and toward economic integration along with more restrained monetary and fiscal policies. By the early 1990s, foreign debts had been renegotiated, trade barriers had been lowered dramatically, public enterprises had been privatized, and deficits and inflation had been reduced or eliminated. Perhaps most striking was the shift away from the commercial closure of the ISI period and a new openness to trade. As an example, between 1965 and 1970 the region's three biggest economies, Argentina, Brazil, and Mexico, were among the most closed in the capitalist world. Exports plus imports were just 12, 13, and 17 percent of their GDPs, respectively. After the shift in policy, between 2000 and 2005, these countries' exports plus imports were respectively 35, 26, and 57 percent of their GDPs, representing a doubling, tripling, or more of their trade ratios.

---

7 In an earlier work, I developed this argument in more detail; see Frieden 1991.
8 For the still-classic treatments, see Díaz Alejandro 1984, 1985.

Again, exchange rate policy played a major role in the new economic policy mix that became standard after 1990. The policy orientation included a general commitment to openness to both trade and capital flows as well as more restrictive fiscal and monetary policies. There were also serious attempts to deepen and more effectively regulate national financial markets in many countries, and to reform social services. By then, the more disastrous macroeconomic conditions of the previous decade were largely past and exchange rate policy was made under more normal circumstances. Private capital flows to the region had also resumed. While commercial banks continued to make syndicated loans, which had been the typical form between 1965 and 1982, bonded (securitized) debt became much more important, and there was also a big upsurge in FDI; eventually even inward equities investment became relevant.

Currency policy after 1990 tended to be of two types. On the one hand, there were governments that kept exchange rates relatively stable against the US dollar (Mexico), including some (Brazil to 1999 and Argentina to 2001) that at times adopted more rigid dollar pegs and a few that even adopted the dollar (Ecuador and El Salvador). The advantages of these relatively fixed-rate policies were obvious, especially in the context of increased openness: they limited inflation, and currency and monetary stability encouraged cross-border trade and investment, reinforcing the new globalizing orientation of economic policy. The disadvantages were those of fixed rates: there was little or no scope for autonomous monetary policy, even in the face of serious national difficulties.

The second type of currency policy was a relatively freely floating exchange rate, albeit with occasional active management. Peru and Chile were quite successful with this regime. The advantages of the floating rate policy were again obvious, particularly in the context of the new open economies: it allowed the authorities to act to maintain the international competitiveness of domestic producers.

Despite the major reform efforts of the 1980s and general stabilization of macroeconomic conditions, Latin America continued to experience exchange rate uncertainties and problems. In addition, almost all the region's nations were now democratic, increasing the importance of electoral considerations. Large real appreciations conflicted with government attempts to increase exports. In some countries, continued inflation led to the use of fixed exchange rates to try to moderate prices, but the resulting real appreciations again conflicted with the new export orientation. The renewed availability of foreign finance made it easier to run fiscal and current account deficits, but these could rapidly become unsustainable. And the greater openness of most Latin American economies left them more susceptible to external financial and commercial shocks.

The result of these tensions was a series of exchange rate crises. These differed from the debt crises of the early 1980s in that they tended to be triggered by runs on currencies rather than by sudden stops in foreign lending—although the currency crises often led to debt crises. The first major one, in 1994 in Mexico, had all the ingredients that soon became familiar. There were substantial capital inflows in the aftermath of the creation of North American Free Trade Agreement (NAFTA), which led to a vigorous economic expansion. This in turn led to a major real appreciation of the peso, which the government was holding relatively stable against the dollar; the strong peso led manufacturers to complain about its impact on their competitiveness. Eventually sentiment turned against the peso and expectations of a devaluation became widespread, reinforced by political unrest in the run-up to the 1994 presidential elections. The government of the Partido Revolucionario Institucional (PRI, the single party that had held office for seventy years) clung desperately to the exchange rate until after the new government was elected and took office, at which point massive speculation against the currency forced a devaluation that turned into a peso collapse and caused a major recession. The reverberations of the Mexican crisis were felt throughout Latin America as the "tequila effect" triggered sell-offs of other Latin American currencies.

The Mexican crisis was followed by other prominent ones that similarly highlighted the difficulties faced by Latin American currency policymakers, and the highly political sources and implications of the crises. The next chapter deals in detail with currency crises, both in general and in relationship to specific Latin American experiences. For now it is enough to note that economic openness and renewed access to international financial markets has hardly insulated Latin America from the vagaries of currency markets or the difficulties of making exchange rate policy.

This historical narrative highlights two factors that are particularly important to understanding Latin American exchange rate policy. First, the region's economies went from being closed—typically with high trade barriers, capital controls, and exchange controls—to open—usually with low trade barriers along with a general freedom of capital movements and currency convertibility. This can dramatically affect policy preferences; for example, a manufacturer with prohibitive protection will be indifferent or even favorable to an appreciated currency, while that same manufacturer exposed to international competition will protest vehemently about an appreciated currency. Second, the region's economies went from having inflation rates that ranged from moderately high to hyperinflation, to having relatively low inflation rates. This, too, affects policy preferences over the exchange rate. For example, some who might support a fixed rate to end high inflation or hyperinflation may abandon this once inflation is defeated.

I now turn to consider the role of factors likely to affect Latin American exchange rate policy. What follows in the next section are simply illustrative indications rather than systematic empirical evidence. Further on, I present more rigorous empirical analyses.

Determinants of Latin American Currency Policy

Currency policies are complex everywhere, and Latin America is no exception. Politicians face many pressures; without claiming to exhaust possibilities, in what follows I catalog the main such pressures I expect to challenge policymakers as they make exchange rate policy.

Interest Groups

Latin American currency policymakers commonly face two sets of economic interest groups with opposing views and substantial political influence. Tradables producers typically press for a depreciated currency, especially when the real exchange rate is strong. Conversely, those in the financial and commercial sector, along with foreign-currency debtors, generally exert pressure to maintain a stable currency and avoid a devaluation.

Tradables producers, particularly manufacturers, often complain that the exchange rate is "too strong" for them to compete on home or foreign markets. This may be due to a prior real appreciation of the currency or some other adverse trend. There is no necessary trigger to complaints about a strong real exchange rate; tradables producers almost always stand to benefit from a depreciation.

Manufacturers are usually the most vocal supporters of depreciation and opponents of appreciation, both because they are likely to be most directly affected as import competers or exporters, and because they are usually influential in Latin American economic policy debates. Brazil's Federação das Indústrias do Estado de São Paulo, Argentina's Unión Industrial Argentina, and the industrialists of Monterrey in northern Mexico have all complained as their respective currencies appreciated—in the case of Argentina and Brazil, often against each other. Before the mid-1980s, industrialists typically demanded steeper trade protection if the currency was not going to be devalued. In that era of high ISI, such protection was almost always granted, so that explicit political action over the exchange rate took second place to trade policy. But since the mid-1980s and the turn toward trade openness—and earlier in Chile and Argentina—manufacturers have known that trade protection is harder to obtain and thus have refocused on the exchange rate.

Manufacturers' concerns to keep the level of the real exchange rate relatively depreciated are frequently associated with a general desire for a more flexible currency. This allows for a depreciation in the case of domestic inflation higher than that of trading partners or any other circumstance (a positive terms of trade shock, for example) that might lead to an appreciation. But there are likely to be some manufacturers—especially those in more product-differentiated lines—for which currency volatility will be costly. Overall, however, given Latin America's manufacturing profile, I expect manufacturers to favor a weak and flexible currency.

Complaints about the impact of an appreciated currency on manufacturers are sometimes echoed by *agriculture*, especially export-oriented farmers. There is little import competition to most of Latin American agriculture (although it matters in some cases, such as in parts of Mexico after NAFTA), and much of the farm sector's output is effectively nontradable—such as truck and dairy farming for local consumption, or near-subsistence agriculture. Nevertheless, some Latin American countries have substantial modern export agricultural sectors: soybeans in Brazil, beef and wheat in Argentina, coffee in Colombia and Brazil, and winter fruits in Chile. These groups often insist on the negative impact on them of an appreciated exchange rate.[9] Their concerns are sometimes more intense than those of manufacturers for reasons associated with pass-through. Farm products are quintessentially simple commodities whose prices are set on world markets and for which pass-through is usually complete; even simple manufactures in Latin America may be complex enough, or traded enough within corporate networks or on longer-term contracts, that pass-through is more limited. In addition, unlike manufacturers, Latin American export-oriented farmers can reap little benefit from trade protection, so that a currency appreciation is hard to counteract. So while manufacturers may be, in general, more organized and influential than farmers, farmers may have more intensely felt preferences over the exchange rate. And in some instances, the agricultural sector has been well organized, such as through Argentina's powerful Sociedad Rural.

Policymakers frequently confront the concerns of manufacturers and farmers, particularly in situations of substantial real appreciations (which often precede currency crises). The reasons for the appreciation can vary widely. One common source is a resource inflow: a positive terms of trade shock such as an increase in oil prices (for oil producers), the discovery of valuable raw materials, or a surge in foreign investment or lending that brings capital into the country. All these can lead to a real appreciation by many channels. If the exchange rate is allowed to vary, the resource inflow can translate into increased demand for the currency and a nominal appreciation. If the currency is fixed, the resource inflow stimulates local demand, increasing imports and driving nontradables prices up, thereby causing a real appreciation. Whatever the cause, the effect for tradables producers is to raise local input prices relative to the price of their output.

Another common cause of a real appreciation is a government decision to fix or lag the nominal exchange rate in order to restrain inflation with a so-called exchange-rate-based stabilization program.[10] This was the case of the policy of preannounced tables of depreciations that were purposely inadequate to compensate for accumulated inflation (the tablitas) that Chile and Argentina adopted in the late 1970s and early 1980s. In other instances, it has taken the form of a currency peg

---

9 Rodrigo Taborda (2013) shows that Colombian interest groups that favored a weak currency, principally manufacturers and coffee growers, manipulated the news media to highlight the negative effects of a currency appreciation.

10 See, for example, Alfaro 2002.

in the context of high inflation; Brazil and Argentina in the 1990s are prominent examples, but there have been many others. In virtually all such circumstances, the fixed or lagged nominal exchange rate combines with inflationary inertia to cause a real appreciation. The real appreciation is indeed frequently regarded as desirable for the task of reducing inflation, as it restrains the price of tradable goods.

Whatever the cause, governments overseeing real appreciations are likely to face serious complaints from industry and sometimes agriculture. The pattern was repeated in Mexico in 1994, Argentina and Brazil after 1997, and other such cases. In all these instances and more, manufacturers and farmers pressed either for a depreciation or other policies (subsidies or emergency temporary protection) to counteract the impact of the strong exchange rate.

The financial sector and foreign-currency debtors. On the other hand, policymakers face demands to avoid depreciation as well as sustain the currency's value and stability. Most important in this camp are typically the financial services industry, especially the internationally oriented portion. Such financial institutions can intermediate between foreign and domestic financial markets, but this business can be impeded by currency volatility. At the same time (and for the same reasons), the local financial sector is closely tied to domestic debtors with substantial foreign-currency liabilities. While the financial (and allied commercial) sector is wary of exchange rate volatility itself, foreign-currency debtors are extra concerned to avoid an unexpected depreciation that increases their real debt burden.

Just as manufacturers and farmers couch their desire for a weaker currency in broader terms—as a way of enhancing local competitiveness or avoiding deindustrialization—support for maintaining a fixed exchange rate, even an appreciated one, is usually cast in terms of monetary stability and predictability. Sometimes supporters of a fixed rate contend that it implicates the credibility of both the government and private borrowers.

In Latin America, these two broad clusters tend to be the most prominent pressure groups—the ones that policymakers are most likely to confront as they attempt to determine their policies. Manufacturers and farmers press for a weaker exchange rate; financial institutions and foreign-currency debtors argue for the government to stay the course with a fixed exchange rate. The more open the economy is, the more economic agents are exposed to currency volatility and the competitive effects of an appreciated exchange rate. Some may be conflicted, wanting both currency flexibility to allow a depreciation and currency predictability to reduce volatility; the weights on both will vary in line with the characteristics of the country, industry, and firm.

Elections

Politicians can use monetary policy for electoral purposes, which can create "political business cycles."[11] One variant of the political business cycle approach emphasizes the government's attempt to attract pivotal voters who value growth and low unemployment; another stresses the government's more partisan attempt to satisfy a segment of the electorate that, for example, weighs low unemployment more heavily than inflation. In both situations, the result is a monetary expansion in the period before an election. There are both theoretical models and empirical evidence supporting the existence of the purely electoral and partisan cycles.

In an open economy, the possibility of political business cycles implies that policymakers can and will use *exchange rate* policy for electoral purposes. Of course, *how* policymakers might use the currency politically would depend on the voters whose favor they are trying to curry. If the target is pivotal or median voters, analogous to the first (electoral) sort of cycle, presumably the strategy would be to encourage a relatively appreciated currency in the run-up to an election. This raises the purchasing power of the population so that it feels (and is) better off. To be sure, the effect is temporary, but the electorate may not be able to figure this out—real exchange rates are complex and appreciate for many reasons—so they may, at the margin, credit incumbents for the good times.[12] In order to achieve this effect, an incumbent government could engineer or allow a preelection real appreciation, either by permitting a pegged currency to appreciate, engineering a nominal appreciation of a floating currency, or lagging a depreciation behind the national inflation rate.

---

11 For a survey, see Franzese and Jusko 2006.
12 There are few rigorous studies of these distributional effects on broad segments of the population. For one, see de Carvalho Filho and Chamon 2008; this work finds that in Brazil, a real appreciation tends to hurt the rural sector especially, while in Mexico it tends to hurt the northern (more export-oriented) states.

What is analogous to the partisan monetary cycle might be an instance in which a particularly powerful interest group—or support group of a political party—had a specific interest in either an appreciated or depreciated real exchange rate. If, for example, import competers were important constituents, the government might aim to depreciate the currency in the preelectoral period.[13]

A final consideration is that politicians in the thick of an election campaign may be motivated to remain on a peg for credibility reasons. Inasmuch as the government's policy credibility is invested in the exchange rate—specifically in a fixed rate—going off such a peg can be costly to the government's reputation. This provides an added electoral incentive for governments to sustain a peg even in the face of a substantial real appreciation.

The exchange rate has often been significant for Latin American election campaigns. At the same time, electoral factors were not major considerations for the US gold standard or European monetary integration periods. In those cases, the choice of exchange rate regime was understood and intended to be a long-lasting one. Certainly the United States eventually did leave the gold standard, and European countries had varying degrees of success fixing against the DM. But the Latin American context is different. Except in the case of full dollarization, a fixed or quasi-fixed (band) regime is seen as something that can be altered as necessary—and in all but the tiny Caribbean economies, this has been the case. So the impact of elections on exchange rate policy—and in particular, choosing to stay on or go off a peg as an election approaches—has been an important decision in Latin America.

I focus on the impact of interest groups and elections on exchange rate policy. In general, tradables producers want a depreciated currency, internationally linked economic actors want a stable currency, and voters want a strong currency. Governments cannot satisfy all these demands at once, and that forces them to trade off among them.

Apart from the relative significance of these interest group and electoral factors, other considerations influence the relevance and strength of these pressures. One crucial consideration is the intensity of policy preferences, which tend to rise, not surprisingly, when the policy choices available have been particularly striking. One such circumstance is when the currency is strong, whatever the reason. A strongly

---

13 For theoretical arguments and some evidence to these effects, see Bonomo and Terra 2005; Stein, Streb, and Ghezzi 2005.

appreciated currency tends to draw the attention of most relevant actors. Foreign-currency debtors are particularly concerned to avoid a potentially devastating devaluation. Tradables producers—whether import competers or exporters—complain bitterly about a strong real exchange rate. What follow are some other features of the Latin American environment that can affect the intensity or character of the political pressures on policy.

Economic Openness

The Latin American shift from general closure to general openness to the world economy allows us to evaluate the implications of this change for the making of currency policy. As discussed in the introduction and chapter 1, there are several dimensions to this. The first is that highlighted by the trilemma and the Mundell-Fleming conditions: as economies opened to financial flows, they were increasingly forced to choose between currency stability and monetary policy autonomy. This in itself would be expected to focus political and policy attention on the exchange rate.

In addition, the more exposed an economy is to international trade and payments, the more sensitive are economic agents to the exchange rate. This means that as a country is integrated into the global economy, the impact of the exchange rate is amplified. This does not change policy preferences, except of producers of goods or services that were previously nontradable and that now have become tradable. Yet increased openness does heighten the impact of movements in the exchange rate on those exposed to it. For example, it amplifies the positive impact of a real appreciation on purchasing power, while expanding the negative impact of currency volatility on some and of a real appreciation on others.

To the extent that economic openness is—as it has been for much of Latin America—the result of a shift in trade policy, it subjects previously protected industries to foreign competition and makes them much more concerned about currency policy. Firms sheltered by trade protection are unconcerned about the exchange rate—and may even favor an overvalued one to cheapen inputs—but the removal of trade barriers makes the currency's value of great importance to them. The contrary trend was at work in the case of late nineteenth-century US manufacturers, whose adamant opposition to gold and a strong currency faded as they obtained higher and higher protective tariffs; in Latin America in the late twentieth century the process went in the opposite direction, as the removal of trade barriers rekindled fears of a strong currency.

Inflation

Domestic and international monetary policies are intricately interwoven. The real exchange rate is, after all, the local inflation rate times the nominal exchange rate—changing either one changes the real rate. Nonetheless, it can be analytically useful to concentrate on how local-currency inflation along with policies toward it affect and are affected by currency policy. Two considerations are primary. First, when the exchange rate lags behind the rate of inflation, the result is an appreciating currency. This outcome is, of course, a result of either the lag or inflation, or both. It may be important to figure out the precise interaction of the two, but it is justifiable to assume that the combination is purposive policy. That is, when policymakers allow the exchange rate to lag inflation, it is reasonable to regard this as a conscious choice of an appreciated currency. Second, currency policies may be chosen in order to affect inflation. Especially after 1980, the use of a currency peg against a low-inflation anchor has been part of many macroeconomic stabilization programs.

All these factors are expected to affect the operation of the basic political pressures on which I wish to focus attention—such interest groups as tradables producers, cross-border financial and commercial institutions, and foreign-currency debtors as well as broad electoral factors. I now turn to more systematic empirical assessments of the significance of these variables in influencing Latin American currency policy.

Analyzing Latin American Currency Policy: A Statistical Assessment of Regime Choice

An attempt to analyze the domestic politics of Latin American currency policy is hampered by the absence of such differentiated, subnational data on domestic decision making as we had in the case of the United States during the gold standard era. The best we can do to consider the impact of the factors of interest, as in the European case, is to use national-level variables as potential sources of national policy choices.

In this section, I attempt to explain the exchange rate policies of Latin American countries with variables that proxy for the explanatory factors explored above. The proxies are far from perfect, but they are just about the best we can do in the absence of much more detailed information at the domestic level about societal actors and governmental decision making. The empirical evaluations presented here can be seen as assessing the plausibility of the arguments made as opposed to establishing their accuracy.

I undertake two types of empirical evaluations. In the first, in this section, I try to explain government choices of an exchange rate regime—the extent to which they fix or float their currencies. While this has, directly, only to do with the *regime* variable, in the Latin American context it is related to the *level* as well: inflation is relatively high in the region, so that the more fixed the exchange rate is, the more appreciated it is likely to be or become. I therefore associate support for a more fixed rate, as usual, with a preference for greater currency stability and predictability, and a more flexible rate with a preference for a weaker currency.

The second type of empirical evaluation, in the following section, looks primarily at the impact of elections. For several reasons, the data and methods in the present section are not well suited to consider electoral considerations. It is not clear, for one, how electoral considerations would be expected to affect choices among the four (or more) possible regimes. Second, inasmuch as the principal effects of elections would be seen over a relatively short time horizon—for example, in the months before and after an election—the annual nature of the regime data does not allow enough of a fine-grained evaluation of electoral considerations.

Latin America has experienced a large range of exchange rate policies over the years. Table 5.1 shows both the range of regimes that countries in the region have adopted and how they have evolved over time. The table is drawn from the widely used classification of de facto exchange rate regimes compiled by Carmen Reinhart and Kenneth Rogoff.[14] It demonstrates that over the course of time, starting from the fixed-rate era of Bretton Woods before 1973, Latin American curren-

14 As used in Reinhart and Rogoff 2009. Data available at http://www.carmenreinhart.com/data/browse-by-topic/topics/11/.

TABLE 5.1
De facto exchange rate regimes in Latin America and the Caribbean, 1960–2004

	Pegs	Bands	Managed	Floats
1960–73	55.6	19.8	16.9	7.7
1974–81	53.9	15.0	12.4	18.7
1982–93	24.2	15.1	25.8	34.9
1994–2000	23.8	47.5	16.6	12.2
2001–10	29.1	44.2	25.5	1.2

Note: Reported are the percent of Latin American and Caribbean countries that had a certain de facto exchange rate regime in a given period, using the Reinhart-Rogoff classification scheme.

cies became increasingly flexible, but since 2000 most countries have moved away from purely (nonmanaged) floating regimes. There nonetheless remains substantial variation among countries.

One important step is to establish the association of a more fixed rate with a more appreciated (stronger) real exchange rate. Table 5.2 shows the relationship between the exchange rate regime, inflation, and REER. Not surprisingly, the more flexible is the regime, the higher is the rate of inflation. It is also not startling that, generally speaking, more flexible currencies are less likely to appreciate and, in fact, likely to depreciate. Pegged currencies do not appreciate as much as those on bands, probably because most pegs have been long lasting enough to bring inflation down dramatically (especially in the small open economies around the Caribbean). But, to take the most striking difference, currencies on bands appreciate on average 1.6 percent a year, while those that float depreciate on average 6.2 percent a year. This is an appreciable difference. This is relevant because it implies that economic actors' views on the fixity or flexibility of the exchange rate is likely to be connected to their preferences with respect to its strength or weakness. All else being equal, those that prefer a strong real exchange rate will prefer a more fixed currency regime, while those that prefer a weak real exchange rate will prefer a more flexible currency regime.

My first empirical evaluation attempts to explain national governments' choices of exchange rate regimes. I examine regime outcomes from 1960 to 2010, although the data for the period before 1973 are scarce. In addition, I look at twenty-six countries, which covers all but a few tiny nations in the region.[15] The dependent variable can be de-

15 The principal excluded countries are those that use the eastern Caribbean dollar—in particular

TABLE 5.2

De facto exchange rate regimes, the real exchange rate, and inflation, 1960–2010

Exchange rate regime	Mean annual REER change	Mean REER	Mean inflation rate
Peg	0.19	120.98	9.1
Band	1.61	110.96	11.2
Managed	−0.67	119.91	13.1
Float	−6.21	106.92	361.7

Note: Reported is the average rate of change of the real effective exchange rate associated with each de facto exchange rate regime, using the Reinhart-Rogoff classification. The data do not include Nicaragua and Suriname. Nicaraguan real exchange rates are nearly nonsensical, reaching an index number of 56,621 in 1987, certainly due to the capital and exchange controls of the Sandinista period from 1979 to 1990. Suriname's REER data are almost as bizarre, with the REER reaching an index number of 1236 in 1993, during a period of political and military unrest.

Sources: On inflation, see World Bank, World Development Indicators. On the real effective exchange rate, see BRUEGEL database, http://www.bruegel.org/publications/publication-detail/publication/716-real-effective-exchange-rates-for-178-countries-a-new-database/.

fined in a variety of different ways, as has been done by other observers. One question is whether the policy evaluated is that *stated* by the government or actually observed. This is particularly relevant when, for example, the government announces that it will allow the currency to float freely but actually intervenes to keep it stable. The question here, then, is whether the de jure or de facto exchange rate policy is relevant. The principal instance in which the difference matters is when exchange rate policy announcements are being used for anti-inflationary purposes. When a government announces a fixed rate in an effort to bring inflation down, it hopes that wage and price setters anticipate that the policy will be followed so as to moderate inflation. In this case, where the actual outcome differs from the announced one, it indicates a failure of government policy, and ex ante economic agents may not fully believe it. On the other hand, inasmuch as economic agents engaged in cross-border trade and investment are making longer-term decisions, and can observe actual outcomes in time to make them, they are not so likely to be influenced by announcements. I thus would ex-

---

Antigua and Barbuda, Dominica, Grenada, Saint Kitts and Nevis, Saint Lucia, and Saint Vincent and the Grenadines. Other English-speaking Caribbean nations (Bahamas, Barbados, Jamaica, etc.) are included, although excluding them does not alter results.

pect the "wedge" between de facto and de jure policies to matter primarily for anti-inflationary purposes.[16]

For my purposes, it makes sense to use the de facto exchange rate regime. Especially in Latin America's high-inflation environment, it is not easy to sustain the pretense of a fixed rate. Yet I also look at de jure classifications. The main dependent variable used is the four-point scale developed by Reinhart and Rogoff.[17] This scale runs from –2 (floating) to +1 (pegged); a positive sign for a variable means that it is correlated with a more fixed exchange rate regime, while a negative sign means that it is associated with a more flexible exchange rate regime.

The principal explanatory factors that I evaluate stand in for the kinds of interests I anticipate to affect policy in Latin America, as follows:

Openness. The openness of the economy—simply, exports plus imports as a share of the GDP—strongly indicates the proportion of economic agents involved in cross-border economic activity. I expect this to be associated with a higher probability of a fixed exchange rate. Expected sign: positive.

Inflation. The higher is inflation, the more difficult it is for the government to sustain a fixed exchange rate, so I expect higher inflation to be associated with a more flexible regime. Expected sign: negative.

Agricultural employment as a share of the total employment. Producers of farm goods are typically exposed to either import or export competition, or both, and hence favorable to a weaker real exchange rate and more flexible regime. Expected sign: negative.

Manufacturing employment as a share of the total employment. Producers of manufactured goods in Latin America are generally in sectors with relatively little product differentiation, and therefore where pass-through is substantial. As a result, manufactures are usually exposed to either import or export competition, or both, and the sector is expected to be favorable to a weaker real exchange rate and more flexible regime. Expected sign: negative.

Two things should be noted. First, unlike in Europe, manufacturers in Latin America are largely in industries with high levels of pass-through, facing a high degree of price competition. Second, as previously mentioned, for something like half the study period, most Latin

16 See, for example, Guisinger and Singer 2010.
17 Details on all data and descriptions of the statistical methods used may be accessed via http://press.princeton.edu/titles/10364.html.

American countries had highly protectionist trade policies. I would not expect manufacturers, who were the primary beneficiaries of this trade protection, to care much about the real exchange rate in a closed economy. In fact, inasmuch as in the typical ISI regime, manufacturers had high protection for their output but none for inputs, a strong real exchange rate would be desirable: they could get their inputs cheaply and not have to worry about foreign competition in their product markets. Agriculture would have been more or less the reverse: in the ISI period, agriculture was strongly *disfavored* by trade policy and would have supported more flexible rates.

For this second reason, I also interact agricultural and manufacturing employment with openness, with expectations as follows:

Agriculture*openness. Farmers in the Latin American closed economies would presumably have wanted more flexible exchange rates, as farmers were among the principal victims of real appreciations (insofar as they did not receive trade protection). In open economies, they should also prefer flexibility if they are competing with foreign producers. Expected sign of the interaction term: negative.

Manufacturing*openness. Manufacturers are expected to have been indifferent or even favorable to a fixed rate in a close economy, but strongly favorable to flexibility in an open one. Expected sign of the interaction term: negative.

I also expect that cross-border investors and debtors will be sensitive to the volatility of the exchange rate, as previously discussed. For this reason I consider:

FDI, specifically FDI liabilities as a share of the GDP. Foreign direct investors are expected to dislike currency volatility and favor a fixed rate. Expected sign: positive.

External debt, specifically external debt as a share of the GDP. Domestic residents with foreign (i.e., foreign-currency) debt are loath to see the currency depreciate and therefore should favor a fixed currency. Expected sign: positive.

Table 5.3 presents the results of a series of statistical analyses with these dependent and explanatory variables. (Table 5.4 displays the correlations among all the variables.) All explanatory variables are lagged one year in a (weak) attempt to reduce endogeneity. Columns 1, 2, and 3 all use the Reinhart and Rogoff classification as a dependent variable; they vary only in including, in columns 2 and 3, respectively, FDI and external debt. Column 4 uses a binary categorization (fixed/flexible) as

TABLE 5.3

Determinants of Latin American exchange rate regimes, 1960–2010

	(1) R + R fine	(2) R + R fine	(3) R + R fine	(4) R + R binary	(5) IMF coarse
Openness	10.71***	9.529**	7.818+	7.386	–7.982+
(M + X/GDP)	(3.91)	(2.75)	(1.85)	(1.24)	(–1.72)
Inflation	–0.0232*	–0.0258*	–0.0219**	–0.00974+	0.00165**
	(–2.22)	(–2.50)	(–2.62)	(–1.83)	(2.76)
Agr	–1.090	–6.498+	–10.93*	–8.656*	0.613
employment	(–0.25)	(–1.80)	(–2.27)	(–1.98)	(0.14)
Mfg	47.70***	68.62***	59.10**	45.57*	–28.83*
employment	(3.40)	(4.17)	(2.83)	(2.13)	(–2.05)
Mfg*openness	–73.26**	–94.28***	–88.66**	–68.77+	66.20**
	(–3.28)	(–3.94)	(–3.18)	(–1.85)	(2.75)
Agr*openness	2.700	16.22**	24.09***	18.36**	–8.418
	(0.39)	(3.16)	(3.42)	(2.66)	(–1.22)
FDI		0.0212*	0.0191+	0.0760**	0.000344
		(2.20)	(1.83)	(3.05)	(0.02)
External debt			–0.0211**	–0.0286*	0.0155*
			(–2.86)	(–2.27)	(2.12)
Constant				–4.978	
				(–1.37)	
Cut1					
constant	4.708*	6.362**	3.233		–4.118
	(2.47)	(2.73)	(0.98)		(–1.28)
Cut2					
constant	6.306**	7.917**	4.890		–3.861
	(3.12)	(3.22)	(1.43)		(–1.21)
Cut3					
constant	7.997***	9.883***	6.987*		–1.889
	(3.99)	(4.13)	(2.13)		(–0.62)
N	442	313	313	305	311
Pseudo R^2	0.181	0.199	0.232	0.347	0.138

t statistics in parentheses

$+ p < 0.1$, $* p < 0.05$, $** p < 0.01$, $*** p < 0.001$

Notes: All explanatory variables are lagged one year. "R + R fine" is the Reinhart and Rogoff four-point de facto exchange rate regime scale in which 1 = peg, 0 = band, –1 = managed float, –2 = float. "R + R binary" collapses 0 and 1 into 1, and –1 and –2 into 0. "IMF coarse" is the IMF's de jure four-point scale on which, importantly for interpretation, 4 is a float and 1 is a peg—in other words, the signs are the opposite of those for the Reinhart and Rogoff classification. The sectoral employment data are as share of total national employment. The FDI is foreign direct investment liabilities as a share of the GDP; external debt is external debt as a share of the GDP.

Sources: The sources of all data, detailed data descriptions, and descriptions of the statistical methods used can be accessed via http://press.princeton.edu/titles/10364.html.

TABLE 5.4
Correlations among all variables

	df_er~2	dfrrbi~y	imf_co~e	L_impo~p	L_infl~n	L_ag_e~l	L_manu~l	fdiliab	L_extd~t
R + R de facto	1.0000								
R + R binary	0.8860	1.0000							
IMF de jure	-0.4565	-0.2868	1.0000						
(X + M)/GDP	0.3464	0.3247	-0.1960	1.0000					
Inflation	-0.1792	-0.1400	0.1267	-0.0995	1.0000				
Agr empl	0.0258	-0.0536	-0.2473	0.0697	0.0738	1.0000			
Mfg empl	-0.1031	-0.1083	0.1958	-0.3922	-0.0941	-0.3979	1.0000		
FDI	0.3662	0.4065	-0.1358	0.5885	-0.0827	-0.0897	-0.5085	1.0000	
External debt	-0.1530	-0.1222	0.1213	0.3941	0.1431	0.0641	-0.3404	0.2370	1.0000

Notes: The variables are (in descending order in the first column: Reinhart-Rogoff classification; Reinhart-Rogoff classification collapsed into two categories; IMF's classification of stated exchange rate regimes; exports plus imports as a share of the GDP; annual inflation rate; employment in agriculture as a share of total employment; employment in manufacturing as a share of total employment; foreign direct investment liabilities as a proportion of the GDP; and external debt liabilities as a proportion of the GDP.

a robustness check, while column 5 employs a different classification—the IMF's coarse classification scheme, which is based on stated (de jure) policy. It should be noted that as the IMF's scheme runs in the reverse order of the Reinhart and Rogoff one (that is, higher numbers mean more flexible), the signs are expected to be reversed.[18]

It can be seen that the explanatory variables are almost all signed as expected and significant. More open economies are more likely to have more fixed exchange rates. This is amenable to many interpretations; the interpretation that I offer is that insofar as more open economies have more economic agents exposed to currency volatility, there is more pressure for more stable exchange rates. Governments of economies experiencing inflation are more likely to have flexible exchange rate regimes, almost certainly due to the serious negative effects of a high inflation on competitiveness with a fixed currency.

The two sectoral variables are of special interest. Manufacturing employment performs as expected. The most directly relevant evidence comes from the interaction term: manufacturing employment is more likely to be associated with a flexible exchange rate, the more open is the economy. This is fully consistent with the idea that in a more open economy, where manufacturers are more exposed to import competition, they will exert more pressure for a flexible rate to sustain their international competitiveness (and oppose a fixed rate that risks a real appreciation). In the sample as a whole, manufacturing employment is actually associated with more fixity, which reflects the fact, mentioned above, that in the closed-economy ISI period, manufacturers were not affected by the exchange rate due to trade protection and may actually have benefited from an appreciated real exchange rate.[19]

Agriculture behaves in more curious ways. It is largely as expected in general: more employment in agriculture is associated with a more flexible exchange rate. ISI policies would not have affected agriculture, as trade protection was almost exclusively provided to industry, so

18 The analysis was also performed with two other commonly used classifications: those of Michael Klein and Jay Shambaugh (2006), and Eduardo Levy Yeyati and Federico Sturzenegger (2003). The results were similar, but many more observations were missing.

19 A further indication of the effect is that when the sample is simply divided between country-years with a trade ratio above and below 0.4 (i.e., exports plus imports greater than 40 percent of the GDP), manufacturing employment increases the likelihood of fixing in the more closed economies, but increases the probability of floating in the more open ones, although the latter results (not reported here) are only of borderline statistical significance.

farmers would have preferred flexibility. The interaction term has unexpected effects, however: in three of the five models, the more open the economy, the more agricultural employment was associated with a fixed rate. One could speculate about the reasons, but it does not really seem consistent with the competitiveness-driven explanation presented here.

FDI also has the expected effect: the more important are international investors, the more likely it is that the currency regime tends toward fixity. This can be taken as evidence that cross-border investors exert influence to stabilize currency values. Yet foreign debt unexpectedly goes in the opposite direction. This may be due to the fact that the vast majority of foreign debt in this period was owed by national governments, not private actors, and public debtors were less concerned about the exchange rate effect on the debt burden, although this is mere conjecture. Stefanie Walter (2008) has provided more detailed and convincing evidence that in general foreign-currency debtors are a force against flexibility.

No other important economic or political variables have any appreciable effect on exchange rate regimes. The results presented here are robust to a large number of permutations and combinations. It is certainly true that measurement error is always a problem, as seen, for example, by the relative low correlation between the Reinhart and Rogoff classification and that of the IMF. It is also certainly true that endogeneity is a serious problem: a country with a long-lasting fixed exchange rate is probably, all else being equal, more likely to be open, have lower inflation and more FDI, and so on. A true fix for this problem does not, to my knowledge, exist; scholars have not yet come up with good instrumental variables for this relationship. Analogous reservations could be voiced about the variables used as proxies for cross-border and sectoral interests: simply measuring the economy's openness or manufacturing employment is a poor substitute for microdata on exchange rate policy preferences, but we have little else to go on.[20]

In any case, the statistical analysis here provides reasonable evidence for the importance of the factors on which this study focuses as sources of private pressures for exchange rate policy. Greater openness to trade and more FDI, and hence greater exposure to currency volatility, are associated with more fixed rates. Larger manufacturing sectors,

---

20 For survey-based evidence on exchange rate policy preferences that tends to confirm the arguments made here, see Broz, Frieden, and Weymouth 2008.

in open economies, are associated with more flexible rates. Other factors seem less critical or of uncertain impact.

Exchange-Rate-Based Electoral Cycles

I now return to consider the role of electoral politics on exchange rate policy. First I present simple descriptive statistics that demonstrate that governments do appear to manipulate exchange rates around elections. Then I report on portions of other work that revolve around how elections affect the durability of currency pegs—and make a similar point.

Figures 5.1 and 5.2 simply plot the movement of nominal exchange rates around elections. Figure 5.1 looks at elections for the executive (typically the president in the mostly presidential Latin American systems). The figure, beginning ten months before an election, is configured so that an increase on the vertical axis is a (monthly) depreciation rate. As can be seen, the exchange rate shows little pattern in the months before an election; given the general tendency to inflation, the monthly depreciation rate is usually between 2 and 5 percent. But two months after the executive election, the currency depreciates *on average* by more than 15 percent. The clear implication is that the government is delaying a greater depreciation until after the elections. This is consistent either with the incumbent government being reelected—in which case it merely delays until it wins reelection—or its being voted out of office and replaced by an opposition that finds it impossible to sustain the appreciated currency's value.

Figure 5.2 presents similar information, but for elections in which only the national legislature was being chosen. A similar pattern is seen—the depreciation is delayed until after the election—although the eventual depreciation is less dramatic. This makes some sense inasmuch as the exchange rate is more likely to be controlled by the executive than the legislature, although of course partisan connections will tie the executive to its legislative supporters. In any case, together the two figures are powerful evidence that governments use the exchange rate for electoral purposes.

There are, as previously discussed, many factors that affect both nominal and real exchange rates, and some might protest that governments do not have direct enough control over these factors to manipu-

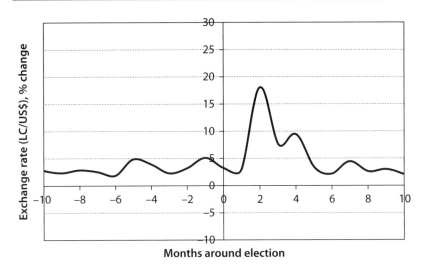

Figure 5.1 Exchange rate movements around executive elections, average for Latin America, 1970–2004. *Sources*: On exchange rates, see IMF, International Financial Statistics; on election timing, see World Bank, Database of Political Institutions.

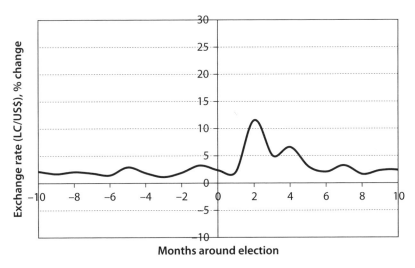

Figure 5.2 Exchange rate movements around legislative elections, average for Latin America, 1970–2004. *Sources*: Same as for figure 5.1.

217

late them for political purposes. This suggests another approach to the problem. While a government may have difficulty directly engineering a depreciation or appreciation, it can certainly directly influence whether the country remains on a publicly declared currency peg.

We can thus restrict our analysis to instances in which Latin American governments have committed themselves to fixing their currencies. The government has chosen to peg the currency in such a situation, and in the periods before and after an election, faces the decision as to whether to maintain the peg. In joint with work Brock Blomberg and Ernesto Stein, I have looked at just this issue by using a hazard (duration) model to evaluate the impact of a variety of factors on the conditional probability that a government will maintain a declared currency peg.[21] The results confirm, incidentally, the impact of manufacturing: countries with larger manufacturing sectors are less likely to sustain a peg. With respect to elections, the work shows that here, too, governments delay going off a peg as elections approach. The results, based on data from 1972 to 1999, indicate that every month before an impending election decreases the conditional likelihood of the peg ending by 1 percent, while every month after an election has taken place increases the conditional probability of the peg ending by 1 percent. Put differently, this implies that over the course of the eight months leading up to an election, the government is 8 percent less likely to leave a peg than otherwise, while over the four months after an election the government is 4 percent more likely to leave the peg.

Together this supplies fairly strong evidence that Latin American governments manage their exchange rates in such a way as to affect electoral outcomes. In particular, they favor a relatively appreciated real exchange rate in the period before an election, which artificially increases the purchasing power of the general population. This, of course, increases the likelihood of a devaluation (and perhaps even a currency crisis) after an election.

The Latin American Currency Experience

The Latin American experience provides us with important evidence about the political economy of exchange rate policy. The region is an

---

21 Blomberg, Frieden, and Stein 2005.

excellent laboratory for the topic's study. Its countries differ in their socioeconomic characteristics, and the countries have experienced an enormous assortment of currency regimes.

This chapter concentrated on how special interest and electoral pressures have influenced currency policy choices. First, it evaluated the impact of the sort of special interest pressures examined in the US and European cases. The evidence presented here reinforces the idea that internationally oriented economic actors favor a more stable currency. The more open to trade is the economy and the greater the significance of foreign investment, the more likely it is to have a more stable currency. The evidence also supports the argument that manufacturers prefer a more flexible currency capable of depreciating to improve their competitive position; this is especially true in more open economies in which manufacturers are exposed to import and export competition.

The second set of political factors is related to elections, which are now common and important in Latin America. Here, unlike in the US and European cases, I explored the potential use of the exchange rate for electoral purposes by incumbent governments. The evidence seems clear that governments do indeed encourage or allow the currency to appreciate in the run-up to an election, and similarly delay going off a currency peg during that period. One implication of this last finding is that governments may delay depreciations for electoral purposes even as a currency becomes unsustainable. This has been known to drive economies into currency crises. I now turn to this very issue in Latin American exchange rate politics: the causes and effects of currency crises.

6

The Political Economy of Latin American Currency Crises

On December 18, 2001, stores in several Argentine cities were looted by citizens furious about government economic policies, including the freezing of bank deposits. The austerity measures were particularly painful after a third straight year of economic stagnation. The next day, the looting spread much more widely throughout the country, and President Fernando de la Rúa declared a state of siege. That evening, de la Rúa—a Radical Party politician elected by coalition with the center-left Frepaso—called on the Peronists who dominated the legislature for unity to face the economic crisis. The Peronists quickly rejected the call. The popular response was even quicker, as hundreds of thousands of middle-class Argentines immediately took to the streets in one of the country's trademark *cacerolazos* (banging of pots and pans) in protest. Later that evening, Domingo Cavallo was forced to step down as economy minister. But the riots spread the next day, including huge crowds surrounding the presidential palace. Violent clashes with the police led to more than two dozen deaths, and at the end of the day de la Rúa resigned—and had to be airlifted by helicopter out of the presidential palace to avoid the hostile populace.

The president of the senate, a Peronist—de la Rúa's vice president had resigned in protest a year earlier—assumed the presidency as an interim measure. Two days later, the Peronists installed provincial governor Adolfo Rodríguez Saá as president until elections could be held in March 2002. Rodríguez Saá implemented some bold economic measures, including the largest default in history, on ninety-seven billion dollars in sovereign debt. But Rodríguez Saá did not receive support from other factions in the Peronist party and resigned a week after taking office. The senate president refused to retake the presidency, and it went to the next in line, the speaker of the house of deputies; almost immediately the legislature met, and after a long debate, appointed Eduardo Duhalde to the presidency. Duhalde was the Peronist candidate who had lost to de la Rúa in the 1999 elections; now he was to serve out the last two years of de la Rúa's term. One of his first moves was to end the currency board established by his Peronist predecessor, Carlos Menem, ten years earlier.

Meanwhile, the country had entered into the deepest economic collapse in its modern history. The Argentine GDP, which had declined by 8 percent over the three previous years of recession, dropped 11 percent in 2002. Unemployment climbed above 20 percent, and inflation—which had virtually disappeared over the previous decade—soared to 80 percent. The government forcibly converted bank accounts denominated in dollars to pesos at a depreciated rate. As the crisis of confidence in the peso continued, Argentine provinces began issuing their own currencies, which proved just as unpopular as the national money.

These extraordinary events—nationwide riots, five presidents in less than two weeks, the biggest default in history, and economic disintegration—could all be traced to the country's exchange rate policies. The government's decade-long commitment to a particularly rigid currency link to the dollar led eventually to everything from the general economic stagnation that was the backdrop to the crisis, to the specific banking policies that provoked such immediate popular outrage. Of course, this currency policy was also responsible for many key economic achievements in Argentina. That is in fact one of the great tragedies of the Argentine events: the country's fortunes rose dramatically and fell even more so with its currency policies.

Argentina is no anomaly. One of the most striking as well as disturbing features of Latin America's political economies over the past thirty years has been the string of currency and financial crises that have affected the region. Almost every country in Latin America has been hit by a run on its currency or debt, or both—sometimes more than once. These crises have devastated national economies and had powerful effects on national political systems. Even when a currency is successfully defended, the defense can require recessionary policies and a host of other unpopular measures. The social costs of these crises can be extraordinary. In Latin America, the fallout from the combined debt and currency crises of the early 1980s in Argentina and Chile led to direct government expenditures equal to 55 and 43 percent of the GDP, respectively.[1]

While scholars have been fascinated by these crises and their effects, they have paid little attention to explaining the currency policies associated with them. This is curious, for exchange rate crises inevitably implicate exchange rate policy. At some level the policies *cause* the crises, for without a government commitment—typically to a fixed exchange rate—there would be nothing for traders to attack. If a government were willing to allow the currency to move with the market, a currency sell-off would simply lead to a depreciation. A crisis occurs when the government has explicitly or implicitly pledged to maintain the currency's value, and investors believe that this promise may not be honored. The government may successfully defend its policy, resisting the depreciation, or it may give in and allow the exchange rate to fall.

The government faces several choices as this process unfolds. Each of them is likely to be political, mobilizing support and opposition. One of the things making crises so difficult is that in many instances the government is left with no good options—only choices among unattractive ones. The policy choices in question suggest a series of analytic questions:

> • What factors affect the likelihood that a government will commit itself to a currency peg (or similarly constraining policy), given that this involves surrendering a policy instrument and is known to be difficult to sustain?

1 Laeven and Valencia 2012.

- What factors influence the probability that a government committed to a currency peg will pursue other economic policies that are inconsistent with the currency peg and that raise doubts about its sustainability?
- What factors affect the probability that a government will stand by a currency peg when it is under attack as opposed to devaluing the currency or allowing the exchange rate to float?

All these are simply subsets of the kinds of policy choices and analytic questions discussed in the previous chapter, but in the case of currency crises they take on particular urgency and sharpness.

The experience of Latin American currency crises over the last thirty years raises an especially striking, important question: Why are depreciations that appear inevitable delayed? This is crucial because much currency crisis damage is done during the period when investors and observers are betting heavily on a depreciation, while the government is steadfastly vowing to avoid one. Typically, the perception becomes widespread that the exchange rate is not sustainable, and people start selling off their currency. The government tries to prop up the currency by buying it, usually borrowing heavily from abroad and raising local interest rates. Eventually the government is forced to let the currency go, but in the interim it may have lost billions of dollars—even tens of billions—trying to shore up the exchange rate, and it may also have driven the economy into a tailspin with high interest rates and a lack of confidence. There are instances in which governments have relatively quickly allowed a peg to be loosened or eliminated, thereby avoiding a serious crisis. But there are many examples of serious delay, and we do not fully understand why they persist.

In this chapter, I look specifically at the political economy of currency crises.[2] This requires attempting to answer the questions listed above, especially the last one. Why do governments so often delay depreciations until it is too late—until the (inevitable) depreciation causes a major crisis? And this question suggests its opposite: Why do governments sometimes choose to depreciate before it is too late?

An arresting example of this set of questions was given by the behavior of the Argentine and Brazilian governments in the late 1990s. Faced with hyperinflation, both governments had adopted a one-to-one currency peg with the US dollar in the early 1990s. Both pegs were

2   For an outstanding analysis of the issue in broad comparative perspective, see Walter 2013.

successful in reducing inflation, such that by 1997 both countries had accomplished the monetary stabilization they sought. Both countries, however, had experienced a substantial real appreciation that put major competitive pressure on tradables producers, who complained about the currency peg; independent economic analysts agreed. Both governments delayed adjusting the exchange rate. But in January 1999, soon after Fernando Henrique Cardoso took office as president for a second term, the Brazilians did in fact devalue substantially. The Argentine government nevertheless held on to its currency board for almost three more years in the face of massive evidence that this was unsustainable. When the Argentine peso eventually was taken off the peg, the result was a catastrophic collapse in the Argentine economy. Argentine delay contrasts vividly with Brazilian action (although the Brazilians might have been better served by depreciating even earlier). How can we explain these divergent policies?

This chapter starts with a general description of how such currency crises unfold. I then provide an in-depth analysis of the Mexican currency crisis of 1994 and of Argentine and Brazilian developments between 1991 and 2001. It would be satisfying to be able to present systematic empirical analyses of currency crises, but there are a number of analytic and empirical problems. First, it is hard to know what the universe of cases of *possible* currency crises might be; if we only looked at actual crises, we would not be able to determine what causes them in some circumstances and not others. Second, while there have been a fair number of currency crises in Latin America, the number is actually relatively small, especially in recent years in the open economy era. It seems more appropriate to provide a detailed analysis of the three cases as illustrations of the broader phenomenon. On that basis, and with the help of the more general analyses in the previous chapter, we can attempt to draw some broader lessons.

Anatomy of a Currency Crisis

A currency crisis is a run on a currency and begins when a government's commitment to a particular exchange rate is challenged by foreign exchange markets. It is analogous to a run on any financial asset, such as a sovereign loan or bank deposits. The ultimate cause of the run is a lack of confidence in the asset or its issuer. Once such a run starts it is self-reinforcing: the withdrawal of deposits weakens the bank and makes its failure more likely, while sales of stocks, bonds, or currency drive their price down and give investors an incentive to get out of the asset as quickly as possible. Yet in all these instances, if the asset is in fact worth its current value—if, for example, the bank is solvent or the monetary authorities are truly committed to the exchange rate—then a successful defense may be mounted, and the asset or institution may emerge strengthened. But such a defense can be extremely costly, and the self-reinforcing nature of the attack can make it too expensive to be practicable.

Currency crises are closely related to financial crises, because a run on a currency and on a national banking system can be effectively the same thing. For investors to get their money out of the national banking system, they have to sell off the local currency; unwinding currency positions typically means calling them in from national financial institutions. These twin crises have recurred throughout the modern era. They were common in the nineteenth century, usually when a country's commitment to the gold standard was in question, such as in the 1893 run on the US dollar. Currency and financial crises played a central part in the collapse of the world economy in the 1930s, as countries were driven off gold and into bank crises by the dozen.[3] They have returned to prominence as world capital markets have become integrated, especially after the 1970s. The developing country debt crisis of the early 1980s and a wave of developing country currency crises after 1994 refocused attention on the problem.

The scholarly literature has presented a variety of potential causes of currency crises—typically divided into three "generations" of crisis models. The first generation focuses on "fundamentals"—that is, macroeconomic policies that are inconsistent with the authorities' exchange rate commitment. The second generation introduces the possibility of multiple equilibria, in particular an exchange rate commitment that might be sustainable if currency markets do not attack it, but that could be abandoned if attacked. The third generation includes models in which the size and speed of financial markets can lead to "runs" on a currency even if it might be fundamentally sound.[4] While the three

---

3 For summaries of the enormous literature on this, see Eichengreen 1992; Bernanke and James 1991.

4 For an excellent survey, see Glick and Hutchison 2013.

generations of models have different implications, they are not mutually exclusive, and it is almost certainly the case that all the factors discussed could conceivably be at play.

My focus is on the willingness and ability of the government to defend a currency that finds itself in crisis. The measures necessary for such a defense will vary from case to case—and the better part of policy valor may be to allow the currency to decline, perhaps preemptively. The analytic question has to do with the factors that might lead a government to take its currency and economy over the brink into full-fledged crisis, rather than either taking preventive measures or allowing the currency to depreciate before a more serious crisis develops. In the context of our broader exploration, this is likely to depend at least in part on the strength of the interests in favor of maintaining the existing exchange rate—whether due to the rate's level or predictability—as opposed to the interests that would be favorable to a depreciation.

To help clarify the issues, it is useful to present a chronology of the typical currency crisis. Of course, there is much variation around these themes, but most currency crises share the features described below.

The government must first have an explicit or implicit commitment to a specific level of the exchange rate. This might be a rigid currency board–style arrangement or a looser target band. But if the government is not constrained to maintain the currency's value, there is no scope for a classic crisis.

The government's commitment to the currency's value could have a variety of sources, all of which were examined in chapter 5. One goal is to reduce exchange rate uncertainty while encouraging cross-border trade and investment—perhaps even going in the direction of a currency union. Another goal might be to reduce inflation by linking the currency to a low-inflation anchor. Still another could be the general "fear of floating" that has been noted in most developing countries.[5] Whatever the reason, the government is committed to sustain the currency at or near a given level.

The path to a currency crisis most commonly begins with an inflow of capital (or, more generally, resources). The inflow could be due to a positive terms-of-trade shock, or a natural resource discovery and boom; in Latin America, it is often related to an accelerated capital inflow as financial markets become enthusiastic about the country. This

---

5 Calvo and Reinhart 2002.

resource inflow leads to an economic expansion. As demand increases, the currency appreciates in real terms. With the exchange rate fixed, this is due to an increase in the price of nontradables (tradables prices are constrained by foreign competition). The boom is therefore concentrated in nontradable sectors, such as finance, real estate, and other services. The economic expansion frequently encourages further capital inflows, especially inasmuch as the appreciated real exchange rate makes foreign borrowing attractive. It also leads to a surge of imports, as foreign producers increasingly satisfy the rising demand; domestic tradables producers face increased costs as nontradables prices rise.

Eventually, the relative price effects of the real appreciation lead to complaints from tradables producers that they are having difficulties competing with foreigners on home and world markets. These become pressures for a loosening of the currency constraint, including for a devaluation. Yet supporters of the peg also mobilize, especially in the financial sector and among those who have accumulated foreign-currency debt. Electoral factors can enter, too, as the consumption boom associated with the real appreciation is normally popular with the voting public. This political jockeying is normal, but it has the effect of raising questions about the viability of the government's exchange rate commitment. As complaints from tradables producers proliferate, fear of a depreciation deepens.

Growing uncertainty about the exchange rate slows the capital inflow, as foreigners become uneasy about the future and national investors start to take their money out of the country. This reinforces pressure on the currency. Over time, devaluation expectations grow and the currency comes under increasingly serious market pressure. As investors sell off the currency, the government can choose to let it depreciate or defend it. There are instances in which governments do not cling to their currency commitments. It is nevertheless more common for the government to attempt to defend the currency with interest rate increases and increased foreign borrowing to fund currency-market intervention. Eventually, however, this becomes unsustainable: foreigners will no longer lend, and the domestic political effects of the real appreciation and high interest rates are too powerful to ignore.

The ultimate fall of the currency has a series of follow-on effects. It causes great distress among foreign-currency debtors, many of whom are bankrupted. This puts strain on the financial system, which is heavily exposed to now-insolvent debtors. The currency crisis may become a banking crisis as well (a "twin crisis" in the phrase of the literature), with compounded effects. The government is also caught in this debt trap, given that its frantic short-term borrowing in the currency defense leaves it with a large foreign-currency debt, now increased by the depreciation. The government is forced to print money, cut spending, or raise taxes—or all three.

The economic, political, and social effects of these crises can be enormous. The debt crises that swept Latin American in the early 1980s, many of which were closely tied to currency crises, led to arguably the most serious economic and political upheavals in the region's modern history. The 1994 currency crisis in Mexico and the 1999–2002 currency crisis in Argentina were among the most traumatic economic and political events in recent Latin American memory. More generally, the costs of currency crises have been estimated to be extremely large. A currency crisis itself in a country is, on average, associated with a decline in output growth of between 5 and 8 percent over a two- to four-year period. When a currency crisis is linked to a banking crisis—which is the case in most instances—the combined output loss is between 13 and 18 percent of output.[6] These are large numbers, especially for developing countries. This makes it all the more important to try to understand the sources of the crises.

Tales of Two Crises: Mexico, 1994–95, and Brazil and Argentina, 1997–2002

Although currency and banking crises have been common in Latin America since the early nineteenth century, more recent experience with them goes back to the debt crisis of the early 1980s. This episode was most often a problem of sovereign indebtedness, and sometimes the currency was not implicated—as in Brazil, whose government had made no explicit exchange rate commitments. The Mexican and Venezuelan crises of 1982 were related to substantial real appreciations of their respective national currencies, and resulted in large depreciations. In Chile and Argentina, there were particularly strong links between debt and currency crises. Both countries began to lag their exchange

6 Hutchison and Noy 2005.

rates behind inflation in 1978 in an attempt to reduce inflation. In February 1979, the Chilean government even fixed the peso against the dollar. The result was real appreciations of well over 25 percent in both countries, followed by spectacular currency collapses that exacerbated the debt problems. The crises of the early 1980s often had currency components, but the exchange rate appeared less significant than the underlying difficulties that Latin America had managing its large sovereign debt.

In the early 1990s, Latin America returned to the international capital markets. The economic reforms of the 1980s transformed what had previously been a financially and commercially closed region into one that was tightly tied into international trade, finance, and direct investment. Open-economy currency dilemmas came to the fore, highlighting tensions between supporters of fixed and floating rates and of strong and weak currencies. In the Latin American context, the typical divisions were exacerbated by the region's long inflationary history, which governments and publics everywhere were eager to put behind them. This additional motivation for fixed rates contributed to the quandaries within which many of the region's nations eventually found themselves.

Mexico and the tequila effect, 1994–95. The first major indication of the new sort of crisis came in Mexico in 1994. Like the rest of the region, Mexico was now open to both trade and financial flows. In addition, on January 1, 1994, NAFTA went into effect, linking the country to the United States and Canada in a far-reaching preferential trade agreement. A few months later, the OECD accepted Mexico as a member, signaling the country's economic success. The Mexican economy was growing rapidly, inflation was lower than it had been in decades, and capital was flowing into the country at the rate of over thirty billion dollars a year. In this context, it did not attract much attention that the peso had appreciated substantially. The currency was held within a narrow band, and its rate of depreciation had not kept up with the inflation differential with the United States. The monetary authorities minimized the problem, maintaining that it simply reflected productivity increases and the impact of capital inflows.[7] Table 6.1 and

---

7   Most of what is presented here is drawn from Edwards and Naím 1997. For a typical ostrich-head-in-the-sand example of the monetary authorities' view—in this case, long after the crisis—see the chapter by Francisco Gil-Diaz and Agustin Carstens.

TABLE 6.1
Macroeconomic variables for Mexico, 1990–96

Year	Real exchange rate	Inflation	External debt / GDP	Trade balance / GDP	CA balance / GDP
1990	82.30	26.65	0.40	−0.01	−0.03
1991	90.02	22.66	0.36	−0.03	−0.05
1992	97.63	15.51	0.31	−0.05	−0.07
1993	104.79	9.75	0.32	−0.04	−0.06
1994	100.54	6.97	0.33	−0.05	−0.07
1995	68.27	35.00	0.58	0.03	−0.01
1996	76.18	34.38	0.47	0.02	−0.01

figure 6.1 summarize the country's macroeconomic developments between 1990 and 1995.

The Mexican picture began to deteriorate in early 1994 for both economic and political reasons. In January, an armed insurgency began in the southern state of Chiapas—a rare indication of political unrest in a country that had been ruled by one party for nearly seventy years. Intimations of instability increased in March, when the ruling party's candidate for the presidency was assassinated (elections were scheduled for August). Capital flows began to slow, while complaints about the real appreciation proliferated. The prominent US macroeconomist Rudiger Dornbusch and a coauthor argued in a widely read paper that the peso was overvalued by at least 30 percent and needed to be devalued to avoid a crisis.[8] Despite an 11 percent devaluation in the aftermath of the assassination, concerns about the exchange rate continued.

The president of Mexico's National Association of Manufacturers told the press in May that "now is the time for the government to accelerate the peso's depreciation ... to allow us to compete and to stop subsidizing foreigners."[9] His demands were echoed by the manufacturing sectors most directly affected—textiles, footwear, furniture, pulp and paper, and others.[10] In June, it was revealed that one of the coun-

8 Dornbusch and Werner 1994.
9 Quoted in *El Financiero*, May 27, 1994, 24. As is customary in many Mexican papers, the line between quotation and paraphrase is not always clear.
10 As indicated in articles in *El Financiero* from January 8 and 23, and June 2, 3, and 10, 1994. It is interesting that the important auto sector was not active in these protests—probably because so much of its business was (and is) in intrafirm and intraindustry trade, which is not so sensitive to the exchange rate.

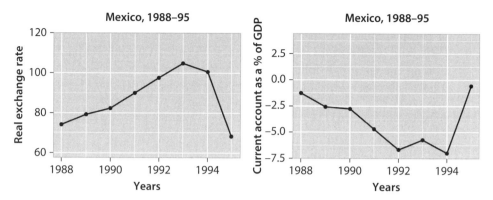

Figure 6.1 Mexico: Real exchange rate and current account deficit, 1988–95

try's largest industrial groups, Grupo Alfa, was in trouble. Alfa's principal problem was that the modest depreciation of the peso had increased the burden of its large dollar debt.[11] This was troubling in its own right, yet also because Alfa's financial difficulties had been a hallmark of the 1982 crisis.

With the presidential election campaign in full swing, the opposition took up the industrialists' complaints. The presidential candidate of the conservative Partido de Acción Nacional (PAN) insisted that "our currency is at least 20 percent overvalued," and while "it is necessary to avoid a brusque devaluation due to the psychological effects this would provoke, we should carry out a gradual decline in the peso to bring its nominal value into line with its real value . . . in order to create better conditions for our exporters."[12] PAN had long-standing ties to the country's leading industrialists in and around the northern city of Monterrey, and its public statements along these lines signaled critical business-community views on the desirability of a weaker exchange rate.

The government faced conflicting pressures. The ruling PRI wanted to ensure the victory of its presidential candidate, Ernesto Zedillo. But Zedillo was a nearly unknown technocrat, and the election promised to be close. A devaluation would have two key negative effects. First, it would substantially reduce the purchasing power of Mexican consum-

11 *El Financiero,* June 10, 1994, 10A.
12 Quoted in *El Financiero,* July 26, 1994, 44.

ers—especially of urban middle-class consumers, for whom the surge of cheap imports had been especially positive—at a point when the PRI could hardly afford to alienate voters. Second, it would risk bankrupting the country's dollar debtors. And while the nation's powerful industrialists were ever more insistent that the strong peso was harming them, the northern industrialists were more closely linked to PAN than to the PRI. As the election campaign wore on, the situation became more difficult, as devaluation fears led investors to sell pesos and the monetary authorities continued to bleed foreign exchange reserves.

The government held on to the peso's exchange rate, and Zedillo and the PRI won the election in August—although, for the first time ever, the PRI candidate did not get an absolute majority of the popular votes. Economic policy problems did not subside, especially after the September 28 assassination of yet another prominent politician—in this case, the PRI's secretary general.[13] Capital continued to flow out of the country, and the country's foreign exchange reserves were drawn even further down. Over the months between the election and Zedillo's inauguration on December 1, the government continued to refuse to devalue, although Zedillo's team apparently encouraged it to do so. While demands for a devaluation proliferated, there were opposing voices: the country's Association of Import-Export Traders (the commercial sector, not the producers) called for a continued commitment to the exchange rate.[14]

Zedillo's inauguration did nothing to reduce demands for a devaluation or the market's expectations that one would take place. PAN's parliamentary delegation railed at the "governmental obsession" that was "bleeding the public treasury dry," and called for a devaluation to stop "subsidizing the dollar."[15] The country continued to lose reserves, and the Zedillo government finally announced a widening of the band on December 20 to allow a depreciation of about 15 percent. This proved inadequate, and soon the peso was allowed to float—whereupon it sank dramatically, reaching 7.59/dollar by March 1995. In three months the peso had gone from 29.4 to 13.2 cents.

13 Raúl Salinas, the brother of the previous president, was eventually convicted of arranging the assassination in order to keep the secretary general from incriminating Salinas in a bribery and corruption scandal.
14 *El Financiero*, November 19, 1994, 4.
15 Quoted in *El Financiero*, December 6, 1994.

The devaluation triggered a massive crisis. The GDP dropped by 7 percent, while inflation soared from just 7 percent in 1994 to 35 percent in 1995. The impact of the crisis—the tequila effect—was felt around the world, since this was the first major developing country crisis since the early 1980s. In an attempt to contain any possible contagion, creditor governments and international financial institutions spent about fifty billion dollars to support the Mexican government. But the damage to the Mexican economy had been done. When the next presidential elections were held in 2000, the PRI went down to defeat for the first time in its history, polling barely one-third of the popular vote and losing to PAN's candidate.

Even as Mexico recovered from its most recent catastrophe, a similar currency and banking crisis hit East Asia. There are many differences between East Asia and Latin America, but the crisis was strikingly familiar to Latin Americans. Just as the Mexican collapse had repercussions elsewhere, the East Asian crisis raised doubts about two South American nations that had, like Mexico, also fixed their currencies in the new commercial and financial environment.

Brazil's real adjustment while Argentina's currency board walks the plank, 1998–2002. In the aftermath of the debt crisis of the early 1980s, Argentina and Brazil were much less successful than Mexico at achieving macroeconomic stability. By 1990, when Mexican inflation was around 20 percent and headed toward the single digits, both Argentina and Brazil were still in the throes of hyperinflation, with inflation rates above 2,000 percent. Both countries had experienced a series of failed stabilization plans that had left the population weary of hyperinflation and wary of government promises.

Perhaps even more worrisome than their continuing macroeconomic problems was the fact that in the aftermath of democratization, both countries had a succession of profoundly disappointing governments. Argentines had elected Radical Raúl Alfonsín in 1983 with high hopes of an alternative to the bitter conflict between Peronists and conservatives that had plagued the country for forty years and had led to a succession of Peronist turmoil followed by anti-Peronist military dictatorships. But by the end of Alfonsín's six-year term, he was so discredited that he left office early to make way for yet another Peronist, Carlos Menem, who appeared to be the product of the worst kind of provincial patronage machine that the Peronists could produce. Conditions in Brazil were just as bad. The first civilian president died before taking office and was succeeded by an ineffectual placeholder; the winner of the first direct elections in 1989 was impeached for corruption and succeeded by another placeholder.

So in 1990, macroeconomic conditions in Argentina and Brazil were bad, and it seemed unlikely that the two political systems would provide leadership to move the countries forward. Yet both nations made major progress during the 1990s. They did so under unlikely presidential leaders, both of whom made central use of fixed exchange rates to achieve their successes.

Menem took office in 1989 in the midst of food riots and intimations of military dissatisfaction. In March 1991, the government instituted a currency board, called a Convertibility Program in Argentina, with a one-to-one, no-margins parity between the peso and the US dollar. This particularly rigid form of a currency peg—in which the monetary authorities were required to hold foreign exchange reserve backing for domestic-currency issue, and the dollar could be used locally at the official rate—was adopted in a last-ditch effort to bring inflation down. Under the supervision of Economy Minister Cavallo, the currency board was accompanied by some fiscal retrenchment and a wave of privatizations. The new policies were very much in line with those pursued by the most enthusiastic economic reformers and strikingly different from traditional Peronist recommendations. Both abroad and at home, the government explicitly promoted the currency board as a symbol of the credibility of the policies.

The international financial community warmly welcomed Argentine stabilization and reform programs, and capital began to flow into (and back into) Argentina. Between 1991 and 1994, the economy grew by one-third and inflation was down to 4 percent (from its 1990 level of 2,300 percent). As the tequila effect of Mexico's crisis hit Latin America, the economy turned down in 1995, but quickly recovered. For the first time in decades, Argentines were enjoying sustained economic growth, macroeconomic stability, and democratic rule—all at the same time. The currency board was a success.

In neighboring Brazil, the transition to stabilization and reform came a bit after Argentina. The government had been immobilized by the collapse of the Collor presidency, which ended in impeachment in December 1992. Soon after Vice President Itamar Franco took over the presidency, he appointed Cardoso to the finance ministry. Cardoso, Brazil's most prominent leftist intellectual, had entered electoral politics in the late 1970s and now headed the center-left Brazilian Social Democratic Party (Partido da Social Democracia Brasileira). In early 1994, Cardoso implemented the Real Plan, a vigorous stabilization program. The plan's centerpiece was an eventual currency peg of the real (the new Brazilian currency) to the US dollar at the rate of one dollar to one real. As in Argentina, the new policies included fiscal retrenchment, privatization, and a further opening of the country to international trade and investment. With the plan a resounding success, Cardoso was elected president of Brazil in December 1994. The economy grew, albeit not so rapidly as in Argentina; inflation also came down, again not quite so rapidly as in Argentina, although by 1997 it was below 7 percent. Like Argentines, Brazilians were experiencing their first sustained episode of simultaneous economic growth, macroeconomic stability, and democratic rule.

At the same time that these currency pegs, stabilization, and reform programs were being put into place, Brazil and Argentina negotiated a preferential trade agreement that came into effect on January 1, 1995. The new Southern Common Market (Mercosur in Spanish, and Mercosul in Portuguese) also included Paraguay and Uruguay, but its centerpiece was the integration of the two economic giants of South America.

By the mid-1990s, then, Argentina and Brazil looked quite similar. They were engaged in a joint effort to integrate their trade and investment; they had stabilized their macroeconomies, controlled inflation, tamed budget deficits, sold off many public enterprises, and substantially opened their economies to foreign trade and investment. And most central for our purposes, both Argentina and Brazil were on hard pegs to the dollar, at the same (one-to-one) exchange rate. But their macroeconomic paths diverged starting in 1998; tables 6.2 and 6.3 provide the basic data for the two countries between 1990 and 2002, which are shown graphically in figures 6.2 and 6.3.

In both countries, the initial currency peg led to the usual real appreciation as inflation continued for a time. Argentina's currency board went into effect in March 1991, and inflation came down relatively quickly. Measured by the consumer price index, inflation was 25 percent in 1992 and 10 percent in 1993. This represented a major victory over inflation—cemented by an average inflation between 1994 and 1998 of under 2 percent a year—but it still led to a substantial real appreciation, as indicated in table 6.2. Much the same happened in Brazil

TABLE 6.2
Macroeconomic variables for Brazil, 1990–2000

Year	Real exchange rate	Inflation	External debt / GDP	Trade balance / GDP	CA balance / GDP
1990	90.49	2947.73	0.26	0.01	–0.01
1991	81.88	432.78	0.30	0.01	–0.00
1992	77.32	951.65	0.33	0.02	0.02
1993	79.80	1927.98	0.33	0.01	0.00
1994	96.42	2075.89	0.28	0.00	–0.00
1995	108.83	66.01	0.21	–0.02	–0.02
1996	114.38	15.76	0.22	–0.02	–0.03
1997	117.37	6.93	0.23	–0.02	–0.03
1998	115.09	3.20	0.29	–0.02	–0.04
1999	76.32	4.86	0.42	–0.01	–0.04
2000	82.94	7.04	0.37	–0.02	–0.04

TABLE 6.3
Macroeconomic variables for Argentina, 1990–2002

Year	Real exchange rate	Inflation	External debt / GDP	Trade balance / GDP	CA balance / GDP
1990	117.21	2313.96	0.44	0.06	0.03
1991	156.12	171.67	0.34	0.02	–0.00
1992	176.65	24.90	0.30	–0.02	–0.02
1993	212.11	10.61	0.27	–0.02	–0.03
1994	212.61	4.18	0.29	–0.03	–0.04
1995	204.43	3.38	0.38	–0.00	–0.02
1996	202.45	0.16	0.41	–0.01	–0.02
1997	211.38	0.53	0.43	–0.02	–0.04
1998	220.01	0.92	0.47	–0.03	–0.05
1999	215.28	–1.17	0.50	–0.02	–0.04
2000	220.31	–0.94	0.50	–0.01	–0.03
2001	221.69	–1.07	0.55	0.01	–0.01
2002	89.34	25.87	1.42	0.15	0.09

Sources (tables 6.1–6.3): World Bank, world development indicators except for real exchange rate; Darvas 2012; http://www.bruegel.org/datasets/real-effective-exchange-rates-for-178-countries-a -new-database/.

after the real was fixed against the dollar on July 1, 1994. Inflation during the month of June was 47 percent (this is a *monthly* rate, not an annualized one); in July it was under 7 percent, and over the last six months of the year prices rose only 18 percent—less than in a typical two weeks before the plan. Inflation did not disappear overnight, how-

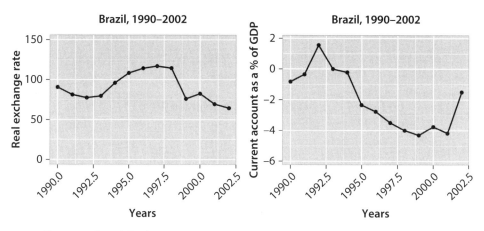

Figure 6.2 Brazil: Real exchange rate and current account deficit, 1990–2002

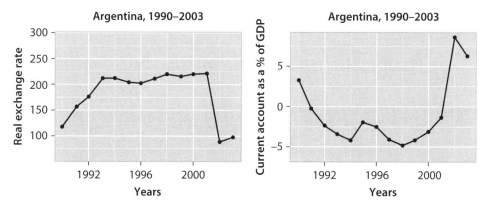

Figure 6.3 Argentina: Real exchange rate and current account deficit, 1990–2002
Source (figures 6.1–6.3): Same as for tables 6.1–6.3.

ever; in 1995 it was 66 percent, and in 1996 it was still almost 16 percent. Again, this implied a significant real appreciation. By one estimate, the REER in 1997 was 47 percent stronger than it had been in 1993 (see table 6.3).

For the first few years of the respective stabilization programs, most attention focused on their success in conquering inflation, which included both the monetary measures and substantial fiscal retrenchment. Almost as striking was the increase in bilateral trade. By 1998, trade among Mercosur member states had risen to over twenty-three billion dollars, up from just four billion dollars at the time of the original treaty's signing in 1991. Even more impressive, the share of intra-Mercosur trade in the two countries' trade had increased dramatically, so that by 1998 Brazil was sending 17 percent of its exports to Mercosur, and Argentina was contributing 36 percent of its exports to Mercosur (up from 4 and 16 percent, respectively, in 1990).[16]

Yet by 1997 the effects of the real appreciation were beginning to be felt. It was clear to most observers. Early in 1997, Dornbusch (1997) flagged a Brazilian real appreciation variously estimated at between 15 and 50 percent over 1993 levels. While inflation had been brought down to single digits, growth was slow, and complaints were starting to be heard in Brazil. Argentine growth remained strong through 1997, but in both countries the real appreciation had led to large current account deficits of about 4 percent of the GDP. Nonetheless, there was little effective incentive for policymakers to review their course.

The 1997–98 East Asian currency crisis heightened pressure on Latin American currencies, including both the peso and real. The peso withstood the pressure with relative ease, although the monetary authorities were forced to raise interest rates, yet investors had less confidence in the real. Brazil's government had not committed to so hard a peg as Argentina's, and the country had a long history of following a flexible (or crawling peg) exchange rate regime.[17] Over the course of 1998, as interest rates shot from below 20 percent to over 40 percent and the Brazilian economy tumbled into recession, complaints rose. These difficulties were compounded by a massive currency crisis and debt default in Russia in the late summer.[18]

All this was happening in the run-up to presidential elections in October 1998. The constitution had been amended to allow Cardoso's reelection, and the Real Plan's designer was running primarily against the left-wing candidate of the Workers' Party, Luíz Inácio ("Lula") da Silva. This made the government reluctant to implement measures that would threaten its electoral position. Cardoso was reelected, and a few weeks later his government negotiated a support package worth more than forty billion dollars from the IMF, World Bank, and creditor

16 Data from https://www.wto.org/english/res_e/statis_e/tradebyregion_e.htm (accessed July 16, 2013).
17 For a good survey, see Bonomo and Terra 2001.
18 On the Real Plan, see Franco 2000.

countries in return for a Brazilian commitment to a more rigorous austerity program, especially in fiscal policy.

Neither the policy changes nor the support package were sufficient to reduce pressure on the currency, both politically and in foreign exchange markets, and on January 15, 1999, the real was allowed to float freely. The currency quickly depreciated dramatically, eventually settling at around two reals to the dollar. Interest rates came down substantially; the economy began to grow, albeit slowly; and despite fears that the devaluation would rekindle inflation, there was only the mildest increase in prices and inflation remained in the single digits. While the crisis was not catastrophic, in its aftermath—from 1998 to 2003—per capita GDP was still stagnant. The fixed exchange rate had accomplished its anti-inflationary purpose, but the cost was a messy exit from the fixed rate followed by five recessionary years.

The Brazilian experience was tame compared to happened in Argentina. Argentina's macroeconomic circumstances were, to be sure, not always easy to analyze.[19] The currency board had worked remarkably well—so well that after 1995 inflation in Argentina was substantially below that of the United States. Indeed, between 1995 and 2001, Argentina's consumer price index actually dropped by nearly 2 percent, while that of the United States rose by about 16 percent. This helped sustain Argentina's external competitiveness, but it was not enough to overcome the substantial initial real appreciation.

In this context, some Argentines began discussing the possibility of relaxing or ending the currency board. As early as summer 1997, the Radical ex-president Alfonsín averred that "some day we will have to think about ending" convertibility, although he hastened to clarify that he was not suggesting that the day was imminent.[20] A year later, as the real appreciation continued to worsen conditions for manufacturers, the head of the country's industrial association (Unión Industrial Argentina) insisted that unless the government protected industry from the mass of imports, "soon we will be talking about changing the exchange rate.... [T]he one-to-one rate cannot last forever."[21]

19 The Argentine crisis has been widely discussed in the literature. For a comprehensive set of articles, see della Paolera and Taylor 2003; de la Torre, Levy Yeyati, and Schmukler 2003; Galiani, Heymann, and Tommasi 2003. For a set of articles on the possibility of dollarization, both in Argentina and general, see Levy Yeyati and Sturzenegger 2003.
20 Quoted in *La Nación*, August 6, 1997.
21 Quoted in *La Nación*, September 2, 1998.

But support for the currency board was strong. In September 1998, before the Brazilian devaluation, 70 percent of those polled wanted the arrangement to continue, and only 12 percent favored abandoning it.[22] There were at least two reasons for opposition to a devaluation. First, many people—both businesspeople and consumers—were benefiting from the real appreciation directly or indirectly. Second, most of the country's debts were now denominated in dollars, and dollar debtors would be hard hit by a devaluation. This included nearly a million holders of mortgages denominated in dollars—beneficiaries of an explosive growth in such mortgage lending.[23] Policymakers, then, found themselves caught between increasing economic and political pressure for a relaxation of the currency constraint on the one hand, and strong support for a maintenance of the existing currency board on the other.

The Argentine crisis began in earnest with the Brazilian devaluation. As the Mercosur agreements were implemented, trade between the two countries had grown dramatically. When the real collapsed, it suddenly made Brazilian goods extremely cheap in Argentina, and Argentine goods super expensive in Brazil. Almost immediately, what had been a booming market for Argentine exports started to contract and instead Argentine producers found their home market flooded with Brazilian imports. Argentina's exports to Brazil fell by over one-third in the year after the real's devaluation, and everyone from textile manufacturers to chicken farmers complained about the blow to the country's trade. Nontrade barriers were imposed on a number of Brazilian products, and the Argentine authorities threatened emergency tariffs—so much so that some observers believed that Mercosur itself might not survive the crisis. Faced with protectionist measures, in October 1999 Brazil's steelmakers agreed to limit their exports to Argentina "voluntarily."[24]

Argentina struggled with the effects of the Brazilian devaluation, compounded by a rising dollar, as 1999 wore on toward the October presidential elections. In May 1999, reports began coming out of the camp of Peronist candidate Duhalde that his economic team was considering ending the hard peg. "The success of the Brazilian devaluation," said one adviser, "has convinced them that they have to devalue

22 Ibid.
23 *La Nación*, June 16, 1998.
24 Quoted in *La Nación*, October 18, 1999.

to improve competitiveness."[25] The impact of the revelations was heightened by the knowledge that the Duhalde camp had been consulting with Cavallo, the architect of the currency board himself, who also seemed to think that it was time to reconsider the policy. Meanwhile, special interest supporters of the currency board—especially the bankers' association (Asociación de Bancos Argentinos)—insisted that fiscal adjustment was preferable to abandoning convertibility, and public opinion polls continued to show support for the fixed rate.

After the Peronists lost the election to de la Rúa, heading a Radical-Frepaso coalition, both verbal and financial speculation against the peso-dollar peg continued. The trade unions insisted on the need for a relaxation of the financial constraints that had driven the country into what was now a serious recession—the GDP fell 4 percent in 1999 and another 1 percent in 2000. The head of the metalworkers' union drew even clearer connections: "When we sit down to talk to businessmen and ask for wage increases, they tell us that we are irresponsible and that we want to destroy convertibility."[26] For their part, industrialists and farmers clamored for protection, and received some emergency measures, including the Brazilian agreement to limit steel exports to Argentina.

And still public opinion backed the currency board. In June 2000, 72 percent of those polled were opposed to a devaluation of the peso; in January 2001, supporters of convertibility were still 67 percent of those surveyed.[27] In any event, the de la Rúa government was extremely weak—a fact indicated by the resignation of the vice president in October 2000. In December, a $40 billion support package from international financial institutions and creditor countries helped the government honor its commitments, both to its creditors and to the exchange rate. Cavallo, called back into government service as the economy minister in April 2001, promised to improve conditions. But the crisis only worsened, and in fact Cavallo's attempts to loosen the currency constraint led only to a further loss of confidence in the peso. Early in December 2001, conditions became so serious that Cavallo announced that bank deposits would be frozen, with account holders restricted to withdrawing $250 a week, in a measure known as the *corralito* (little corral). The measure enraged the middle classes: not only did they not

25 Quoted in *La Nación*, May 20, 1999.
26 Quoted in *La Nación*, July 21, 2000.
27 *La Nación*, June 12, 2000; Galiani, Heymann, and Tommasi 2003, 135.

have access to their money, but they also anticipated that the government would soon force them to convert it from pesos into dollars at an unfavorable (devalued) rate. And indeed, after the mid-December crisis described above, the currency board came to an ignominious end. As previously mentioned, the GDP dropped, unemployment and inflation soared, and Argentina was off to another swing of its economic policy pendulum.

Implications and Interpretation

We can draw some conclusions from these three episodes, especially in the context of the much broader analyses in the previous chapter. Both the narrative of the three cases and statistical analyses point to several important considerations.

Elections. In all three cases, there is evidence that the governments in office were looking for a way to make the exchange rate more flexible and to depreciate in a relatively orderly fashion. Nevertheless, all three faced national elections, and the electorate was not favorable to a depreciation. This is consistent with the more general evidence presented in chapter 5, in which Latin American governments typically postpone depreciations until after elections. Both qualitative and quantitative evidence suggest that the public's support for the appreciated real exchange rate is a function of its impact on purchasing power and the benefit to consumers. In some cases—in particular Argentina in the late 1990s—it was also clearly the case that middle-income voters were opposed to a depreciation because they had incurred substantial dollar-indexed debts, especially mortgages.

The implication of both the case studies and statistical analysis is that impending elections can delay a government's response to an unsustainable currency policy. This in turn may increase the likelihood of a currency crisis.

Manufacturers. The case studies and statistical analyses all point to the central role of manufacturers in exerting pressure for a realistic real exchange rate, and thus for an adjustment of a strongly appreciated currency before it collapses. Brazil's manufacturing sector has an almost-mythological reputation for political and economic influence, and it clearly pressed the government for a depreciation and eventually achieved its goal. Mexico's northern industrialists are economically important, but as they have tended to support PAN, they were less influential in the PRI governments of the late 1990s and had less influence on exchange rate policy. Argentina's manufacturing sector had been weakened by decades of crises; its farmers, while supportive of a depreciation, had little influence over the traditionally antiagricultural Peronists who controlled the government.

Foreign-currency debtors. Until the 1980s, almost all foreign (and foreign-currency borrowing) by Latin American countries was done by governments or public enterprises. Yet as the region became more open to international financial flows, it was increasingly common for private banks and corporations to borrow abroad. In addition, as financial institutions drew more funds from foreign sources, they often lent them to domestic residents, including households, in dollars or a dollar-indexed form. Whether directly or indirectly, then, more Latin American firms and households had liabilities denominated in foreign currencies, and would suffer substantial losses in the event of a depreciation. While this is hard to document (or does not seem to come through) in the statistical analyses, it is a constant theme in narratives of currency crises in the region and elsewhere. The reason for the disjuncture between the statistics and the narratives is that the former typically do not indicate the extent to which households have incurred foreign-currency debt but rather only the aggregate level of foreign liabilities. Banks and corporations with foreign liabilities may be able to hedge against the impact of a devaluation, while households cannot. But this is purely speculative. What much of the secondary literature seems to make clear is that foreign-currency liabilities are a powerful force against a devaluation.[28]

International exposure. Throughout my analyses, it appears that internationally oriented economic actors—in particular, banks and corporations with important cross-border interests—have been a powerful (perhaps the most powerful) force for stable exchange rates. This preference is relevant to currency crises, of course, as those who want stable or fixed exchange rates will resist any attempts to make the currency more flexible.

Argentina provides a textbook example of how political pressures can force a government to delay a depreciation that it knows is inevitable and to attempt to sustain a currency that it knows to be unsus-

---

28 See especially Walter 2008, 2013.

tainable. Consumers appreciated the enhanced purchasing power of an overvalued peso; households with debts denominated in dollars strenuously opposed a depreciation; supporters of the fixed exchange rate for trade and investment-facilitating reasons were similarly against any loosening of the fixed rate. Meanwhile, the principal losers from the appreciated peso, manufacturers and farmers, were not politically powerful. In this context, it seems likely that any Argentine government that tried to manage a (precrisis) depreciation would have been thrown out of office—so that in some sense the crisis was politically inevitable.

By the same token, this survey suggests the factors that we would expect to be associated with more successful efforts to avoid a currency crisis. A government faced with politically powerful manufacturers, farmers, and miners exposed to import or export competition would be pressed to adjust the exchange rate sooner rather than later. Where consumers were less powerful, their desire for enhanced purchasing power would be less politically relevant. And where the internationally oriented financial and commercial sectors were less economically or politically important, again, pressure to maintain a fixed rate would be less insistent. It may not be a coincidence that East Asian governments tend to look more like this than do those in Latin America: they tend to confront less political pressure from consumers (especially among authoritarian regimes) and more political pressure from export-oriented producers.

Understanding Currency Crises

Currency crises are likely to be a continuing feature of the modern international economy, for they may be an inevitable result of contemporary levels of international financial integration. There are two senses in which this is the case: in the direct effect of financial globalization on borrowing nations and in its broader impact on the transmission of crises.

First, today's global capital markets give both governments and firms powerful incentives to borrow abroad, as they can mobilize enormous sums quickly and inexpensively. By the same token, governments whose economies are open to the rest of the world—especially on capital account—have strong incentives to avoid major changes in the exchange rate. These factors can come together to set the stage for the typical course of a currency crisis: capital flows into a country, leading to a strong real appreciation of the currency. If this real appreciation is politically popular, the government has little reason to avoid or counteract it, even as warning signs accumulate that the exchange rate may be unsustainable.

Second, integrated international financial markets mean that crises can be transmitted rapidly from country to country. As was the case in the aftermath of the Mexican crisis of 1994 and East Asian crisis of 1997–98, the collapse of one currency can lead investors to flee other currencies, thereby precipitating a cascade of crises.

Currency crises, like financial ones, may be a necessary concomitant of an integrated world economy; after all, they were as common under the gold standard as they are today. The benefits of financial and commercial integration presumably outweigh the costs of periodic currency crises. Nonetheless, it is helpful—perhaps even valuable—to understand the political economy factors that might make such crises more or less likely. In this chapter, building both on my more general analysis and on a few prominent Latin American cases, I have emphasized the factors that can encourage governments to address an unsustainable exchange rate before it collapses—or that can press it to delay until it is too late. Strong tradables producers can exert pressure on policymakers to relieve them from a real appreciation by depreciating the currency; those with important cross-border interests, including foreign-currency debts, can strenuously oppose a depreciation. An impending election typically leads governments to postpone adjustment. While these factors certainly do not exhaust the sources of currency crises, they definitely appear to be part of the picture. Given the enormous social costs of currency crises, both scholars and policymakers might benefit from paying attention to them.

The Politics of Exchange Rates: Implications and Extensions

The previous chapters provide an empirical evaluation of the theoretical propositions put forth in chapter 1 about the expected policy preferences of economic groups in society. These investigations, however, also suggest a series of related observations— some of which harken back to points made in chapter 1—that are worth making explicit. These include the relationship between currency politics and the level of economic integration, trade policy, international cooperation, and economic development. After exploring some of the implications of my main results, in this chapter I address these broader questions.

Exchange Rate Politics in Perspective

As noted early on, the exchange rate is the most significant single price in any economy, as it affects all other prices. We have seen throughout this study how central exchange rates can be to national political debates. By the same token, the political economy of exchange rate policy is often emblematic of broader and deeper trends in national political economies. A national decision as to the exchange rate regime, in its starkest presentation, forces a choice between stability in cross-border economic exchange, on the one hand, and the ability to affect national monetary conditions, on the other. In many instances, this pits those favorable to integration into the world economy against those who would like to be protected from it. It is not surprising that the authoritarian autarkies of the 1930s, from Nazi Germany to the Soviet Union and all points in between, chose to shut their currencies, like their economies, off from the rest of the world. Nor is it surprising that one of the first successful cooperative measures among the Western democracies, after the shock of the first few years of the Great Depression faded, was the Tripartite Monetary Agreement of 1936, which eventually brought together most of the countries interested in reviving international economic activity. Neither is it coincidental that the attempts to restore an open world economy after World War II were centered around blueprints for a new, stable international monetary order.

To be sure, none of these relationships is pure or unproblematic, in particular because of the other dimension of currency policy: the level of the real exchange rate. For example, as discussed in detail above, a flexible (and depreciated) currency can give national producers a leg up in international competition, so that an interest in economic integration could be associated with a weak and flexible exchange rate. On this dimension, the level of the exchange rate can express a government's position on the trade-off between domestic consumers and domestic producers. A stronger real exchange rate helps national consumers by boosting purchasing power; a weaker one benefits national producers in home and foreign markets.

A government's exchange rate policies tell us a great deal about its priorities, both international and domestic. This is true in a broader perspective as well. These more general trends may not have been obvious in the previous, narrower chapters, but they do emerge if we consider both the historical and comparative context.

This chapter discusses some of the broad patterns of interest as a partial antidote to the narrower empirical implementations that have preceded it. It considers some general trends in the politics of exchange rates over the past 150 years and across a wide range of countries. It cannot but do this discursively and somewhat superficially. Nonetheless, the breadth of the comparisons may compensate for their lack of depth.

Globalization and Exchange Rate Policy

In chapter 1, I suggested that the exchange rate should be more politically contentious in open economies than in closed ones. This is for two reasons. First, in line with the trilemma, in financially open economies the choice of exchange rate regime directly implicates the influence of national monetary policy; in particular, a country with a fixed currency has given up its monetary independence and has to follow the monetary policy of the country to which its currency is fixed. Second, in an open economy, more economic agents are exposed to both currency volatility and the relative price effects of currency movements.

We can only assess this argument by comparing the politics of monetary and exchange rate policy in open and closed economies. Since economic openness—especially financial openness, which is of special relevance here—tends to ebb and flow at the global level as well as over long periods of time, the most relevant comparison is probably among eras, not between two countries at a point in time or one country over a relatively short time period. There are several ways, direct and indirect, to evaluate the evidence.[1]

In the first era of globalization, before 1914, the exchange rate regime—the gold standard—was controversial. The US experience is perhaps extreme, but similar battles were played out in many other countries. Debates raged even in the European core of the gold standard about whether to embrace gold and whether to stay on it—typically, with proponents victorious. On the system's "periphery" of commodity producers from the New World to eastern Europe, from Asia to

---

1 For a discussion of this in the US context, see Frieden 1996. For a more general exploration, see Frieden 2008.

Africa, similarly heated battles raged over the desirability of the gold standard—but here, opponents were more likely to win the debate.

These conflicts culminated with the collapse of the international gold standard in the early 1930s, as the world economy shut down (discussed in more detail below). Even after the Bretton Woods order was established in the 1940s and the world economy began reopening gradually, the degree of economic integration was limited enough that currency policy was largely uncontroversial. Domestic groups rarely questioned the Bretton Woods system of fixed yet adjustable rates— which is not surprising, since the arrangement rarely threatened the interests of many economic actors.

By the 1980s, however, currency policy had come back toward the center of economic policy debates. This is indicated by European developments and also by attempts at international monetary policy cooperation. Exchange rate politics has remained important since then.

More recent Latin American experience provides another illustration. In the relatively closed economies that prevailed in the region from the 1930s until the 1980s, currency policy was hardly ever the focus of much attention. The only exception was a brief period in the late 1970s and early 1980s, but this was in the context of the broader collapse of the region's reigning economic model along with the beginning of the region's lost decade of the 1980s. By 1990, as most of Latin America emerged from crisis into economic integration, the exchange rate was central to the region's policy debates. Chapter 6's narrative of the region's currency crises shows this to some extent. Similarly, the results in chapter 5 reinforce this point: manufacturing employment is strongly associated with more flexible exchange rates, but only when economies are relatively open.

The European process of monetary integration might also be invoked in this regard. As the region's economies became more tightly integrated on commercial and financial accounts, pressures for—and against—some form of monetary integration grew. Since the 1980s, in fact, monetary and exchange rate policy issues have been at the center of the region's political economy.

All this is reasonably strong evidence that the more open an economy is, the more politically controversial its currency policy is likely to be. This is probably true for the world as a whole: the more integrated the world (or a regional) economy is, the more currency policies are likely to be a topic of domestic and international political controversy. Inasmuch as this is the case and contemporary levels of globalization persist, we can expect currency policy to remain politically important and contentious. This does not necessarily lead to predictions about who will win these debates, and in fact the gold standard era of economic integration includes important instances in which progold forces were victorious, as well as cases in which they failed.

The End of the First Era of Globalization

The integrated world economy that prevailed from the 1870s until 1914, and that was more or less rebuilt by the early 1920s, collapsed definitively in the 1930s. There is by now widespread agreement that the reigning exchange rate regime, the interwar gold standard, played a major role in deepening, broadening, and lengthening the Great Depression.[2] The gold standard unraveled, thereby undermining international trade and payments. And as it came undone, some countries seriously delayed leaving gold, which made their economic decline much more severe. This raises three questions: How did the gold standard hold together for so long? Why did it fall apart? And why were some countries so much slower than others to delink from a dysfunctional monetary order?

The classical gold standard of the nineteenth and early twentieth century reflected, and relied on, the prevailing political economies of the major powers of the time.[3] In particular, it was predicated on a broad consensus among elites that the preservation of an integrated world economy was crucial, and that, in general, national economies could and should adapt themselves to the requirements of the global economy rather than the other way around. This was implicit in the operation of the "rules" of the gold standard, by which a national economy facing macroeconomic imbalances would be driven back toward balance—even if this involved recession and deflation. We saw the operation of this expectation in the US case, in which supporters of the gold standard insisted on deflationary policies in the 1860s and 1870s,

---

2 For the classic statements, see Bernanke and James 1991; Eichengreen 1992. See also Frieden 1993.

3 Again, the presentation here follows closely Eichengreen 1992. See also the treatment in Frieden 2006, 173–250; Frieden 1993.

and on not pursuing expansionary policies in the face of the depression of the early 1890s.

How was it possible for national governments to sustain an exchange rate regime that took such a single-minded, often brutal approach to the trilemma, subordinating national concerns to the requirements of the gold standard? For one thing, the economies of the nineteenth century were flexible enough—characterized as they were by family firms and farms, and without organized labor—that prices and wages could in fact be pushed down rapidly.

The approach taken here spotlights the political economy of gold, especially the sources of support for and opposition to a nation's adherence to the gold standard. We saw in the United States how the internationally connected commercial and financial sectors were able to defeat their opponents—although with difficulty. Elsewhere in the advanced industrialized world the battles were less fierce and more easily won by gold supporters. One reason was the general predominance of financial, commercial, and industrial elites whose fortunes were closely tied to the world economy. Recall that the United States was unusual in having *both* a thriving industrial economy and dynamic commodity-exporting economy within its borders. There were farmers in western Europe, and many of them opposed gold, but they were relatively insignificant compared to the leading industrial, commercial, and financial sectors. Perhaps more important, few of the leading gold standard countries were democratic, and even those that were democratic were only imperfectly so. This meant that the principal victims of gold standard austerity were either entirely absent from or only weakly represented in national political systems.

By the 1920s, the political economies of the major financial centers had changed, and these shifts had powerful effects on the currency regime. Large national and international corporations, frequently with oligopolistic characteristics, increasingly dominated the economies themselves. Labor was increasingly organized in powerful unions. This meant that neither prices nor wages were so flexible, which fundamentally undercut the gold standard adjustment mechanism. Furthermore, the prevailing political systems had changed utterly. Now the urban middle and working classes as well as poor farmers were well represented in politics; indeed, socialist parties were the largest ones in many countries and were often in government. This made it impossible to simply shunt the adjustment burden onto those who had previously borne most of it: the working and middle classes along with the farmers. Profound transformations in the political economies of the developed nations so weakened the bases of support for the gold standard that it could not withstand the economic downturn that began in 1929.

Why, then, did some countries take so long to leave gold? It is generally accepted that those countries that went off the gold standard recovered more quickly.[4] Again, the approach here would suggest looking at those who stood to gain the most from a depreciation and those who stood to lose the most from abandoning gold—exporters and import competers in the first case, and international financial institutions and investors in the second. Beth Simmons (1994) has explored the issue, but there is certainly much more work to be done before we understand the political economy of the period and the answer to this third question.

Trade and Exchange Rate Policy

One of the reasons that currencies are more controversial in an open economy than in a closed one is because of their impact on and interaction with trade policy. A 10 percent devaluation is equivalent to a 10 percent tariff and a 10 percent export subsidy, and the substitutability of trade and exchange rate policy indicates that they will be tightly linked in political debates. This can be seen in several ways.

First, the potential for exchange rate policy to substitute for trade policy means that as governments reduce trade barriers they are likely to find themselves under greater pressure to manipulate exchange rates instead. After all, the removal of one policy instrument does not remove the political pressures previously exerted on policymakers. This is seen in many studies of individual countries that have undertaken trade liberalization, in which political pressures on the exchange rate rise dramatically as trade barriers are removed.[5]

Second, and closely related to this experience, is the broader sense that the willingness and political ability of countries to reduce trade barriers among themselves is challenged by the use of active exchange rate policy. A government that has agreed to reduce trade protection

---

4 For the pioneering statement, see Eichengreen and Sachs 1985.
5 See, for example, Frieden and Stein 2001.

with a partner is unlikely to look favorably on the partner's engineering a substantial devaluation that leads to a major import surge. We saw that Mercosur was nearly subverted by the Brazilian devaluation of 1999, which in fact led to substantial emergency protective measures on Argentina's part. It seems that flexible exchange rates may challenge attempts to sustain bilateral or regional trade agreements. While the NAFTA and Mercosur experiences hardly point to so definitive a conclusion, they also demonstrate how large-scale currency movements can threaten commercial ties.

Understanding the Euro

Most economic commentary on the euro has concentrated on the generally accepted fact that the eurozone did not constitute an OCA when it was created and does not constitute one now.[6] When looked at in this light, it is hard to see why the EMU happened at all. Certainly, the economic analysis of currency areas provides valuable insights into the underlying weaknesses of the euro, as seen in the crisis that erupted in 2007 and as discussed in chapter 4. But the purely economic approach is left with a puzzle, for it clearly does not go far in explaining why these countries created a common currency.

In the absence of purely economic arguments for currency union, many analysts have defaulted to purely political explanations: the EMU was a "trade" for German unification, a counterbalance to US monetary power, and an exercise in ideological fervor.[7] The notion underlying these explanations is that the principal alternative to a purely economic source of the EMU is a purely political source.

A *political economy* approach can in fact explain the EMU. As examined in chapter 4 and throughout this book, there are clear political economy connections between commercial and financial ties, on the one hand, and exchange rate policy, on the other. In countries that have eliminated trade barriers among themselves, depreciations can be expected to give rise to protests from affected groups in other countries. This was seen, as mentioned, in Mercosur in 1999. It was also apparent in the European Union. With the completion of the single market,

6　For a useful compendium and assessment, see Jonung and Drea 2010.
7　See, for example, Garrett 2001; McNamara 1998.

member governments needed to avoid competitive depreciations. Again, there is no purely economic, aggregate welfare assertion along these lines: a trading partner's depreciation is an economic benefit, not a cost, providing consumers with cheaper goods. But from a *political economy* standpoint, as example after example makes clear in this study, a trading partner's depreciation almost always gives rise to powerful protectionist pressures. And in the case of the European Union, such protectionist pressures would threaten the very foundation of the single market.

Indeed, many in northern Europe interpreted the various rounds of devaluations that occurred in 1992–93 as unfair attempts to gain competitive advantage for national producers. There were even threats of emergency protective measures, especially in France. In this context, many northern European producers felt that drawing such countries as Italy and Spain into the euro was necessary to avoid further competitive depreciations. The European experience in fact is read by some to imply that commercial integration requires monetary integration— again, not for purely economic reasons but instead for political economy ones.

Evaluations of the euro, then, should take the appropriate alternatives into account. The purely economic view misses many of the crucial points. A single market for goods and capital *without* monetary integration would almost certainly have given rise to powerful political pressures that could have threatened European integration more generally. Conversely, there was evidence that currency union would accelerate economic integration more broadly and help create further constituencies in favor of a continuation of the process. This is not to say that the euro was a good idea or a bad one; it is only to hold that it has to be evaluated—and explained—in political economy terms, not just economic ones. And this fact may have implications beyond Europe—indeed for international economic cooperation more generally.

Macro Is the New Trade

For most of the postwar period, the focus on attempts to increase economic ties among countries was on reducing trade barriers. Accordingly, the most strenuous efforts to encourage cooperation among governments were in the commercial realm, whether under the auspices of the General Agreement on Tariffs and Trade and the World Trade Organization, or in bilateral and multilateral trading agreements. There were some attempts to reduce barriers to capital movements, especially among developed countries, but these were never so controversial and therefore rarely required any particular interstate coordination.

For decades, neither scholars nor politicians have shown much enthusiasm for coordination in macroeconomic, especially monetary, policies. There has been a long-standing academic view that the benefits of international monetary policy coordination are limited: individual countries have every incentive to adopt the appropriate national policies, and little is gained by attempting to coordinate. One prominent macroeconomist was categorical: "A solution can only consist in each individual country's keeping its own house in order and maintaining a stable domestic price level."[8] In practice, virtually the only potential success of international monetary policy cooperation was the Plaza Accord of 1985.[9] And even then, the agreement had clear political economy roots: the soaring dollar had given rise to the strongest protectionist pressures in postwar US history. But more recent experiences have suggested that the run-up to the Plaza Accord was no fluke, and that in a globalized economy, monetary policy cooperation actually may be both desirable and even necessary.

In fact, one country's exchange rate policy may impose what we could call political economy externalities on other countries. The most common example would be of a currency purposely kept weak for competitive reasons. When one government acts to maintain a depreciated real exchange rate, the result is often an upsurge of protectionist measures in its trading partners. This in turn can lead to commercial conflicts and even trade wars. One study found, for example, that a 10 percent real appreciation of the dollar was associated with a greater than 25 percent increase in antidumping complaints in the United States, and that a standard deviation appreciation of the Argentine peso increased antidumping filings in Argentina by nearly one-third.[10] The fact that national currency policies can exacerbate conflict on other dimensions means that coordination on exchange rate policy could be Pareto improving.

8 Siebert 1999, 146.
9 Funabashi 1988.
10 Broz and Frieden 2013, 84–85. See also Frieden 2009; Frieden et al. 2012.

The implication is that there may be both normative reasons and political pressures for governments to work together to arrive at a common approach to currency policies. Seventy years of trade liberalization have almost eliminated trade barriers among developed countries, and most developing countries have been following suit. While there are still important international commercial issues, both theory and history suggest that this second era of globalization may resemble the first in the centrality of international interactions over macroeconomic policy, specifically with respect to international monetary relations.

Development and Exchange Rate Policy

The experience of the past fifty years is a strong argument for development strategies that encourage national firms to export into world markets. The precise mechanisms by which export promotion stimulates growth remain controversial: they may involve developing the expertise to tap foreign markets, pressures to adapt the latest technologies or quality standards, or something else. Nonetheless, the examples of a string of East Asian (and some other) countries leaves little question that export promotion has been more successful than import substitution.

Exchange rate policy is typically a critical component of export promotion: most successful export-promoting experiences have involved government policies that keep the exchange rate artificially weak. Indeed, many development experts regard a realistic, even depreciated currency as a powerful stimulant to economic growth more generally.[11] Certainly the opposite—strongly appreciated (overvalued) real exchange rates—have a bad track record. They are associated with stop-and-go, crisis-ridden, and generally stagnant development experiences, especially in Latin America.

This raises an analytic question: Why do some governments seem strongly inclined to keep the real exchange rate depreciated, while others seem to want it appreciated? Even if we do not accept that a depreciated real exchange rate is superior for developmental performance, it seems that some countries—even regions—tend to have depreciated currencies even as others have appreciated ones. Again, the East Asia–Latin America comparison is obvious: East Asian countries have

11 For one powerful statement, see Rodrik 2008.

tended to have realistic or depreciated currencies, while Latin American countries have tended to have overvalued currencies.[12]

The analyses in the preceding chapters, particularly those devoted to Latin America, help explain these cross-national (and cross-regional) differences. Recall that the main source of pressure for a weaker exchange rate is typically tradables producers; the sources of pressure for a stronger exchange rate are cross-border financial and investing interests, consumers, and foreign-currency debtors. In the East Asia–Latin America comparison, two broad differences suggest themselves. East Asian countries have tended to be more authoritarian than Latin American ones and have shown little concern for consumers. In the Latin American democracies, urban consumers have typically been politically crucial; even when there have been authoritarian regimes in Latin America, they have generally been careful to try to keep urban middle-class consumers happy. By the same token, the East Asian development strategy has relied on manufactured exporters, often promoting their activities and frequently subsidizing their production.

The archetypical East Asian political economy can be thought of as one dominated by powerful export-oriented manufacturing firms, usually large conglomerates, in which consumers have little role. The typical Latin American political economy is much more domestically oriented, and the urban middle and working classes have a great deal more political power. These are exaggerated stereotypes, of course, but there appears to be something to them. China and Brazil, as the two giants of the two regions, come close to fitting these stereotypes. Certainly consumers are not irrelevant to the Chinese government, and large export manufacturers are not irrelevant to the Brazilian government. It seems apparent, however, that the Chinese regime puts greater weight on export manufacturing than on consumption, while successive Brazilian governments have had to pay a great deal of attention to the concerns of urban consumers.

There are obvious macroeconomic concomitants to the East Asia–Latin America comparison as well. The East Asian tendency to restrain domestic wages and consumption as well as to provide a minimal social safety net tends to raise the savings rate: corporations save to invest out of profits, and households save for emergencies and for retirement.

12 For an early observation of this and attempt to explain it, see Sachs 1985.

High savings rates in turn reduce the propensity to attract large-scale capital inflows that can appreciate the currency and create a group of foreign-currency debtors. On the other hand, the Latin American propensity to encourage consumption and support for populist spending policies lowered the savings rate yet raised the inflation rate. Scarce domestic savings encouraged foreign borrowing and subsequent real appreciations, exacerbated by chronic inflation. Many analysts regard the resultant real exchange rates—weak in East Asia and strong in Latin America—as an unintended consequence of other macroeconomic trends. Still, as some of the Latin American cases discussed here make clear, the national political economies clearly permitted and even encouraged these divergent strategies. Exchange rate policy was not an afterthought; it was central to the development policies.

Might the changing nature of developing societies affect the political economy of their exchange rate policies? As East Asian societies develop, their urban middle and working classes grow, and their political influence is likely to grow apace. This is certainly the case for those countries that democratize, but it is also likely to be the case even for authoritarian regimes that cannot afford to ignore the concerns of growing urban populations. Similarly, Latin American governments have had to pay more attention to the concerns of their export producers—a major change from the years of import substitution. Whether the export producers in question are Colombian coffee growers, Chilean fruit farmers, or Brazilian and Mexican manufacturers, Latin American governments cannot afford to ignore the impact of appreciated exchange rates on increasingly important segments of their economies.

The China Syndrome

China's exchange rate policy has been the most politically contentious national currency policy for years.[13] There is little question that the Chinese government has purposely kept the renminbi artificially weak at least since the early 1990s, and that this has played a major role in stimulating China's manufactured exports to the rest of the world.

---

13 For an influential set of studies, see Goldstein and Lardy 2007.

Many producers in North America and Europe see the weak renminbi as one of the more important sources of distress in developed-country industries. Studies have suggested that Chinese imports, heavily promoted by the weak currency, have had substantial effects on labor market conditions in the United States.[14] This has led to insistent demands that China reduce the currency's undervaluation and permit it to appreciate.

There is substantial foreign pressure on China to allow its currency to rise in value; in purely economic terms, this would offer great benefits to the country, as it would raise the national purchasing power. After all, an appreciation of the renminbi would improve the country's terms of trade and make it cheaper to obtain the raw materials that the country imports in huge quantities. Why, then, has there been so much Chinese resistance to a stronger currency?

A political economy analysis helps explain why the Chinese government resists a stronger currency. Since 1979, the country's economic and social order has been constructed around the export-led development model. The principal beneficiaries of the manufactured-export drive, especially the major industrial zones in the coastal regions, have not only been at the center of Chinese economic development, but they also have dominated the country's politics. Although Chinese domestic politics is opaque, there is strong evidence that exchange rate policy has been highly political.[15] The exporters who have benefited so much from the weak exchange rate are politically powerful; Chinese consumers are politically weak.

Certainly a confluence of domestic and international pressures—both economic and political—can and will bring about a policy evolution. The Chinese government is not oblivious to the potential sociopolitical impact of suppressing consumption, including by an artificially weak currency, nor is it immune to foreign pressure. At the same time, economic trends over time make it harder and harder to sustain the weak renminbi. All these push in the direction of a strengthening of the currency. Nonetheless, we could never understand Chinese currency policy without a clear picture of the political pressures on Chinese policymakers.

14 Autor, Dorn, and Hanson 2013.
15 See, for example, Steinberg and Shih 2012.

The Exchange Rate as Residual?

Discussions of currency policy rarely *start* with political economy considerations, especially among policymakers. They should. To be sure, a currency's value responds to many forces, which raises a variety of objections to a focus on political economy. For one, there is the question of whether we should interpret observed currency outcomes as the result of purposive government policy. A restrictive monetary policy aimed at reducing inflation raises interest rates, attracts foreign capital, and drives up the real exchange rate (if the currency is fixed) or nominal exchange rate (if it is not). An expansionary fiscal policy, similarly, draws in foreign funds and drives up the real and/or nominal exchange rate. In these instances, one might argue, the movement of the exchange rate is an unintended consequence of another set of policies; we should concentrate on explaining *those* tools, not currency policy. Instead, in this study, I have simply assumed that whatever currency value we observe is the result of an intentional effort on the government's part. But currency values are notorious for moving in unexpected ways. What if the government did not intend the exchange rate to end up where it did? Then trying to explain exchange rate policy on the basis of the currency's observed value might be misplaced.

There are two ways to address this concern. The first is to note that it applies only to the actual *level* of the exchange rate rather than the regime. Governments typically make explicit their currency regime, although they also sometimes deviate from their statements.[16] Yet we can be quite confident that the choice of regime is intentional. That is not the case with the currency's value, however.

In the case of the observed exchange rate, it is of course true that there are many factors that influence currency movements. Changes in the terms of trade, foreign economic conditions, and trends on international capital markets—all these and more can eventually profoundly affect the real or nominal exchange rate. This is simply to say that an emphasis on the exchange rate as a policy instrument in isolation is an exercise in partial equilibrium analysis. But in this the exchange rate is hardly alone; virtually every macroeconomic trend has many sources,

---

16 Alesina and Wagner 2006; Guisinger and Singer 2010.

and we certainly would like to be able to explain *all* aspects of national macroeconomic policy simultaneously, in general equilibrium. We are nonetheless far from being able to do this, and so a partial equilibrium approach seems a reasonable starting point.

In addition, I would challenge the notion that the exchange rate can be regarded as a residual result of other policies. Not to intervene to affect the currency is also a policy choice, after all, and when we observe a currency movement that *could* have been affected by government policy, it is reasonable to infer that at the margin the government either wanted that movement or was unwilling to act to forestall it. This is analogous to other macroeconomic policies. When oil prices skyrocket, domestic inflation may rise, but only if the monetary authorities are willing to allow it to do so—that is, if they are (perhaps wisely) unwilling to apply restrictive policies to avoid inflation. When a recession causes an increase in the budget deficit, this is because the government (perhaps wisely) is unwilling to respond to the recession with fiscal austerity.

The exchange rate is, similarly, always an implicit or explicit policy variable. If a central bank raises its policy interest rate and the currency appreciates as a result, this can be taken to mean that the central bank either wants the exchange rate to appreciate or cares less about the appreciation than it does about the domestic effects of the interest rate increase. Either way, it has made an implicit or explicit choice as to currency policy. If a country experiences a resource discovery or borrowing boom that drives up its real or nominal exchange rate, the government always has alternative responses: it could sterilize the capital inflow, expand foreign-currency reserves, tax foreign borrowing, or do any number of things to address the appreciation. If it does not, it has made a decision. A policy *not* to intervene is, after all, a policy.

Certainly it would be desirable to have a fully formed, general equilibrium model of all macroeconomic policies, including those toward the exchange rate. But we are far from that. In the meantime, it is instructive and valuable to examine policies that indirectly or directly affect the currency, and to assume—with much justification—that their impact on the currency is in line with the government's preferences, or at least that the government is unwilling to do what would be necessary to counteract the outcome.

Understanding Exchange Rate Policy

All these considerations highlight the great importance of understanding the sources of national currency policy. In a world that is ever more tightly economically integrated, we can expect exchange rates to be increasingly key instruments of policy and sources of political conflict. As world trade grows, its relationship to currency policies will become ever more complex and critical. As developing countries strive to catch up with the advanced economies—and with the more successful emerging markets—their exchange rate policies will be important tools in their arsenals.

Currency policies are central to today's globalized world. This highlights the significance of scholarly attempts to understand and explain national decisions about the exchange rate regime and level. This study has suggested a series of factors that influence the making of exchange rate policy. It emphasizes the role of economic interests and of broader macroeconomic considerations. There are certainly other forces that are at play in discussions of exchange rate policy that have not been assessed here.

One consideration that deserves more explicit attention is strategic interaction among countries. This has been central to the process of European monetary integration, but my analysis did not provide a systematic interpretation of the strategic component of the path to the EMU. This would require a much more complex and complete exploration of the role of various governments, their potential choices, and how they interacted with one another.[17] One obvious implication of a focus on strategic interaction is that governments may be driven to particular exchange rate policies by the policies of the countries with which they are competing for trade or investment.[18] In this case, it would be hard to explain national policy solely on the basis of domestic political economy developments alone.

Some explanations might move even further from economic or political economy motivations to stress that governments learn from, or

---

[17] In an earlier work (Frieden 2004), I considered the trade-offs involved generally in delegating national decision making to an EU-wide agency. The argument made in this article is easily applicable to the EMU, but its application would require substantial additional information and analysis.

[18] For clear and convincing findings in this regard, see Simmons 2000; Simmons and Elkins 2004.

imitate, other governments they regard as successful. By the same token, economic advice—whether from foreign advisers, international organizations, or national experts—can have a powerful impact on the policy agenda and how it is decided.[19]

It is also often suggested that nationalistic or other culturally determined sentiments enter into decisions about exchange rate policy. This was a common observation in the course of European monetary integrations—Germans were attached to their DM, and Italians were not attached to their lira—and extends to common assertions that associate a strong currency with a strong country. These are undoubtedly powerful forces, although they seem to vary among countries: just as many nations might see the currency's value as a symbol of their prestige, East Asian exporters seem strongly favorable to keeping their currencies relatively weak.

All these forces and more are at play in determining national exchange rate policy, and eventually in shaping both regional and international monetary orders. They deserve continued and enhanced study from scholars.

Conclusions

Exchange rate policy plays a central part in a country's relationship with the rest of the world economy. It affects and is affected by every aspect of a nation's international economic interactions. A government's exchange rate policy, in turn, both reflects and is determined by the country's social as well as political structures and relations. The political economy of exchange rates not only helps us explain a government policy that is increasingly important in today's globalized economy; it also provides powerful insights into a host of economic and political decisions and processes at the domestic and international levels.

---

19 For a detailed assessment of this process related to the role of US-trained economists in Latin America, see Biglaiser 2002.

Conclusions

E xchange rate policy is crucial to the international economy. Economic analysts recognize this, and recognize that currency policy is highly political, but their analyses typically focus on purely economic considerations, judging macroeconomic policy from the standpoint of a "representative agent." However, politics is not made by representative agents but rather by representatives of powerful groups in society, of voters, or of political parties. A full understanding of currency policy must take these powerful political pressures into account—and even purely economic analyses would benefit from a recognition of their significance.

This book makes a simple theoretical argument about the distributional implications of exchange rate policy. I suggest that economic actors with important cross-border interests, exposed to currency volatility, will tend to prefer more stable and predictable exchange rates. I also claim that tradables producers will, all else being equal, tend to prefer a depreciated real exchange rate. These concerns will be tempered by the extent of exchange rate pass-through—that is, the degree to which currency movements affect domestic prices.

I have applied this reasoning to a series of highly varied currency experiences. I start with an analysis of the contentious US politics of the gold standard. The first episode in this saga was the battle over whether and how to return to gold after the American Civil War ended, which went on from 1865 until 1879. The second episode was the resurgence of antigold sentiment in the 1890s. I correlated the economic characteristics of the constituencies of members of Congress with their voting behavior on major currency policy legislation. Partisan and other political considerations were always critical and make a "clean" evaluation of economic interests difficult. Nonetheless, it seems that most tradables producers were particularly hostile to the gold standard, which would have stymied the ability to depreciate the dollar. This was especially true for manufacturers facing significant import competition, such as Pennsylvania's iron producers. By the 1890s, with prohibitive trade protection in place, they were indifferent to or supportive of gold. But farmers, especially those producing tradable farm products, were strongly opposed to gold. I found no support for the received wisdom about debt as motivating opposition to the gold standard.

I next turned to the decades-long process of European monetary integration, which eventually led to the creation of the euro. Different European countries demonstrated different levels of willingness and ability to stabilize their currencies, in particular against the DM, and ultimately to join the eurozone. In this instance, I found that countries whose manufactured exports were more oriented toward markets in Germany and its near neighbors were more likely to successfully stabilize their currencies with that of Germany. I also discovered that countries facing an import surge were less likely to bind their exchange rates and more likely to allow their currencies to depreciate, which is consistent with the expectation that tradables producers will oppose a fixed rate in order to maintain the ability to devalue the currency and improve their competitive position.

Latin America has an extraordinarily varied history of currency policies, and its economic fortunes have often been linked to the success or failure of its exchange rate policies. An analysis of nearly fifty years of Latin American exchange rate policies led to a number of conclusions. Some are with respect to the choice of exchange rate regime. First, countries with economies more open to trade—hence with, presumably, more economic agents exposed to exchange rate volatility—tend to have more stable or fixed exchange rates. Second, countries with larger manufacturing sectors tend to have more flexible exchange rates, which permit currency depreciation—but only when they are relatively open. That is, manufacturers' desire for depreciation is not present in highly protected economies, such as those pursuing ISI. I then examined the impact of electoral considerations. This demonstrates that governments tend to permit or encourage an appreciation of the currency before an election, likely to increase the purchasing power of potential voters. Further analysis indicates that for similar reasons, governments tend to delay going off a peg until after an election, but depreciate strongly in an election's aftermath.

These results, across time and space, give credence to my principal theoretical arguments. Countries whose economic agents are more involved in cross-border trade are more likely to fix their exchange rates in order to reduce currency volatility. Countries with large groups susceptible to import or export competition—import-competing manufacturers and export farmers—are more likely to choose flexible exchange rates that allow currency depreciations. Governments facing an election encourage or allow currency appreciation that increases the purchasing power of consumers.

There are many other factors that affect currency policy, such as trends on international markets, the policies of trading and financial partners, regional agreements, bureaucratic preferences, and more. Still, this study makes a case for paying systematic attention to the distributional impact of exchange rate regimes and exchange rate levels, and the consequences of this impact on the politics of currency policy.

REFERENCES

Aizenman, Joshua, Menzie Chinn, and Hiro Ito. 2010. "The Emerging Global Financial Architecture: Tracing and Evaluating the New Patterns of the Trilemma's Configurations." *Journal of International Money and Finance* 29 (4): 615–41.

Alesina, Alberto. 1989. "Politics and Business Cycles in Industrial Democracies." *Economic Policy* 8: 57–98.

Alesina, Alberto, and Andrea Stella. 2011. "The Politics of Monetary Policy." In *Handbook of Monetary Economics*, edited by Benjamin Friedman and Michael Woodford, 3: 1000–1054. Amsterdam: North-Holland.

Alesina, Alberto, and Alexander Wagner. 2006. "Choosing (and Reneging on) Exchange Rate Regimes." *Journal of the European Economic Association* 4: 770–99.

Alfaro, Laura. 2002. "On the Political Economy of Temporary Stabilization Programs." *Economics and Politics* 14 (2): 133–61.

Alogoskoufis, George. 1990. "Traded Goods, Competitiveness, and Aggregate Fluctuations in the United Kingdom." *Economic Journal* 100 (March): 141–63.

Anderton, Bob. 2003. "Extra-Euro Area Manufacturing Import Prices and Exchange Rate Pass-Through." Working paper 219. Frankfurt: European Central Bank.

Autor, David, David Dorn, and Gordon H. Hanson. 2013. "The China Syndrome: Local Labor Market Effects of Import Competition in the United States." *American Economic Review* 103 (6): 2121–68.

Bacchetta, Philippe, and Eric van Wincoop. 2005. "A Theory of the Currency Denomination of International Trade." *Journal of International Economics* 67 (2): 295–319.

Barnhart, John. 1925. "Rainfall and the Populist Party in Nebraska." *American Political Science Review* 19 (3): 527–40.

Barrett, Don C. 1931. *The Greenbacks and the Resumption of Specie Payments, 1862–1879.* Cambridge, MA: Harvard University Press.

Bauchard, Philippe. 1986. *La guerre des deux roses: Du rêve à la réalité, 1981–1985.* Paris: Bernard Grasset.

Bayoumi, Tamim, and Barry Eichengreen. 1993. "Shocking Aspects of European Monetary Unification." In *Adjustment and Growth in the European Monetary Union*, edited by Francisco Torres and Francesco Giavazzi, 193–240. Cambridge: Cambridge University Press.

Bearce, David. 2003. "Societal Principals, Partisan Agents, and Monetary Policy Outcomes." *International Organization* 57 (2): 373–410.

———. 2008. "Not Complements, but Substitutes: Fixed Exchange Rate Commitments, Central Bank Independence, and External Currency Stability." *International Studies Quarterly* 52 (4): 807–24.

Bearce, David, and Mark Hallerberg. 2011. "Democracy and De Facto Exchange Rate Regimes." *Economics and Politics* 23 (2): 172–94.

Bensel, Richard. 2000. *The Political Economy of American Industrialization, 1877–1900.* Cambridge: Cambridge University Press.

Bernanke, Ben, and Harold James. 1991. "The Gold Standard, Deflation, and Financial Crisis in the Great Depression: An International Comparison." In *Financial Markets and Financial Crises*, edited by R. Glenn Hubbard, 33–68. Chicago: University of Chicago Press.

Bernhard, William, Lawrence Broz, and William Clark. 2002. "The Political Economy of Monetary Institutions: An Introduction." *International Organization* 56 (4): 693–723.

———, eds. 2003. *The Political Economy of Monetary Institutions.* Cambridge, MA: MIT Press.

Bernhard, William, and David Leblang. 1999. "Democratic Institutions and Exchange Rate Commitments." *International Organization* 53 (1): 71–97.

Besnard, Denis, and Michel Redon. 1985. *La monnaie: Politique et institutions.* Paris: Dunod.

Bhalla, Surjit S. 2012. *Devaluing to Prosperity: Misaligned Currencies and Their Growth Consequences.* Washington, DC: Peterson Institute.

Biglaiser, Glen. 2002. *Guardians of the Nation? Economists, Generals, and Economic Reform in Latin America.* Notre Dame, IN: University of Notre Dame Press.

Blackburn, Keith, and Michael Christensen. 1989. "Macroeconomic Policy and Policy Credibility: Theories and Evidence." *Journal of Economic Literature* 27 (1): 1–45.

Blomberg, S. Brock, Jeffry A. Frieden, and Ernesto Stein. 2005. "Sustaining Fixed Rates: The Political Economy of Currency Pegs in Latin America." *Journal of Applied Economics* 8 (2): 203–25.

Bodea, Cristina. 2010. "Exchange Rate Regimes and Independent Central Banks: A Correlated Choice of Imperfectly Credible Institutions." *International Organization* 64 (3): 411–42.

Bodnar, Gordon, and William Gentry. 1993. "Exchange Rate Exposure and Industry Characteristics: Evidence from Canada, Japan, and the USA." *Journal of International Money and Finance* 12:29–45.

Bonomo, Marco, and Maria Cristina Terra. 2001. "The Dilemma of Inflation vs. Balance of Payments: Crawling Pegs in Brazil, 1964–98." In *The Currency Game: Exchange Rate Politics in Latin America*, edited by Jeffry A. Frieden and Ernesto Stein, 119–55. Baltimore: Johns Hopkins University Press.

———. 2005. "Elections and Exchange Rate Policy Cycles." *Economics and Politics* 17 (2): 151–76.

Bordo, Michael, and Barry Eichengreen, eds. 1993. *A Retrospective on the Bretton Woods System.* Chicago: University of Chicago Press.

Bordo, Michael, and Finn Kydland. 1995. "The Gold Standard as a Rule: An Essay in Exploration." *Explorations in Economic History* 32: 423–64.

Bordo, Michael, and Hugh Rockoff. 1996. "The Gold Standard as a 'Good Housekeeping Seal of Approval.'" *Journal of Economic History* 56 (3): 389–428.

Bowman, John D. 1965. "Economic Analysis of Midwestern Farm Land Values and Farm Land Income, 1860 to 1900." *Yale Economic Essays* 5 (2): 317–52.

Bowman, John, and Richard Keehn. 1974. "Agricultural Terms of Trade in Four Midwestern States, 1870–1900." *Journal of Economic History* 34: 592–609.

Branson, William, and James Love. 1988. "U.S. Manufacturing and the Real Exchange Rate." In *Misalignment of Exchange Rates: Effects on Trade and Industry*, edited by Richard C. Martson, 241–70. Chicago: University of Chicago Press.

Broz, J. Lawrence. 2002. "Political System Transparency and Monetary Commitment Regimes." *International Organization* 56 (4): 863–89.

Broz, J. Lawrence, and Jeffry A. Frieden. 2001. "The Political Economy of International Monetary Relations." *Annual Review of Political Science* 4 (1): 317–43.

———. 2006. "The Political Economy of Exchange Rates." In *The Oxford Handbook of Political Economy*, edited by Barry Weingast and Donald Wittman, 587–97. New York: Oxford University Press.

———. 2013. "The Political Economy of International Monetary Policy Coordination." In *Handbook of Safeguarding Global Financial Stability*, edited by Gerard Caprio, 81–91. London: Elsevier.

Broz, J. Lawrence, Jeffry A. Frieden, and Stephen Weymouth. 2008. "Exchange-Rate Policy Attitudes: Direct Evidence from Survey Data." *IMF Staff Papers* 55 (3): 417–44.

Brun-Aguerre, Raphael, Ana-Maria Fuertes, and Matthew Greenwood-Nimmo. 2013. "Heads I Win, Tails You Lose: New Evidence of Long-Run Asymmetry in Exchange Rate Pass-Through by Exporting Firms." Working paper. Melbourne, Australia.

Burstein, Ariel, and Gita Gopinath. 2014. "International Prices and Exchange Rates." In *Handbook of International Economics*, edited by Gita Gopinath, Elhanan Helpman, and Kenneth S. Rogoff, 4: 391–452. New York: North-Holland.

Calomiris, Charles. 1988. "Prices and Exchange Rate Determination during the Greenback Suspension." *Oxford Economic Papers*, new series 40 (4): 719–50.

Calvo, Guillermo, and Carmen Reinhart. 2002. "Fear of Floating." *Quarterly Journal of Economics* 117 (2): 379–408.

Cameron, David. 1992. "The Franc, the EMS, Rigueur, and 'l'Autre Politique': The Regime-Defining Choices of the Mitterrand Presidency." Unpublished paper, New Haven, CT.

Campa, José, and Linda Goldberg. 1995. "Investment in Manufacturing, Exchange Rates, and External Exposure." *Journal of International Economics* 38: 297–320.

———. 1999. "Investment, Pass-Through, and Exchange Rates: A Cross-Country Comparison." *International Economic Review* 40 (2): 287–314.

———. 2005. "Exchange Rate Pass-Through into Import Prices." *Review of Economics and Statistics* 87:679–90.

Canzoneri, Matthew, and Carol Ann Rogers. 1990. "Is the European Community an

Optimal Currency Area? Optimal Taxation versus the Cost of Multiple Currencies." *American Economic Review* 80 (3): 419–33.

Caranza, Cesare, and Antonio Fazio. 1983. "L'evoluzione dei metodi di controllo monetario in Italia: 1974–1983." *Bancaria* (September): 819–33.

Chinn, Menzie, and Jeffry A. Frieden. 2012. "The Eurozone in Crisis: Origins and Prospects." La Follette Policy Report 21, no. 2 (Spring): 1–5.

Clarida, Richard, and Jordi Gali. 1994. "Sources of Real Exchange Rate Fluctuations: How Important Are Nominal Shocks?" NBER working paper no. 4658. Cambridge, MA: National Bureau of Economic Research.

Coffey, Peter. 1987. *The European Monetary System—Past, Present, and Future*. Amsterdam: Kluwer.

Cohen, Benjamin J. 1977. *Organizing the World's Money: The Political Economy of International Monetary Relations*. New York: Basic Books.

———. 1994. "Beyond EMU: The Problem of Sustainability." In *The Political Economy of European Monetary Unification*, edited by Barry Eichengreen and Jeffry A. Frieden, 179–96. Boulder, CO: Westview Press.

Copelovitch, Mark S., and Jon Pevehouse. 2013. "Ties That Bind? Preferential Trade Agreements and Exchange Rate Policy Choice." *International Studies Quarterly* 57 (2): 385–99.

Corden, Max. 2002. *Too Sensational: On the Choice of Exchange Rate Regimes*. Cambridge, MA: MIT Press.

Croly, Herbert D. 1912. *Marcus Alonzo Hanna*. New York: Macmillan.

Cukierman, Alex, Steven Webb, and Bilin Neyapti. 1992. "Measuring the Independence of Central Banks and Its Effect on Policy Outcomes." *World Bank Economic Review* 4: 353–98.

Cumby, Robert, and Maurice Obstfeld. 1984. "International Interest-Rate and Price-Level Linkages under Flexible Exchange Rates: A Review of Recent Evidence." In *Exchange Rate Theory and Practice*, edited by John F. O. Bilson and Richard C. Marston, 121–52. Chicago: University of Chicago Press.

Dam, Kenneth W. 1981. "The Legal Tender Cases." *Supreme Court Review*, 367–412.

Darvas, Zsolt. 2012. "Real Effective Exchange Rates for 178 Countries: A New Database." Bruegel working paper 2012/06, March 15.

de Carvalho Filho, Irineu, and Marcos Chamon. 2008. "A Micro-Empirical Foundation for the Political Economy of Exchange Rate Populism." *IMF Staff Papers* 55 (3): 481–510.

De Grauwe, Paul. 1988. Exchange rate variability and the slowdown in growth of international trade. *IMF Staff Papers* 35: 63–84.

De Grauwe, Paul, and Wim Vanhaverbeke. 1993. "Is Europe an Optimum Currency Area? Evidence from Regional Data." In *Policy Issues in the Operation of Currency Unions*, edited by Paul Masson and Mark Taylor, 111–29. Cambridge: Cambridge University Press.

de la Torre, Augusto, Eduardo Levy Yeyati, and Sergio Schmukler. 2003. "Living and Dying with Hard Pegs: The Rise and Fall of Argentina's Currency Board." *Economia* (Spring): 43–107.

della Paolera, Gerardo, and Alan Taylor. 2003. "Gaucho Banking Redux." *Economia* (Spring): 1–42.

Devereux, Michael, and Charles Engel. 2002. "Exchange Rate Pass-Through, Exchange Rate Volatility, and Exchange Rate Disconnect." *Journal of Monetary Economics* (June): 913–40.

Díaz Alejandro, Carlos F. 1982. "Latin America in Depression, 1929–39." In *The Theory and Experience of Economic Development: Essays in Honour of Sir Arthur Lewis*, edited by Mark Gersovitz, Carlos F. Díaz Alejandro, Gustav Ranis, and Mark R. Rosenzweig, 334–55. London: George Allen and Unwin.

———. 1983. "Stories of the 1930s for the 1980s." In *Financial Policies and the World Capital Market: The Problem of Latin American Countries*, edited by Pedro Aspe Armella, Rudiger Dornbusch, and Maurice Obstfeld, 5–35. Chicago: University of Chicago Press.

———. 1984. "Latin American Debt: I Don't Think We Are in Kansas Anymore." *Brookings Papers on Economic Activity* 2: 335–403.

———. 1985. "Good-bye Financial Repression, Hello Financial Crash." *Journal of Development Economics* 19 (1–2): 1–24.

Dornbusch, Rudiger. 1973a. "Currency Depreciation, Hoarding, and Relative Prices." *Journal of Political Economy* 81 (4): 893–915.

———. 1973b. "Devaluation, Money, and Nontraded Goods." *American Economic Review* 63 (1): 871–80.

———. 1976. "Expectations and Exchange Rate Dynamics." *Journal of Political Economy* 84 (6): 1161–76.

———. 1987. "Exchange Rates and Prices." *American Economic Review* 77 (March): 93–106.

———. 1997. "Brazil's Incomplete Stabilization and Reform." *Brookings Papers on Economic Activity* 1: 367–404.

Dornbusch, Rudiger, and Alejandro Werner. 1994. "Mexico: Stabilization, Reform, and No Growth." *Brookings Papers on Economic Activity* 1: 253–97.

Duckenfield, Mark. 2006. *Business and the Euro: Business Groups and the Politics of EMU in Germany and the United Kingdom*. London: Palgrave.

Edwards, Sebastian, and Moisés Naím. 1998. *Mexico 1994: Anatomy of an Emerging-Market Crash*. Washington, DC: Carnegie Endowment for International Peace.

Eglene, Ophelia. 2011. *Banking on Sterling: Britain's Independence from the Euro Zone*. Lanham, MD: Lexington Books.

Eichenbaum, Martin, and Charles Evans. 1995. "Some Empirical Evidence on the Effects of Shocks to Monetary Policy on Exchange Rates." *Quarterly Journal of Economics* 110 (4): 975–1009.

Eichengreen, Barry. 1989. "Hegemonic Stability Theories of the International Monetary System." In *Can Nations Agree?* edited by Richard N. Cooper, Barry Eichengreen, Gerald Holtham, Robert D. Putnam, and C. Randall Henning, 255–98. Washington, DC: Brookings Institution.

———. 1992. *Golden Fetters: The Gold Standard and the Great Depression, 1919–1939*. New York: Oxford University Press.

Eichengreen, Barry. 1993. "European Monetary Unification." *Journal of Economic Literature* 31 (3): 1321–57.

———. 1996. *A More Perfect Union? The Logic of Economic Integration.* Princeton Essays in International Finance no. 198. Princeton, NJ: International Finance Section, Department of Economics.

———. 2009. *Globalizing Capital: A History of the International Monetary System.* 2nd ed. Princeton, NJ: Princeton University Press.

Eichengreen, Barry, and Jeffry A. Frieden. 1994. "The Political Economy of European Monetary Unification: An Analytical Introduction." In *The Political Economy of European Monetary Unification,* edited by Barry Eichengreen and Jeffry A. Frieden, 1–21. Boulder, CO: Westview Press.

Eichengreen, Barry, and Jeffrey Sachs. 1985. "Exchange Rates and Economic Recovery in the 1930s." *Journal of Economic History* 45 (December): 925–46.

Eichengreen, Barry, and Charles Wyplosz. 1993. "The Unstable EMS." *Brookings Papers on Economic Activity* 24 (1): 51–143.

Elliott, E. A., ed. 1889. *Proceedings of the First National Silver Convention, Held at St. Louis, November 26, 27, and 28.* Saint Louis: Buxton and Skinner.

Ellison, Thomas. (1886) 1968. *The Cotton Trade of Great Britain.* New York: Augustus Kelley.

Engel, Charles. 2000. "Local-Currency Pricing and the Choice of Exchange-Rate Regime." *European Economic Review* 44 (August): 1149–472.

———. 2002. "Expenditure Switching and Exchange Rate Policy." *NBER Macroeconomics Annual* 17: 231–72.

———. 2006. "Equivalence Results for Optimal Pass-Through, Optimal Indexing to Exchange Rates, and Optimal Choice of Currency for Export Pricing." *Journal of the European Economic Association* 4: 1249–60.

———. 2014. "Exchange Rates and Interest Parity." In *Handbook of International Economics,* edited by Gita Gopinath, Elhanan Helpman, and Kenneth S. Rogoff, 4: 453–522. New York: North-Holland.

Engel, Charles, and John Rogers. 2001. "Deviations from Purchasing Power Parity: Causes and Welfare Costs." *Journal of International Economics* 55: 29–57.

Epstein, Gerald. 1991. "Profit Squeeze, Rentier Squeeze, and Macroeconomic Policy under Fixed and Flexible Exchange Rates." *Economies et Sociétés* 8 (November–December): 219–57.

Estevadeordal, Antoni, Brian Frantz, and Alan M. Taylor. 2003. "The Rise and Fall of World Trade, 1870–1939." *Quarterly Journal of Economics* 118 (May): 359–407.

Eusufzai, Zaki. 1997. "Instability in the Production and Employment Effects of Real Exchange Rate Changes." Unpublished paper, Loyola Marymount University, Los Angeles.

Farmer, Hattie. 1924. "The Economic Background of Frontier Populism." *Mississippi Valley Historical Review* 10 (4): 406–27.

Favier, Pierre, and Michel Martin-Roland. 1990. *La décennie Mitterrand 1. Les ruptures (1981–1984).* Paris: Seuil.

Fazio, Antonio. 1979. "La politica monetaria in Italia dal 1947 al 1978." *Moneta e Credito* (September): 269–319.

Feenstra, Robert. 1989. "Systematic Pass-Through of Tariffs and Exchange Rates under Imperfect Competition." *Journal of International Economics* 27 (1–2): 25–45.

Feinberg, Robert. 1989. "The Effects of Foreign Exchange Movements on United States Domestic Prices." *Review of Economics and Statistics* 71 (August): 505–11.

Fisher, Eric. 1989. "A Model of Exchange Rate Pass-Through." *Journal of International Economics* 26 (February): 119–37.

Fleming, Marcus. 1962. "Domestic Financial Policies under Fixed and Floating Exchange Rates." *IMF Staff Papers* 9 (November): 369–79.

Forbes, Kristin. 2002a. "Cheap Labor Meets Costly Capital: The Impact of Devaluations on Commodity Firms." *Journal of Development Economics* 69 (2): 335–65.

———. 2002b. "How Do Large Depreciations Affect Firm Performance?" *IMF Staff Papers* 49: 214–38.

Franco, Gustavo. 2000. *The Real Plan and the Exchange Rate*. Essays in International Finance, no. 217. Princeton, NJ: International Finance Section.

Frankel, Jeffrey A., and Andrew Rose. 1998. "The Endogeneity of the Optimum Currency Area Criteria." *Economic Journal* 108 (449): 1009–25.

Franzese, Robert, and Karen Jusko. 2006. "Political-Economic Cycles." In *The Oxford Handbook of Political Economy*, edited by Barry Weingast and Donald Wittman, 545–64. New York: Oxford University Press.

Fratianni, Michele, and Jürgen von Hagen. 1991. *The European Monetary System and European Monetary Union*. Boulder, CO: Westview Press.

Frieden, Jeffry A. 1991. "Invested Interests: The Politics of National Economic Policies in a World of Global Finance." *International Organization* 45 (4): 425–51.

———. 1993. "The Dynamics of International Monetary Systems: International and Domestic Factors in the Rise, Reign, and Demise of the Classical Gold Standard." In *Coping with Complexity in the International System*, edited by Robert Jervis and Jack Snyder, 137–62. Boulder, CO: Westview Press.

———. 1994a. "Exchange Rate Politics: Contemporary Lessons from American History." *Review of International Political Economy* 1 (1): 81–103.

———. 1994b. "Making Commitments: France and Italy in the European Monetary System, 1979–1985." In *The Political Economy of European Monetary Unification*, edited by Barry Eichengreen and Jeffry A. Frieden, 25–46. Boulder, CO: Westview Press.

———. 1996. "Economic Integration and the Politics of Monetary Policy in the United States." In *Internationalization and Domestic Politics*, edited by Robert Keohane and Helen Milner, 108–36. Cambridge: Cambridge University Press.

———. 1997. "Monetary Populism in Nineteenth-Century America: An Open Economy Interpretation." *Journal of Economic History* 57 (2): 367–95.

———. 2004. "One Europe, One Vote? The Political Economy of European Union Representation in International Organizations." *European Union Politics* 5 (2): 261–76.

———. 2006. *Global Capitalism: Its Fall and Rise in the Twentieth Century*. New York: W. W. Norton.

———. 2008. "Globalization and Exchange Rate Policy." In *The Future of Globalization*, edited by Ernesto Zedillo, 344–57. New York: Routledge.

Frieden, Jeffry A. 2009. "Global Governance of Global Monetary Relations: Rationale and Feasibility." *Economics* 3 (6): 1–13.

Frieden, Jeffry A., David Leblang, and Neven Valev. 2010. "The Political Economy of Exchange Rate Regimes in Transition Economies." *Review of International Organizations* 5 (1): 1–25.

Frieden, Jeffry A., Michael Pettis, Dani Rodrik, and Ernesto Zedillo. 2012. *After the Fall: The Future of Global Cooperation*. Geneva Report no. 14. London: Center for Economic Policy Research.

Frieden, Jeffry A., and Ernesto Stein, eds. 2001. *The Currency Game: Exchange Rate Politics in Latin America*. Baltimore: Johns Hopkins University Press.

Friedman, Milton. 1990. "The Crime of 1873." *Journal of Political Economy* 98 (6): 1159–94.

Friedman, Milton, and Anna Jacobson Schwartz. 1963. *A Monetary History of the United States, 1867–1960*. Princeton, NJ: Princeton University Press.

Froot, Kenneth, and Paul Klemperer. 1989. "Exchange Rate Pass-Through When Market Share Matters." *American Economic Review* (September): 637–54.

Froot, Kenneth, and Kenneth S. Rogoff. 1995. "Perspectives on PPP and Long-Run Real Exchange Rates." In *Handbook of International Economics*, edited by Gene Grossman and Kenneth S. Rogoff, 3: 1647–88. Amsterdam: North-Holland.

Funabashi, Yoichi. 1988. *Managing the Dollar: From the Plaza to the Louvre*. Washington, DC: Institute for International Economics.

Galiani, Sebastián, Daniel Heymann, and Mariano Tommasi. 2003. "Great Expectations and Hard Times: The Argentine Convertibility Plan." *Economia* 3 (2): 109–47.

Gallarotti, Giulio M. 1995. *The Anatomy of an International Monetary Regime: The Classical Gold Standard, 1880–1914*. New York: Oxford University Press.

Gallman, Robert. 1960. "Commodity Output, 1839–1899." In *Trends in the American Economy in the Nineteenth Century,* edited by William N. Parker, 24: 13–71. Princeton, NJ: Princeton University Press.

Garber, Peter, and Vittorio Grilli. 1986. "The Belmont-Morgan Syndicate as an Optimal Investment Banking Contract." *European Economic Review* 30 (3): 649–77.

Garrett, Geoffrey. 2001. "The Politics of Maastricht." In *The Political Economy of European Monetary Unification*, edited by Barry Eichengreen and Jeffry A. Frieden, 111–30. 2nd ed. Boulder, CO: Westview Press.

Giavazzi, Francesco, and Alberto Giovannini. 1989. *Limiting Exchange Rate Flexibility: The European Monetary System*. Cambridge, MA: MIT Press.

Giavazzi, Francesco, and Marco Pagano. 1988. "The Advantage of Tying One's Hands: EMS Discipline and Central Bank Credibility." *European Economic Review* 32 (5): 1055–75.

Giovannini, Alberto. 1988. "Exchange Rates and Traded Goods Prices." *Journal of International Economics* 24: 45–68.

Glick, Reuven, and Michael Hutchison. 2012. "Models of Currency Crises." In *The Evidence and Impact of Financial Globalization, Handbooks in Financial Globalization*, edited by Gerard Caprio, 3: 485–97. London: Academic Press.

Goldberg, Linda. 1993. "Exchange Rates and Investment in United States Industry." *Review of Economics and Statistics* 75 (4): 575–88.

———. 1997. "Exchange Rates and Investment Response in Latin America." In *International Trade and Finance: New Frontiers for Research*, edited by Benjamin J. Cohen, 157–83. Cambridge: Cambridge University Press.

Goldberg, Linda, and José Campa. 1996. "Investment, Pass-Through, and Exchange Rates: A Cross-Country Comparison." Federal Reserve Bank of New York Staff Reports no. 14 (June).

Goldberg, Linda, and Charles D. Kolstad. 1995. "Foreign Direct Investment, Exchange Rate Variability, and Demand Uncertainty." *International Economic Review* 36 (4): 855–73.

Goldberg, Linda, and Cédric Tille. 2008. "Vehicle Currency Use in International Trade." *Journal of International Economics* 76: 177–92.

———. 2013. "A Bargaining Theory of Trade Invoicing and Pricing." NBER working paper no. 18985. Cambridge, MA: National Bureau of Economic Research.

Goldberg, Pinelopi, and Michael Knetter. 1997. "Goods Prices and Exchange Rates: What Have We Learned?" *Journal of Economic Literature* 35 (3): 1243–72.

Goldstein, Morris, and Nicholas S. Lardy, eds. 2007. *Debating China's Exchange Rate Policy*. Washington, DC: Peterson Institute for International Economics.

Goodhart, Charles. 1995. "The Political Economy of Monetary Union." In *Understanding Interdependence: The Macroeconomics of the Open Economy*, edited by Peter Kenen, 448–506. Princeton, NJ: Princeton University Press.

Goodman, John. 1992. *Monetary Sovereignty: The Politics of Central Banking in Western Europe*. Ithaca, NY: Cornell University Press.

Goodwyn, Lawrence. 1976. *Democratic Promise: The Populist Moment in America*. New York: Oxford University Press.

Gopinath, Gita, and Oleg Itskhoki. 2010. "Frequency of Price Adjustment and Pass-Through." *Quarterly Journal of Economics* 125 (2): 675–727.

Gopinath, Gita, Oleg Itskhoki, and Roberto Rigobon. 2010. "Currency Choice and Exchange Rate Pass-Through." *American Economic Review* 100 (1): 304–36.

Gowa, Joanne. 1983. *Closing the Gold Window: Domestic Politics and the End of Bretton Woods*. Ithaca, NY: Cornell University Press.

———. 1988. "Public Goods and Political Institutions: Trade and Monetary Policy Processes in the United States." *International Organization* 42: 15–32.

Graham, Frank D. 1922. "International Trade under Depreciated Paper: The United States, 1862–1879." *Quarterly Journal of Economics* 36 (2): 220–73.

Grilli, Vittorio, Donato Masciandaro, and Guido Tabellini. 1991. "Political and Monetary Institutions and Public Financial Policies in the Industrial Countries." *Economic Policy* 13 (October): 342–92.

Gros, Daniel. 1996. *Towards Economic and Monetary Union: Problems and Prospects*. Brussels: Centre for European Policy Studies.

Gros, Daniel, and Niels Thygesen. 1998. *European Monetary Integration from the European Monetary System to Economic and Monetary Union*. 2nd ed. London: Longman.

Guerrieri, Paolo, and Pier Carlo Padoan. 1989. "Two-Level Games and Structural Adjustment: The Italian Case." *International Spectator* 24 (3–4): 128–40.

Guisinger, Alexandra, and David Singer. 2010. "Exchange Rate Proclamations and Inflation-Fighting Credibility." *International Organization* 64 (2): 313–37.

Harley, C. Knick. 1980. "Transportation, the World Wheat Trade, and the Kuznets Cycle, 1850–1913." *Explorations in Economic History* 17 (3): 218–50.

Harvey, William. (1894) 1963. *Coin's Financial School*. Edited by Richard Hofstadter. Cambridge, MA: Harvard University Press.

Hefeker, Carsten. 1997. *Interest Groups and Monetary Integration: The Political Economy of Exchange Regime Choice*. Boulder, CO: Westview Press.

Helleiner, Eric. 2003. *The Making of National Money: Territorial Currencies in Historical Perspective*. Ithaca, NY: Cornell University Press.

Henning, C. Randall. 1994. *Currencies and Politics in the United States, Germany, and Japan*. Washington, DC: Institute for International Economics.

Hicks, John D. 1921. "The Political Career of Ignatius Donnelly." *Mississippi Valley Historical Review* 8 (1–2): 80–132.

———. 1931. *The Populist Revolt*. Minneapolis: University of Minnesota Press.

Hoffman, Charles. 1956. "The Depression of the Nineties." *Journal of Economic History* 16 (2): 137–64.

Hollingsworth, J. Rogers. 1963. *The Whirligig of Politics: The Democracy of Cleveland and Bryan*. Chicago: University of Chicago Press.

Hooper, Peter, and Catherine Mann. 1989. "Exchange Rate Pass-Through in the 1980s: The Case of U.S. Imports of Manufactures." *Brookings Papers on Economic Activity* 1: 297–329.

Hutchison, Michael, and Ilan Noy. 2005. "How Bad Are Twins? Output Costs of Currency and Banking Crises." *Journal of Money, Credit, and Banking* 37 (4): 725–52.

Isard, Peter. 1995. *Exchange Rate Economics*. Cambridge: Cambridge University Press.

James, Harold. 2012. *Making the European Monetary Union: The Role of the Committee of Central Bank Governors and the Origins of the European Central Bank*. Cambridge, MA: Harvard University Press.

Jones, Stanley. 1964. *The Presidential Election of 1896*. Madison: University of Wisconsin Press.

Jonung, Lars, and Eoin Drea, eds. 2010. "It Can't Happen, It's a Bad Idea, It Won't Last: U.S. Economists on the European Monetary Union and the Euro, 1989–2002." Special issue, *Econ Journal Watch* 7 (1): 4–52.

July, Serge. 1986. *Les années Mitterrand*. Paris: Bernard Grasset.

Kandil, Magda, and Aghdas Mirzaei. 2002. "Exchange Rate Fluctuations and Disaggregated Economic Activity in the US: Theory and Evidence." *Journal of International Money and Finance* 21: 1–31.

Kenen, Peter. 1969. "The Theory of Optimum Currency Areas: An Eclectic View." In *Monetary Problems of the International Economy*, edited by Robert Mundell and Alexander K. Swoboda, 41–60. Chicago: University of Chicago Press.

Kinderman, Daniel. 2008. "The Political Economy of Sectoral Exchange Rate Preferences and Lobbying: Germany from 1960–2008, and Beyond. *Review of International Political Economy* 15 (5): 851–80.

Kirshner, Jonathan. 1995. *Currency and Coercion: The Political Economy of International Monetary Power*. Princeton, NJ: Princeton University Press.

———, ed. 2003. *Monetary Orders: Ambiguous Economics, Ubiquitous Politics*. Ithaca, NY: Cornell University Press.

Klein, Michael, and Nancy Marion. 1997. "Explaining the Duration of Exchange-Rate Pegs." *Journal of Development Economics* 54 (2): 387–404.

Klein, Michael, and Jay Shambaugh. 2006. "Fixed Exchange Rates and Trade." *Journal of International Economics* 70: 359–83.

———. 2008. "The Dynamics of Exchange Rate Regimes: Fixes, Floats, and Flips." *Journal of International Economics* 75 (1): 70–92.

Knetter, Michael. 1989. "Price Discrimination by U.S. and German Exporters." *American Economic Review* 79 (March): 198–210.

———. 1993. "International Comparisons of Pricing-to-Market Behavior." *American Economic Review* 83 (June): 473–86.

Krugman, Paul. 1987. "Pricing to Market When the Exchange Rate Changes." In *Real-Financial Linkages among Open Economies*, edited by Sven Arndt and J. David Richardson, 49–70. Cambridge, MA: MIT Press.

Laeven, Luc, and Fabián Valencia. 2012. "Systemic Banking Crises Database: An Update." International Monetary Fund Working Paper 12/163. Washington, DC: International Monetary Fund.

Lake, David A. 1988. *Power, Protection, and Free Trade*. Ithaca, NY: Cornell University Press.

———. 2009. "Open Economy Politics: A Critical Review." *Review of International Organizations* 4 (3): 219–44.

Lauber, Volkmar. 1983. *The Political Economy of France: From Pompidou to Mitterrand*. New York: Praeger.

Lause, Mark A. 2001. *The Civil War's Last Campaign: James B. Weaver, the Greenback-Labor Party, and the Politics of Race and Section*. New York: University Press of America.

Lee, Jaewoo. 1997. "The Response of Exchange Rate Pass-Through to Market Concentration in a Small Economy: The Evidence from Korea." *Review of Economics and Statistics* 79 (February): 142–45.

Lee, Susan Previant, and Peter Passell. 1979. *A New Economic View of American History*. New York: W. W. Norton.

Levy Yayati, Eduardo, and Federico Sturzenegger, eds. 2003. *Dollarization: Debates and Policy Alternatives*. Cambridge, MA: MIT Press.

Lohmann, Susanne. 2006. "The Non-Politics of Monetary Policy." In *The Oxford Handbook of Political Economy*, edited by Barry Weingast and Donald Wittman, 523–44. New York: Oxford University Press.

López-Córdova, J. Ernesto, and Christopher Meissner. 2003. "Exchange-Rate Regimes and International Trade: Evidence from the Classical Gold Standard Era." *American Economic Review* 93 (1): 344–53.

Ludlow, Peter. 1982. *The Making of the European Monetary System*. London: Butterworth.

Mackie, Thomas T., and Richard Rose. 1991. *International Almanac of Electoral History*. Washington DC: Congressional Quarterly.

Markiewicz, Agnieszka. 2006. "Choice of Exchange Rate Regime in Transition Economies: An Empirical Analysis." *Journal of Comparative Economics* 34: 484–98.

Marston, Richard. 1990. "Pricing to Market in Japanese Manufacturing." *Journal of International Economics* 29 (3–4): 217–36.

Masson, Paul, and Mark Taylor. 1993. "Currency Unions: A Survey of the Issues." In *Policy Issues in the Operation of Currency Areas*, edited by Paul Masson and Mark Taylor, 3–54. Cambridge: Cambridge University Press.

Mayhew, Anne. 1972. "A Reappraisal of the Causes of Farm Protest in the United States, 1870–1900." *Journal of Economic History* 32: 464–75.

McGuire, Robert. 1981. "Economic Causes of Late-Nineteenth Century Agrarian Unrest: New Evidence." *Journal of Economic History* 41 (4): 835–52.

McKinnon, Ronald. 1963. "Optimum Currency Areas." *American Economic Review* 53: 717–25.

McNall, Scott. 1988. *The Road to Rebellion: Class Formation and Kansas Populism, 1865–1900*. Chicago: University of Chicago Press.

McNamara, Kathleen. 1998. *The Currency of Ideas: Monetary Politics in the European Union*. Ithaca, NY: Cornell University Press.

Milesi-Ferretti, Gian Maria. 1995. "The Disadvantage of Tying Their Hands: On the Political Economy of Policy Commitments." *Economic Journal* 105: 1381–402.

Miller, Raymond. 1925. "The Background of Populism in Kansas." *Mississippi Valley Historical Review* 11 (4): 469–89.

Milner, Helen. 1999. "The Political Economy of International Trade." *Annual Review of Political Science* 2: 91–114.

———. 2013. "International Trade." In *Handbook of International Relations*, edited by Walter Carlsnaes, Thomas Risse, and Beth A. Simmons, 720–45. 2nd ed. Thousand Oaks, CA: SAGE Publications.

Moravcsik, Andrew. 1991. "Negotiating the Single Act: National Interests and Conventional Statecraft in the European Community." *International Organization* 45 (1): 19–56.

Mundell, Robert. 1960. "The Monetary Dynamics of International Adjustment under Fixed and Flexible Exchange Rates." *Quarterly Journal of Economics* 74 (May): 227–57.

———. 1961. "A Theory of Optimum Currency Areas." *American Economic Review* 51 (4): 657–65.

———. 1963. "Capital Mobility and Stabilization Policy under Fixed and Flexible Exchange Rates." *Canadian Journal of Economics and Political Science* 29 (4): 475–85.

Mussa, Michael. 1979. "Macroeconomic Interdependence and the Exchange Rate Regime." In *International Economic Policy: Theory and Evidence*, edited by Rudiger Dornbusch and Jacob Frenkel, 160–204. Baltimore: Johns Hopkins University Press.

———. 1984. "The Theory of Exchange Rate Determination." In *Exchange Rate Theory and Practice*, edited by John Bilson and Richard Marston, 13–58. Chicago: University of Chicago Press.

Neumeyer, Pablo Andrés. 1998. "Currencies and the Allocation of Risk: The Welfare Effects of a Monetary Union." *American Economic Review* 88 (1): 246–59.

Nugent, Walter. 1966. "Some Parameters of Populism." *Agricultural History* 40 (4): 255–70.

Obstfeld, Maurice, Jay Shambaugh, and Alan Taylor. 2005. "The Trilemma in History: Tradeoffs among Exchange Rates, Monetary Policies, and Capital Mobility." *Review of Economics and Statistics* 87 (August): 423–38.

Officer, Lawrence. 1981. "The Floating Dollar in the Greenback Period." *Journal of Economic History* 41 (3): 629–50.

O'Leary, Paul. 1960. "The Scene of the Crime of 1873 Revisited: A Note." *Journal of Political Economy* 60 (4): 388–92.

Oudiz, Gilles, and Henri Sterdyniak. 1985. "Inflation, Employment, and External Constraints: An Overview of the French Economy during the Seventies." In *The French Economy: Theory and Policy*, edited by Jacques Melitz and Charles Wyplosz, 9–50. Boulder, CO: Westview Press.

Oye, Kenneth A. 1992. *Economic Discrimination and Political Exchange: World Political Economy in the 1930s and 1980s*. Princeton, NJ: Princeton University Press.

Parsley, David. 1995. "Exchange Rate Pass-Through with Intertemporal Linkages: Evidence at the Commodity Level." *Review of International Economics* 3 (3): 330–41.

Persson, Torsten, and Guido Tabellini. 1990. *Macroeconomic Policy Credibility and Politics*. New York: Harwood.

"Policy Coordination in the European Monetary System." 1988. IMF Occasional Paper 61. Washington, DC: International Monetary Fund.

Powell, G. Bingham, Jr., and Guy D. Whitten. 1993. "A Cross-National Analysis of Economic Voting." *American Journal of Political Science* 37 (2): 391–414.

Quinn, Dennis. 1997. "The Correlates of Change in International Financial Regulation." *American Political Science Review* 91 (3): 531–52.

Reinhart, Carmen, and Kenneth S. Rogoff. 2009. *This Time Is Different: Eight Centuries of Financial Folly*. Princeton, NJ: Princeton University Press.

Reti, Steven P. 1998. *Silver and Gold: The Political Economy of International Monetary Conferences, 1867–1892*. Westport, CT: Greenwood Press.

Ritter, Gretchen. 1997. *Goldbugs and Greenbacks: The Antimonopoly Tradition and the Politics of American Finance, 1865–1896*. New York: Cambridge University Press.

Rockoff, Hugh. 1990. "The 'Wizard of Oz' as a Monetary Allegory." *Journal of Political Economy* 98 (4): 739–60.

Rodrik, Dani. 1995. "The Political Economy of Trade Policy." In *Handbook of International Economics*, edited by Elhanan Grossman and Kenneth S. Rogoff, 3: 1457–94. Amsterdam: Elsevier Science.

———. 2008. "The Real Exchange Rate and Economic Growth." *Brookings Papers on Economic Activity* 39 (2): 365–439.

Roett, Riordan, and Carol Wise, eds. 2000. *Exchange Rate Politics in Latin America*. Washington, DC: Brookings Institution.

Rose, Andrew. 2000. "One Money, One Market: Estimating the Effect of Common Currencies on Trade." *Economic Policy* 30: 7–46.

Sachs, Jeffrey D. 1985. "External Debt and Macroeconomic Performance in Latin America and East Asia." *Brookings Papers on Economic Activity* 16 (2): 523–73.

Sachs, Jeffrey D., and Charles Wyplosz. 1986. "The Economic Consequences of President Mitterrand." *Economic Policy* 2 (April): 262–322.

Sandholtz, Wayne, and John Zysman. 1989. "1992: Recasting the European Bargain." *World Politics* 42 (1): 95–128.

Sarno, Lucio, and Mark Taylor. 2002. *The Economics of Exchange Rates*. Cambridge: Cambridge University Press.

Sharkey, Robert P. 1959. *Money, Class, and Party: An Economic Study of Civil War and Reconstruction*. Baltimore: John Hopkins University Press.

Siebert, Horst. 1999. *The World Economy*. London: Routledge.

Simmons, Beth. 1994. *Who Adjusts? Domestic Sources of Foreign Economic Policy during the Interwar Years*. Princeton, NJ: Princeton University Press.

———. 2000. "International Law and State Behavior: Commitment and Compliance in International Monetary Affairs." *American Political Science Review* 94 (4): 819–35.

Simmons, Beth, and Zachary Elkins. 2004. "The Globalization of Liberalization: Policy Diffusion in the International Political Economy." *American Political Science Review* 98 (1): 171–89.

Singer, David A. 2010. "Migrant Remittances and Exchange Rate Regimes in the Developing World." *American Political Science Review* 104 (2): 307–23.

Snowden, Kenneth. 1987. "Mortgage Rates and American Capital Market Development in the Late Nineteenth Century." *Journal of Economic History* 47 (3): 671–91.

———. 1988. "Mortgage Lending and American Urbanization, 1880–1890." *Journal of Economic History* 48 (2): 273–85.

Stein, Ernesto, Jorge Streb, and Piero Ghezzi. 2005. "Real Exchange Rate Cycles around Elections." *Economics and Politics* 17 (3): 297–330.

Steinberg, David A., and Krishan Malhotra. 2014. "The Effect of Authoritarian Regime Type on Exchange Rate Policy." *World Politics* 66 (3).

Steinberg, David A., and Victor C. Shih. 2012. "Interest Group Influence in Authoritarian States: The Political Determinants of Chinese Exchange Rate Policy." *Comparative Political Studies* 45 (November): 1405–34.

Stevans, Charles McClellan. 1896. *Free Silver and the People: A Campaign Handbook for the Struggling Millions against the Gold-Hoarding Millionaires*. New York: F. T. Neely.

Stock, James. 1984. "Real Estate Mortgages, Foreclosures, and Midwestern Agrarian Unrest, 1865–1920." *Journal of Economic History* 44 (1): 89–105.

Sundquist, James L. 1983. *Dynamics of the Party System*. Washington, DC: Brookings Institution.

Swoboda, Alexander K. 1968. *The Euro-Dollar Market: An Interpretation*. Essays in

International Finance 64. Princeton, NJ: International Finance Section, Department of Economics, Princeton University.

Taborda, Rodrigo. 2013. "Bias in Economic News: The Reporting of the Nominal Exchange Rate Behavior in Colombia." *Economia* 14 (1): 103–47.

Tavlas, George S. 1993. "The 'New' Theory of Optimum Currency Areas." *World Economy* 16 (6): 663–85.

———. 1994. "The Theory of Monetary Integration." *Open Economies Review* 5 (2): 211–30.

Timberlake, Richard. 1978. "Repeal of Silver Monetization in the Late Nineteenth Century." *Journal of Money, Credit, and Banking* 10 (1): 27–45.

Tsoukalis, Loukas. 1977. *The Politics and Economics of European Monetary Integration.* London: George Allen and Unwin.

Unger, Irwin. 1959. "Business Men and Specie Resumption." *Political Science Quarterly* 74 (1): 46–70.

———. 1964. *The Greenback Era: A Social and Political History of American Finance, 1865–1879.* Princeton, NJ: Princeton University Press.

Ungerer, Horst. 1983. "The European Monetary System: The Experience, 1979–82." IMF Occasional Paper 19. Washington, DC: International Monetary Fund.

Walter, Stefanie. 2008. "A New Approach for Determining Exchange-Rate Level Preferences." *International Organization* 62 (3): 405–38.

———. 2013. *Financial Crises and the Politics of Macroeconomic Adjustments.* Cambridge: Cambridge University Press.

Warren, George, and Frank Pearson. 1935. *Gold and Prices.* New York: John Wiley and Sons.

Weber, Axel. 1991. "Reputation and Credibility in the European Monetary System." *Economic Policy* 12 (April): 57–102.

Wegner, John M. 1995. "Remembering the 'Rag Baby': Toledo and the Greenback-National Movement in the 1870s." *Northwest Ohio Quarterly* 67 (3): 118–45.

Weinstein, Allen. 1970. *Prelude to Populism: Origins of the Silver Issue, 1867–1878.* New Haven, CT: Yale University Press.

Williams, Jeffrey C. 1981. "Economics and Politics: Voting Behavior in Kansas during the Populist Decade." *Explorations in Economic History* 18: 233–56.

Ypersele, Jacques van. 1985. *The European Monetary System: Origins, Operation, and Outlook.* Brussels: Commission of the European Communities.

A page number followed by f refers to a figure and a page number followed by t indicates a table.